AMC'S BEST DAY HIKES IN THE
BERKSHIRES

Four-Season Guide to 50 of the Best T̶r̶a̶i̶l̶s̶
in Western Massachusetts

Third Edition

RENÉ LAUBACH & JOHN S. BURK

Appalachian Mountain Club Books
Boston, Massachusetts

AMC is a nonprofit organization, and sales of AMC Books fund our mission of protecting the Northeast outdoors. If you appreciate our efforts and would like to become a member or make a donation to AMC, visit outdoors.org, call 800-372-1758, or contact us at Appalachian Mountain Club, 10 City Square, Boston, MA 02129.

outdoors.org/books-maps

Distributed by National Book Network.

Front cover photograph of Hoosac Range Trail by Matthew Grymek © Appalachian Mountain Club
Back cover photographs (left to right) of Mount Greylock by Nina Paus-Weiler and Harish Janardhan, both © Appalachian Mountain Club
Title page photograph of Spruce Hill © John S. Burk
Interior photographs by René Laubach and John S. Burk
Maps by Ken Dumas © Appalachian Mountain Club
Book design by Abigail Coyle

Library of Congress Cataloging-in-Publication Data

Names: Laubach, René, author. | Burk, John S., author. | Appalachian
   Mountain Club, issuing body.
Title: AMC's best day hikes in the Berkshires : four-season guide to 50 of
   the best trails in western Massachusetts / René Laubach & John S. Burk
Description: Third edition. | Boston, Massachusetts : Appalachian Mountain
   Club Books, 2020. | Includes index. |
   Summary: "A four-season guide to 50 of the best day hikes in the
   Berkshire Mountain region of Massachusetts"—Provided by publisher.
Identifiers: LCCN 2020013875 (print) | LCCN 2020013876 (ebook) | ISBN
   9781628421217 (trade paperback) | ISBN 9781628421231 (mobi) | ISBN
   9781628421224 (epub)
Subjects: LCSH: Hiking—Massachusetts—Berkshire Hills—Guidebooks. |
   Walking—Massachusetts—Berkshire Hills—Guidebooks. |
   Trails—Massachusetts—Berkshire Hills—Guidebooks. | Berkshire Hills
   (Mass.)—Guidebooks.
Classification: LCC GV199.42.M42 B474 2020 (print) | LCC GV199.42.M42
   (ebook) | DDC 796.5109744/1—dc23
LC record available at https://lccn.loc.gov/2020013875
LC ebook record available at https://lccn.loc.gov/2020013876

The paper used in this publication meets the minimum requirements of the American National Standard for Information Sciences-Permanence of Paper for Printed Library Materials, ANSI Z39.48-1984. ∞

Outdoor recreation activities by their very nature are potentially hazardous. This book is not a substitute for good personal judgment and training in outdoor skills. Due to changes in conditions, use of the information in this book is at the sole risk of the user. The author and the Appalachian Mountain Club assume no liability for accidents happening to, or injuries sustained by, readers who engage in the activities described in this book.

Interior pages and cover are printed on responsibly harvested paper stock certified by The Forest Stewardship Council,® an independent auditor of responsible forestry practices. Printed in the United States of America, using vegetable-based inks.

5 4 3 2 1   20 21 22 23 24

MIX
Paper from responsible sources
FSC® C005010

*This book is dedicated to my late, good friend Don Reid,
who loved the outdoors.*
—René Laubach

And to Esin Atil, who appreciated scenic places.
—John Burk

LOCATOR MAP

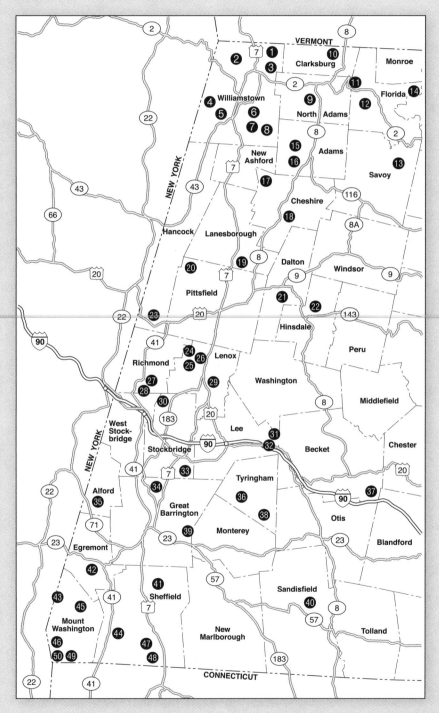

CONTENTS

ESSAYS

AT-A-GLANCE TRIP PLANNER

TRIP NUMBER	TRIP	LOCATION	RATING	ROUND-TRIP DISTANCE	ELEVATION GAIN
NORTHERN BERKSHIRES					
1	Mountain Meadow Preserve	Williamstown, MA; Pownal, VT	Moderate	4 mi	690 ft
2	Hopkins Memorial Forest and Taconic Crest Trail	Williamstown, MA; Petersburg, NY; Pownal, VT	Strenuous	10.4 mi	1,650 ft
3	Pine Cobble and East Mountain	Williamstown and Clarksburg, MA	Moderate	4.8 mi	1,340 ft
4	Berlin Mountain	Williamstown, MA; Berlin, NY	Strenuous	4.7 mi	1,545 ft
5	Field Farm Reservation	Williamstown, MA	Easy	2.9 mi	120 ft
6	Greylock Range Traverse	Williamstown, Adams, and North Adams, MA	Strenuous	12.1 mi	2,390 ft
7	Hopper Trail to Mount Greylock Summit	Williamstown and Adams, MA	Strenuous	9 mi	2,390 ft
8	Stony Ledge via Haley Farm Trail	Williamstown, MA	Moderate-Strenuous	5.6 mi	1,460 ft
9	Mount Greylock and Ragged Mountain via Bellows Pipe Trail	North Adams and Adams, MA	Strenuous	8.8 mi	2,140 ft
10	Clarksburg State Park	Clarksburg, MA	Easy-Moderate	4.1 mi	340 ft
11	Hoosac Range Trail to Spruce Hill	North Adams, MA	Moderate	5.4 mi	540 ft
12	Spruce Hill via Busby Trail	Florida and North Adams, MA	Moderate	2.6 mi	670 ft
13	Tannery Falls and Parker Brook Falls	Savoy, MA	Easy-Moderate	0.6 mi (round trip) or 4.5 mi (loop)	200 ft (round trip) or 615 ft (loop)
14	Dunbar Brook	Florida and Monroe, MA	Moderate-Strenuous	6.8 mi	1,010 ft
15	Saddle Ball Mountain	Adams, Cheshire, New Ashford, and Williamstown, MA	Strenuous	10.4 mi	1,675 ft
16	Mount Greylock State Reservation: East Side	Adams, MA	Moderate-Strenuous	6.6 mi	1,930 ft
17	Mount Greylock State Reservation: Jones Nose and Rounds Rock	Cheshire and New Ashford, MA	Easy-Moderate	2.6 mi	235 ft
18	Cheshire Cobbles and Gore Pond	Cheshire and Dalton, MA	Moderate	7.6 mi	1,250 ft

Estimated Time	Trip Highlights	Fee	Good for Kids	Dogs Allowed	X-C Skiing	Snowshoeing
2.5 hrs	Wildflower meadow and panoramic views		✓	✓		✓
5.5 hrs	Taconic ridgeline vistas, Snow Hole			✓		✓
3 hrs	Stunning views			✓		✓
2.5–3.5 hrs	Views from summit			✓		✓
1.5–2 hrs	Meadows with bucolic mountain vistas		✓	✓	✓	✓
6.5–8 hrs	Four summits, spectacular vista at Stony Ledge			✓		✓
5–6 hrs	Boreal forest and Greylock summit			✓		✓
2.5–3 hrs	One of Massachusetts's most outstanding vistas			✓		✓
5 hrs	Magnificent view of Greylock's east face			✓		✓
2–2.5 hrs	Scenic pond views, wetlands, birding		✓	✓	✓	✓
2.5–3.5 hrs	Stunning vistas			✓		✓
1.5–2 hrs	Fabulous views, migrating hawks in fall			✓		✓
30 minutes (round trip); 2.5 hrs (loop)	Ravine with twin waterfalls, cascading brook, fall foliage, wildflowers			✓	✓	✓
4 hrs	Old-growth trees and roaring brook			✓		✓
6–7 hrs	Flower-filled meadow with wonderful views, boggy wetlands			✓		✓
4–4.5 hrs	State's highest summit			✓		✓
1.5–2 hrs	Great vistas, prolific blueberries in season		✓	✓		✓
4 hrs	Fantastic vista point, scenic pond			✓		✓

TRIP NUMBER
TRIP
LOCATION
RATING
ROUND-TRIP DISTANCE
ELEVATION GAIN

CENTRAL BERKSHIRES

Trip Number	Trip	Location	Rating	Round-Trip Distance	Elevation Gain
19	Ashuwillticook Rail Trail: Lanesborough to Cheshire	Lanesborough and Cheshire, MA	Easy-Moderate	7.4 mi	20 ft
20	Pittsfield State Forest: Lulu Cascade, Berry Pond, Tilden Swamp	Pittsfield, Lanesborough, and Hancock, MA	Moderate	5.4 mi	1,000 ft
21	Warner Hill	Dalton and Hinsdale, MA	Moderate	6.3 mi	430 ft
22	Old Mill Trail	Hinsdale and Dalton, MA	Easy	3 mi	155 ft
23	Shaker Mountain	Hancock, MA	Moderate	5.8 mi	790 ft
24	Pleasant Valley Wildlife Sanctuary: Fire Tower Loop	Lenox, MA	Strenuous	3 mi	825 ft
25	Pleasant Valley Wildlife Sanctuary: Beaver Ponds Loop	Lenox, MA	Easy	1.5 mi	115 ft
26	John Drummond Kennedy Park	Lenox, MA	Easy-Moderate	4.8 mi	355 ft
27	Lenox Mountain: Burbank Trail	Richmond and Lenox, MA	Easy-Moderate	3.2 mi	540 ft
28	West Stockbridge Mountain: Charcoal Trail	Stockbridge, West Stockbridge, and Richmond, MA	Moderate	1.6 mi	530 ft
29	Schermerhorn Gorge	Lenox, Lee, and Washington, MA	Moderate-Strenuous	3.7 mi	620 ft
30	Stevens Glen	West Stockbridge and Richmond, MA	Easy-Moderate	1.2 mi	320 ft
31	October Mountain State Forest: Finerty Pond	Becket and Washington, MA	Moderate	6 mi	870 ft
32	Upper Goose Pond	Becket, Lee, and Tyringham, MA	Moderate	3.7 mi	385 ft

SOUTHERN BERKSHIRES

Trip Number	Trip	Location	Rating	Round-Trip Distance	Elevation Gain
33	Ice Glen and Laura's Tower	Stockbridge, MA	Moderate	1.9 mi	580 ft
34	Monument Mountain Reservation	Great Barrington, MA	Moderate	2.7 mi	765 ft
35	Alford Springs	Alford, MA	Moderate	5.1 mi	940 ft
36	Tyringham Cobble Reservation	Tyringham, MA	Easy-Moderate	2 mi	380 ft
37	Becket Land Trust Historic Quarry and Forest	Becket, MA	Easy-Moderate	3 mi	400 ft

Estimated Time	Trip Highlights	Fee	Good for Kids	Dogs Allowed	X-C Skiing	Snowshoeing
3 hrs	Wildlife-rich wetlands		✓	✓	✓	✓
3–3.5 hrs	Trifecta of water attractions	$		✓		✓
3–3.5 hrs	Attractive northern hardwoods, evergreen stands, Greylock view		✓	✓	✓	✓
1.5–2 hrs	Industrial history		✓	✓	✓	✓
3–4 hrs	Sojourn back in time					✓
2 hrs	Fine summit views	$				✓
1 hr	Active and easily observed beaver colony	$	✓			✓
2.5–3 hrs	Interesting local history, views		✓	✓	✓	✓
1.5–2 hrs	Attractive woodland, pleasing lookout		✓	✓		✓
1–1.5 hrs	Mature woodland, pleasing vistas			✓		✓
2–2.5 hrs	Cascading brook and massive trees			✓		✓
1–1.5 hrs	Towering trees, cascading brook		✓	✓		✓
3.5 hrs	Serene pond ringed by mountain laurel			✓		✓
2.5 hrs	Serene and scenic Upper Goose Pond		✓	✓		
1.5 hrs	Magical rocky cleft, ancient evergreens			✓		✓
2 hrs	Picturesque summit of quartzite boulders	$		✓		
2.5–3 hrs	Views, quiet trails, great for skiing			✓	✓	✓
1.5 hrs	Bucolic pastures, lovely views		✓	✓	✓	✓
1.5–2 hrs	Former granite quarry artifacts	$	✓	✓	✓	✓

TRIP NUMBER	TRIP	LOCATION	RATING	ROUND-TRIP DISTANCE	ELEVATION GAIN
38	McLennan Reservation	Tyringham and Otis, MA	Easy-Moderate	2.5 mi	448 ft
39	Benedict Pond and the Ledges	Great Barrington and Monetery, MA	Easy-Moderate	3 mi	240 ft
40	Clam River Reserve	Sandisfield, MA	Easy-Moderate	5.5 mi	860 ft
41	East Mountain and Ice Gulch	Sheffield and Great Barrington, MA	Moderate	7.2 mi	680 ft
42	Jug End State Reservation and Wildlife Management Area	Egremont, MA	Easy	2.9 mi	365 ft
43	Bash Bish Falls	Mount Washington, MA; Copake Falls, NY	Easy-Moderate or Moderate	2 mi or 3.8 mi	470 ft or 900 ft
44	Upper Race Brook Falls and Mount Race	Sheffield and Mount Washington, MA	Strenuous	6.2 mi	1,625 ft
45	Guilder Pond and Mount Everett	Mount Washington, MA	Moderate	4.2 mi	825 ft
46	Alander Mountain Trail	Mount Washington, MA	Moderate	5 mi	790 ft
47	Lime Kiln Farm Wildlife Sanctuary	Sheffield, MA	Easy	1.8 mi	135 ft
48	Bartholomew's Cobble Reservation	Sheffield, MA	Moderate	3.5 mi	310 ft
49	Sages Ravine and Bear Mountain	Mount Washington, MA; Salisbury, CT	Strenuous	3.9 mi	915 ft
50	Round Mountain, Mount Frissell, and Brace Mountain	Mount Washington, MA; Salisbury, CT; Millertown, NY	Moderate-Strenuous	4.4 mi	1,425 ft

ACKNOWLEDGMENTS

Many people and organizations provided helpful updates, feedback, and resources for this third edition of *AMC's Best Day Hikes in the Berkshires* including Mariah Auman, Berkshire Natural Resources Council; Biodrawversity Ecological Consulting and Communications; Cosmo Catalano, AMC Berkshire Chapter; Maribeth Cellana, Hancock Shaker Village; Copake Iron Works National Heritage Area; Caitlin Davis, The Trustees of Reservations Western Regional Office; Olivia Dorrance, Massachusetts Department of Conservation and Recreation; Pat Flinn and Shelby Marshall, Laurel Hill Association; Dustin Griffin, Dan Gura, Williamstown Rural Lands Foundation; Marianne Hall, Pleasant Valley Wildlife Sanctuary; Massachusetts Department of Conservation and Recreation state forest and parks staff; David Orwig, Harvard Forest; James Pelletier, Massachusetts Appalachian Trail Management Committee; Chris Pryor, New England Forestry Foundation; Ken Smith, Becket Land Trust; Cathy Talarico, Williamstown Rural Land Foundation; and Ruth Wheeler, Kennedy Park Committee.

John Burk would like to thank the AMC Books staff, including former editorial director Jennifer Wehunt, books project editor Tim Mudie, production manager Abigail Coyle, mapmaker Ken Dumas, copyeditor Lenore Howard, proofreader Ken Krause, and former books project editor Shannon Smith.

Finally, this book would not have been possible were it not for all the hard-working people who protect open spaces and construct and maintain the wonderful system of trails that we are so fortunate to have in the Berkshires. Thank you all!

INTRODUCTION

The Berkshires have long been renowned as one of the nation's premier outdoor and cultural destinations. From the summit of Mount Greylock to the cascades of Bash Bish Falls, the region boasts an outstanding variety of natural areas, trails, flora, and fauna. A 90-mile segment of the Appalachian Trail runs through the heart of the area, linking both well-known landmarks and hidden treasures.

I've enjoyed exploring the region and reading René Laubach's well-written guides for many years, and it was a pleasure to revise this third edition of *AMC's Best Day Hikes in the Berkshires*. We have added five diverse new hikes at destinations across the region, including recently established Berkshire Natural Resources Council properties at Alford Springs in the Taconic Mountains and the Clam River valley of Sandisfield. Waterfall enthusiasts will enjoy the dramatic twin cascades and hemlock-lined brooks of Savoy Mountain State Forest. Mausert Pond in Clarksburg State Park offers an easy loop trail with views of surrounding mountains and hills. And on the Mount Frissell Trail in the southwestern Taconics, you can traverse three summits in three states—all within roughly 2 miles.

Two new essays detail the arrival and effects of the emerald ash borer on the region's forests and, on a more positive note, the development of the Mahican-Mohawk Trail along the Mohawk Trail corridor. All hikes from the previous edition have been fully revised and updated with feedback from land managers. The appendix includes listings and contact information for the region's campgrounds, state forests and parks, ski areas, and outfitters.

Whether you're looking for a rugged mountain trek or an easy, family-friendly outing, you'll find a choice of trails to explore. A wealth of interesting natural features, such as the botanically rich limestone knolls of Bartholomew's Cobble, giant old-growth trees sheltered in the Ice Glen and along Dunbar Brook, rare old pitch pines capping Mount Everett's summit, and Berry Mountain's colorful wild azalea fields, await your discovery. There are also many artifacts of the region's long and rich history, including the well-preserved Becket Quarry and Copake Iron Works, remains of an elaborate nineteenth-century hilltop hotel at Kennedy Park, old mill sites along the Housatonic River, and former railroad and trolley lines that have been converted into popular recreational paths. And, of course, there are plenty of scenic views overlooking mountains, rolling hills, and unbroken forests.

In addition to enjoying the attractions, we encourage readers to treat these areas with respect, and to support the region's many land protection and trail organizations.

John Burk, October 2019

HOW TO USE THIS BOOK

With 50 hikes to choose from, you may wonder how to decide where to go. The locator map at the front of this book will help you narrow down the trips by location, and the at-a-glance trip planner that follows the table of contents will provide more information to guide you toward a decision. Once you settle on a destination and turn to a trip in this guide, you will find a series of icons that indicate whether there are fees, whether the hike is good for kids, whether dogs are allowed, and whether the trail is good for snowshoeing.

(For those hikes with the "good for kids" icon, the authors have used the designation conservatively, basing suggestions on hikes we feel are appropriate for children whose families hike together regularly. Some of the hikes designated for kids visit waterfalls or cliffy lookouts; these can be great rewards for kids' efforts to get there but can also be hazardous. Ultimately, to determine whether a hike is appropriate for your family, gauge your children's level of interest, motivation, and ability.)

Information on the basics follows: location, rating, distance, elevation gain, estimated time, and maps. The ratings are based on the authors' perception and are estimates of what the average hiker will experience. You may find them to be easier or more difficult than stated. The distance and estimated hiking time shown are for the whole trip, whether it's an out-and-back hike (with distance noted as "round trip") or a loop. The estimated time is also based on the authors' perception. Consider your own pace when planning a trip. The elevation gain is calculated from measurements and information from U.S. Geological Survey (USGS) topographic maps, landowner maps, and Google Earth. Information is included about the relevant USGS maps, as well as where you can find trail maps.

The boldface summary that follows the list of basics provides an overview of what you will see on your hike. The directions explain how to reach the trailhead by car and include Global Positioning System (GPS) coordinates for parking lots. In the trail description, you will find instructions on where to hike, the trails on which to hike, and where to turn. You will also learn about the natural and human history along your hike, as well as about flora, fauna, and any landmarks or objects you will encounter. The trail maps that accompany each trip will help guide you along your hike, but it would be wise to take an official trail map, which will show additional details of side trails and other information for the area, with you as well. Official maps are often—but not always—available for download or purchase online, at the trailhead, or at the visitor center. Each hike description also lists the best available topographic map of the area. We highly recommend that hikers purchase these maps.

Each trip ends with a "More Information" section that provides details about access times and fees, the property's rules and regulations, and contact information for the place where you will be hiking. The "Nearby" section offers suggestions for places to continue the experience when the hike is done and where to find the closest restaurants.

TRIP PLANNING AND SAFETY

Planning your trip well is the first step to having a safe hike. Some of the trips in this book ascend to higher elevations or summits where winds and lower temperatures necessitate extra clothing. Other hikes visit clifftops or waterfalls or have rocky stretches where you'll need to use extra caution with children and dogs. Learn about the terrain you will travel through so you can pack the right gear and prepare for the experience. Allow extra time in case you get lost. You will be more likely to have an enjoyable, safe hike if you plan ahead and take proper precautions. Before heading out for your hike, consider the following:

- Select a hike that everyone in your group is comfortable taking. Match the hike to the abilities of the least capable person in the group. If anyone is uncomfortable with the weather or is tired, turn around and complete the hike another day.

- Plan to be back at the trailhead before dark. Before beginning your hike, determine a turnaround time. Don't diverge from it, even if you have not reached your intended destination.

- Check the weather and assume it will be cooler and windier on the mountain than at the base. If you are planning a ridge or summit hike, start early so that you will be off the exposed area before the afternoon hours, when thunderstorms most often strike, especially in summer. Weather conditions can change quickly, and any changes are likely to be more severe the higher you are on the mountain.

- Bring a pack with the following items:

    ✓ Water: Two quarts per person is usually adequate, depending on the weather and the length of the trip. On extended day hikes, consider carrying some method of water purification so you can refill your water bottles en route.

    ✓ Food: Even if you are planning just an hour-long hike, bring some high-energy snacks such as nuts, dried fruit, or snack bars. Pack a lunch for longer trips.

    ✓ Map and compass: Be sure you know how to use them. A handheld GPS device may also be helpful but it is not always reliable.

    ✓ Headlamp or flashlight, with spare batteries.

✓ Extra clothing: Waterproof/breathable rain gear, synthetic fleece or wool jacket, hat, and mittens or gloves.

✓ Sunscreen.

✓ First-aid kit, including adhesive bandages, gauze, nonprescription pain-killers, moleskin, and any necessary prescription medication in case you are on the trail longer than expected.

✓ Pocketknife or multitool.

✓ Waterproof matches and a lighter.

✓ Trash bag.

✓ Toilet paper and double plastic bag to pack it out.

✓ Whistle.

✓ Insect repellent.

✓ Sunglasses.

✓ Cell phone: Be aware that cell phone service is unreliable in rural areas. If you are receiving a signal, use the phone only for emergencies to avoid disturbing the backcountry experience for other hikers.

✓ Trekking poles (optional).

✓ Binoculars (optional).

✓ Camera (optional).

• Wear appropriate footwear and clothing. Wool or synthetic hiking socks will keep your feet dry and help prevent blisters. Comfortable waterproof hiking boots or shoes will provide support and good traction. Avoid wearing cotton clothing, which absorbs sweat and rain and contributes to an unpleasant hiking experience. A synthetic or wool base layer (T-shirt, or underwear tops and bottoms) will wick moisture away from your body and keep you warm in wet or cold conditions. Synthetic zip-off pants that convert to shorts are popular. To help avoid bug bites, you may want to wear synthetic pants and a long-sleeve shirt.

• When you are ahead of the rest of your hiking group, wait at all trail junctions until the others catch up. This avoids confusion and keeps people from getting separated or lost.

• If you see downed wood that appears to be purposely covering a trail, it probably means the trail is closed due to overuse or hazardous conditions. If a trail is muddy, walk through the mud or on rocks, never on tree roots or plants. Water-resistant boots or shoes will keep your feet comfortable. Staying in the center of the trail will keep it from eroding into a wide hiking highway.

- Leave your itinerary and the time you expect to return with someone you trust. If you see a logbook at a trailhead, be sure to sign in when you arrive and sign out when you finish your hike.

- After you complete your hike, check for deer ticks, which carry the dangerous bacteria that causes Lyme disease.

- Poison ivy is always a threat when hiking. To identify the plant, look for clusters of three leaves that shine in the sun but are dull in the shade. If you do come into contact with poison ivy, wash the affected area with soap as soon as possible.

- Wear blaze-orange items in hunting season. Hunting seasons vary. Check with state game commissions: mass.gov/hunting-in-the-parks.

Check on trail or road closures with land managers prior to heading out in any season, particularly in winter. Certain forest roads may also be closed in the winter months; check with the relevant park agency to get updated information on gaining access to certain trailheads.

Winter hiking can be an enjoyable way to experience the Berkshires, but it requires extra gear and planning. All winter hikers need to bring more food and warm layers than they would in summer, and exercise more caution; fewer daylight hours, colder temperatures, and slower travel times magnify any problems that may occur, like getting lost or twisting an ankle. Near-freezing temperatures freeze hoses on hydration systems. Consider using insulated water bottles and packing them as close as possible to your body heat to keep your water from freezing during the day. Small-mouthed water bottles tend to freeze faster. Traction devices—such as Microspikes—can help you navigate icy stretches. Prudent winter travelers do not go out alone and make sure at least one person in the group has a sleeping bag and a small camp stove in case of emergency. When properly prepared, hikers can safely and comfortably experience the deep quiet and spectacular beauty of the Berkshires in winter.

When the weather warms up, the bugs start to come out. Mosquitoes can be a nuisance in some places, depending on seasonal and daily conditions. West Nile virus and eastern equine encephalitis (EEE) virus can be transmitted to humans by infected mosquitoes and cause rare but serious diseases. More prevalent, however, are deer ticks, which can transmit Lyme disease. Reduce your risk of being bitten by using insect repellent and wearing long sleeves and pants. Check yourself carefully for ticks when you finish your hike. A variety of options are available for dealing with bugs, ranging from sprays that include the active ingredient DEET, which can potentially cause skin or eye irritation, to more skin-friendly products. Head nets, which often can be purchased more cheaply than a can of repellent, are useful during especially buggy conditions.

LEAVE NO TRACE

The Appalachian Mountain Club (AMC) is a national educational partner of Leave No Trace, a nonprofit organization dedicated to promoting and inspiring responsible outdoor recreation through education, research, and partnerships.  The Leave No Trace program seeks to develop wildland ethics—ways in which people think and act in the outdoors to minimize their impact on the areas they visit and to protect our natural resources for future enjoyment. Leave No Trace unites four federal land management agencies—U.S. Forest Service, National Park Service, Bureau of Land Management, and U.S. Fish and Wildlife Service—with manufacturers, outdoor retailers, user groups, educators, organizations such as AMC, and individuals.

The Leave No Trace ethic is guided by the following seven principles:

1. **Plan Ahead and Prepare.** Know the terrain and any regulations applicable to the area you're planning to visit, and be prepared for extreme weather or other emergencies. This will enhance your enjoyment and ensure that you've chosen an appropriate destination. Small groups have less impact on resources and on the experiences of other backcountry visitors.

2. **Travel and Camp on Durable Surfaces.** Travel and camp on established trails and campsites, rock, gravel, dry grasses, or snow. Good campsites are found, not made. Camp at least 200 feet from lakes and streams, and focus activities on areas where vegetation is absent. In pristine areas, disperse use to prevent the creation of campsites and trails.

3. **Dispose of Waste Properly.** Pack it in, pack it out. Inspect your camp for trash or food scraps. Deposit solid human waste in cat holes dug 6 to 8 inches deep, at least 200 feet from water, camps, and trails. Pack out toilet paper and hygiene products. To wash yourself or your dishes, carry water 200 feet from streams or lakes and use small amounts of biodegradable soap. Scatter strained dishwater.

4. **Leave What You Find.** Cultural or historical artifacts, as well as natural objects such as plants and rocks, should be left as found.

5. **Minimize Campfire Impacts.** Cook on a stove. Use established fire rings, fire pans, or mound fires. If you build a campfire, keep it small and use dead sticks found on the ground.

6. **Respect Wildlife.** Observe wildlife from a distance. Feeding animals alters their natural behavior. Protect wildlife from your food by storing rations and trash securely.

7. **Be Considerate of Other Visitors.** Be courteous, respect the quality of other visitors' backcountry experience, and let nature's sounds prevail.

AMC is a national provider of the Leave No Trace Master Educator course. AMC offers this five-day course, designed especially for outdoor professionals and land managers, as well as the shorter two-day Leave No Trace Trainer course, at locations throughout the Northeast.

For Leave No Trace information and materials, contact the Leave No Trace Center for Outdoor Ethics, P.O. Box 997, Boulder, CO 80306; 800-332-4100 or 302-442-8222; lnt.org. For a schedule of AMC Leave No Trace courses, see outdoors.org/education/lnt.

SECTION 1
NORTHERN
BERKSHIRES

The northern Berkshires comprise some of the highest and most remote lands in Berkshire County. The area boasts the only true boreal forest in Massachusetts, the only summits above 3,000 feet elevation, craggy out-croppings yielding splendid vistas, and sphag-num-filled bogs. Eighteen of the excursions in this guide are in this region. Mount Greylock State Reser-vation is the centerpiece and includes a sizable section of the Appalachian Trail as well as miles of blue-blazed side routes. This area beckons hikers with many fine trails that range in difficulty from easy to strenuous. The reservation is home to several interesting natural and historical features, including waterfalls, old for-ests, Stony Ledge, and the Hopper, a dramatic cirque, or ravine, carved by glaciers.

Hikes in this northern section, including Hopkins Memorial Forest and Taconic Crest Trail (Trip 2), run along the spine of the Taconic Range. Berlin Mountain (Trip 4) borders New York. Trail-rich Greylock Range (Trips 6, 7, 8, 9, 15, 16, and 18) boasts Massachusetts's loftiest peak. The Hoosac Range, includ-ing Hoosac Range Trail to Spruce Hill (Trip 11) and Spruce Hill via Busby Trail (Trip 12), is east of the marble valley. The northernmost hikes, including Pine Cobble and East Mountain (Trip 3) and Clarksburg State Park (Trip 10), are an extension of Vermont's Green Mountains. This area contains the longest, most arduous hikes but also a moderate walk to the Cheshire Cobbles and Gore Pond (Trip 18) and a stroll through bucolic Field Farm (Trip 5).

1

MOUNTAIN MEADOW PRESERVE

Straddling two states, this string of small loop trails begins with one of the most evocative panoramic views in the Berkshires. The Greylock and Taconic ranges are stunning backdrops to a meadow that in summer is filled with colorful wildflowers and butterflies. A few short, steep climbs and the ruins of former habitations add interest.

DIRECTIONS

From the intersection of US 7 and MA 2 in Williamstown, follow US 7 north for 1.7 miles, crossing the Hoosic River and Broad Brook along the way. Turn right onto gravel Mason Street and follow it 0.1 mile to where it terminates at the preserve entrance and parking area. *GPS coordinates*: 42° 44.314′ N, 73° 12.452′ W.

TRAIL DESCRIPTION

A kiosk with a large trail map stands just beyond the parking area; paper copies of maps may also be available here. Trail intersections are signed. Main trails are blazed yellow; other trails are blazed blue. Follow mowed Niles Trail across a field of goldenrod, yellow hawkweed, and robin plantain, bordered by autumn olive, apple trees, honeysuckle, and dogwood. Autumn olive, now considered an invasive exotic, was planted to control erosion. Its yellowish blossoms fill the air with a sweet perfume in late spring. The trail rises into a wooded strip and then enters another small field. Quaking aspens and cottonwoods line the left perimeter. As the trail steepens, young white ashes with compound leaves and white pines appear.

Turn right at the trail split to follow Niles Trail, still an obvious mowed path, along the margin of a large meadow, the preserve's namesake. At this low end of the hillside

LOCATION
Williamstown, MA;
Pownal, VT

RATING
Moderate

DISTANCE
4 miles round trip

ELEVATION GAIN
690 feet

ESTIMATED TIME
2.5 hours

MAPS
USGS Williamstown,
USGS Berlin; The Trustees
of Reservations map:
thetrustees.org/assets/
documents/places-to-visit/
trailmaps/Mountain-Meadow
-Preserve-Trail-Map.pdf

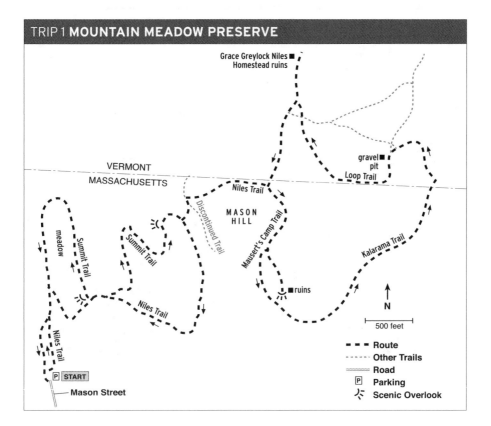

Grace Greylock Niles ■
Homestead ruins

gravel ■
pit
Loop Trail

VERMONT
MASSACHUSETTS

Niles Trail

MASON
HILL

Discontinued Trail

Summit Trail

Summit Trail

meadow

Mauser's Camp Trail

Kalarama Trail

■ ruins

N

500 feet

Niles Trail

Niles Trail

P START

Mason Street

- - - Route
----- Other Trails
=== Road
P Parking
Scenic Overlook

meadow, various field flowers add dashes of color from late spring to fall. This 20-acre grassland is alive with a bountiful array of butterflies in summer. The wood satyr, a small, brown butterfly with a row of black bull's-eye spots, is abundant in late spring. The path soon bears left and climbs the modest slope. The panoramic vista of the Greylock Range to the right is without a doubt the highlight of this hike. Glance over your shoulder and be treated to a view of the Taconic Range.

Turn right to enter the forest on yellow-blazed Niles Trail and cross a short boardwalk over a trickling flow. At the signed trail junction at 0.4 mile, turn left off of Niles Trail onto Summit Trail. White pine, red maple, witch hazel, and striped maple predominate. Oaks are present too. Reach a low stone wall of water-tumbled quartzite and follow along it, keeping it to your left. The narrow trail becomes steeper and passes a spreading white oak with three trunks. (White oak leaves have rounded lobes, unlike the bristle-tipped lobes of red and black oaks. White oak acorns are sweet and mature in the fall of their first year, but red and black oaks require two years to mature.) After passing the three-trunked oak, the trail climbs the slope on switchbacks. The last 200 yards are at quite an acute angle leading to the 1,120-foot summit at

The Taconic Range along the Massachusetts–New York border forms a backdrop to the 20-acre meadow encircled by the footpath.

0.7 mile. This U-shaped hill is the result of glacial deposition. Wild geraniums bloom pink in late spring along the ridgeline path. Only a limited view is possible due to encroaching trees. An interesting small tree here is a multitrunked hop hornbeam, with thin, light-brown, shredding bark. Its wood is extremely hard and durable.

Bear right and descend to an intersection on the left. Turn left and descend past low maple-leaf viburnum shrubs under a canopy of oaks and red maples. At a junction with a woods road, bear left onto the roadway to continue on Niles Trail, then almost immediately right at the preserve's boundary, in the direction of the preserve's Vermont parking area. Mature red pines, characterized by scaly pinkish bark, were probably planted along the road, which skirts Mason Hill, during the Great Depression. Enjoy the wide path that parallels the Vermont state line for a brief time. When you reach a green metal gate along the preserve boundary, continue straight ahead to another green metal gate. Walk around it to reach a T intersection with another woods road. Turn right onto yellow-blazed Mausert's Camp Trail.

During damp conditions in late spring and summer, be alert for fiery-orange-red efts traversing the road. The eft, the terrestrial stage of the aquatic red-spotted newt, spends between two and seven years roaming woodlands before returning to water as a breeding adult. The red skin warns potential predators that it is poisonous when eaten. Young regenerating trees and decaying stumps speak of past logging here. Watch for a patch of wild geraniums on the left in late spring.

Bear left at the intersection with Kalarama Trail, continuing to follow the yellow blazes; you'll return here shortly. Ahead stand the remains of Mausert's Camp, a rustic family retreat that was destroyed by fire in the 1970s. All that is left are two stone chimneys at either end of a clearing. Indigo buntings nest along the edges of the clearing.

Retrace your steps to the intersection and turn left on Kalarama Trail. Descend on this old roadway cut into the side slope past a gravel borrow pit. Black birches and oaks with lowbush blueberries below dot the rising slope. A couple of beech trees on the right show faint black scars from having been climbed by bears that relish the nuts. Cross a pile of quartzite cobbles (cobble is a New England word for "hill") gathered during field clearing, and marvel at the huge twin-trunked oak on the right that exhibits the scars of a wire fence. Watch out for a bit of poison ivy that borders the path before it bisects a handsome patch of spinulose wood fern, and then stroll easily downhill.

Look for a cluster of delicate maidenhair fern on the left shortly after the trail climbs again. Before long, reach a junction on the right with a narrow path. Leave the road and continue on Kalarama Trail. A couple of dogwood trees at this intersection sport large, white, four-petaled blossoms in spring, but young white birches are generally more noticeable near the trail. Descend into a shallow hemlock ravine cut by a modest brook. Reach a woods road and bear left to remain on Kalarama Trail, and soon turn right to cross the brook. After the crossing, a yellow marker on the right indicates the boundary of Williamstown conservation land. A massive white pine towers behind it.

Bear left and climb past nearly 5-foot-tall bracken fern to an intersection with another woods road at the end of Kalarama Trail. You are now in Vermont. Bear left and follow the old road that is cut into the slope. Arrive at the clearing and bear left through an old gravel pit, where rock was removed for road and railroad bed construction in the 1950s and '60s. White pines and quaking aspens, species that thrive in human-disturbed areas, colonized the edge of the pit, which is now carpeted by grass. Reenter the woodland of oaks and a variety of birches on a gravelly track. This was once a multilayered forest dominated by white pines and American chestnuts. Pass through another small old gravel pit by a glacial boulder on the left, along Loop Trail, before emerging into a meadow where boxes provide nesting spaces for bluebirds. Follow the mowed path across it.

At a T intersection with Niles Trail, turn right for a brief walk to the old concrete foundation of the Grace Greylock Niles Homestead on the left at 2.3 miles, then retrace your steps to the intersection. Continue straight ahead this time and arrive back at the intersection with the trail on the left leading to Mausert's

Camp. Turn right on Niles Trail to retrace your steps back to Massachusetts along the base of Mason Hill, and turn right again to climb back to the intersection just below the summit. But rather than return to the summit, turn left to continue on Niles Trail, descending moderately along the ridgeline under a canopy of oaks. White pines soon become numerous above a sapling layer of maples, beeches, and birches. In summer, listen for the sweet, languid trill of pine warblers high in the pine boughs.

Continue walking steadily downhill, steeply at times, on Niles Trail, and bear right as the trail levels out in closely spaced pine groves. Pass the path on the right leading to the summit, and when you reach the large meadow (1.0 mile from the Niles homestead site), turn right to explore the north end of the field. Here, you have a second chance to admire the stunning views and numerous butterflies, and you might see tawny-coated white-tailed deer in summer. A rusty hay rack sits idly along the path. Follow the mowed treadway around the field's perimeter. When you reach the trail intersection, bear right to return to your vehicle.

DID YOU KNOW?

Botanist and author Grace Greylock Niles, a native of Pownal, wrote *Bog-Trotting for Orchids* (1904) and *The Hoosac Valley: Its Legends and Its History* (1912). She died in 1943 at age 78.

MORE INFORMATION

Open sunrise to sunset, year-round. Free access; membership in and donations to The Trustees of Reservations are welcomed. Dogs are permitted but must be on leash at all times. Mountain biking, horseback riding, motorized vehicles, hunting, and firearms are not permitted. The Trustees of Reservations, Berkshires Regional Office, 1 Sergeant Street, Stockbridge, MA 01262 (413-298-3239; thetrustees.org/places-to-visit/berkshires/mountain-meadow.html).

NEARBY

Boat access to the nearby Hoosic River is available at Lauren's Launch in Williamstown, about 3.1 miles away from Mountain Meadow Preserve. Paddlers can travel 4.8 miles north (downstream) to Clayton Park in Pownal. Some tricky rips lie along the route (hoorwa.org/recreation/paddling-the-hoosic). From the junction of US 7 and MA 2 at the Williamstown rotary (traffic circle), follow US 7 for 1.2 miles to an unnamed road on the left at a sign for Hoosic River access. Follow the unnamed road for 0.2 mile, across railroad tracks, to a sign for Lauren's Launch. Park in the pullout opposite the entrance to the transfer station.

2

HOPKINS MEMORIAL FOREST AND TACONIC CREST TRAIL

This excursion features monumental hardwood trees, babbling brooks, thrilling vistas, and a geologic curiosity: the Snow Hole, a 50-foot chasm where snow and ice may linger throughout the year.

LOCATION
Williamstown, MA;
Petersburg, NY; Pownal, VT

RATING
Strenuous

DISTANCE
10.4 miles round trip

ELEVATION GAIN
1,650 feet

ESTIMATED TIME
5.5 hours

MAPS
AMC Massachusetts Trail Map 1: B1; USGS Williamstown, USGS Berlin, NY; Hopkins Memorial Forest map: hmf.williams.edu/public/trail-map/?dts=1

DIRECTIONS

From the intersection of US 7 and MA 2 at the rotary in Williamstown, follow US 7 north 0.4 miles to Bulkley Street on the left. Drive down Bulkley Street for 0.75 mile to gravel Northwest Hill Road. Turn right and drive for 0.1 mile, bearing left onto the gravel drive to enter Hopkins Memorial Forest (at the carved wooden sign). Park in the small gravel lot on the left, which has room for eight vehicles. *GPS coordinates*: 42° 43.408′ N, 73° 13.402′ W.

TRAIL DESCRIPTION

Amble up the gravel drive between apple trees and a small meadow, where tree swallows and bluebirds nest in boxes that have been erected for them. The Rosenburg Visitor Center (once a carriage house) serves as forest headquarters. Excellent trail maps are available at the kiosk here, which also features a posted trail map and historical information. Bear right past Buxton Garden onto a gravel carriage road. The relocated former Moon Farm barn stands on the left.

Tread beneath a canopy of sugar maple, black locust, and white ash, passing the Williams Outing Club cabin. A bit beyond this stands a maple sugar processing shed. An adjacent field hosts the forest's main weather station. (*Note*: Numerous research projects are under way on the property's 2,600 acres; visitors are asked to stay on trails and not interfere with research sites.) Cross the field and continue above Ford Glen Brook, which soon reveals itself 60 feet below in the ravine to your right. The forest changes

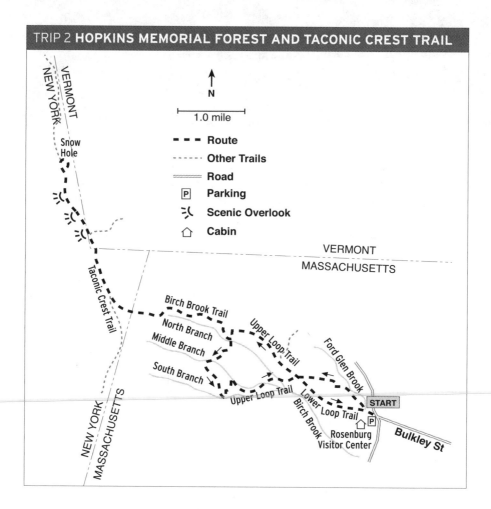

after the road bears left, with the addition of black birch, beech, oak, and hop hornbeam—easy to identify by its flaky, tan bark.

As you bear right, a canopy walkway may be partially visible. The walkway (off-limits to visitors, unfortunately) enables scientists to reach a world usually hidden from human eyes. Soon, gigantic oaks dating from the 1860s tower above; their first branches start 40 feet up. As you continue, beeches, yellow birches, and black birches increase in an obviously younger forest. Starflower and Canada mayflower bloom here in spring, while lowbush blueberry, prince's pine, and shining and cedar club mosses spread largely by runners in the acidic soil. In June, watch for pink lady's slipper orchids just before reaching a four-way intersection with Upper Loop Trail at a stone bench, at 0.7 mile.

Turn right on the north fork of Upper Loop Trail. On your way to Birch Brook, ignore several side paths. As the trail climbs gently, a forest of red maple changes to one dominated by oak. Tiny lowbush blueberry shrubs thrive beneath

Immediately upon entering the cool, damp fissure known as the Snow Hole, you'll feel a radical drop in temperature, especially during summer.

the trees. A significant number of these oaks have more than one trunk—a sure sign that these woods were logged. (*Note*: The yellow paint marks on the trees here are not blazes; these demarcate forest study plots, which you should avoid.) At the North Branch of Birch Brook, bear right onto signed and blue-blazed Birch Brook Trail. From here, walk 1.5 miles up to meet Taconic Crest Trail.

Now the real hiking begins. Follow Birch Brook Trail past the end of a fallen stone wall indicating former pasturing. Then bear right and pass knee- to waist-high blueberry and huckleberry bushes. The grade of this old woods road increases under mixed northern hardwoods and oaks. On a more moderate slope, notice the dying paper birches—pioneering trees that sprouted after logging and were later shaded out by species whose seeds required less sunlight to germinate. About three-quarters of the way to the ridge (1.1 miles from the junction with Upper Loop Trail), you'll cross into New York.

Log steps help you ascend the eastern slope past glades of yellow-green ferns—most notably hay-scented fern, also called boulder fern, which characteristically forms dense stands. Hopkins Forest researchers are trying to determine whether it secretes a substance that inhibits the growth of competing species. This path along the ferns ends at obviously well-trodden and undulating Taconic Crest Trail, which is blazed by a white diamond in a blue square for 35 miles along the spine of the Taconic Range. The Snow Hole is 1.6 miles north. Up here, where soils are shallow, the forest is reduced in height but boasts a thick sapling layer, consisting mostly of American beech, which is a prolific sprouter.

Turn right and enter an area where much of the small, woody vegetation has been cut, creating an early successional habitat for species not able to live in dense woodland. At a three-way intersection in a waist-high fern glade, continue straight. Shortly after the trail leaves Hopkins Memorial Forest property and passes onto New York State Forest land, you arrive at the first of three shrubby clearings where scenic vistas abound. Gaze out on rolling hills running toward the western horizon. Close at hand, shiny-leafed bilberry shrubs thrive in the sunny gap, as do a few red spruces. Bilberries and less common huckleberries fill the second clearing. Enjoy fine views from the third clearing, and then reenter the woods. Many beech trees have black bark lesions, symptoms of beech bark disease. Continue past these trees, and less than ten minutes after leaving the third clearing, reach the first of two signed and red-blazed side trails on the right. These are the ends of a short loop leading to a geologic and meteorologic wonder—the Snow Hole.

Continue to the second red-blazed path; turn right past patches of shining club moss, and walk downhill about 250 feet to the narrow entrance on the right. Old graffiti—some dating to 1865—is carved into the relatively soft phyllite bedrock near the entrance. As you descend into the crevice to explore it from within, watch your footing, as the rock may be slick. Immediately you'll feel a radical drop in temperature, especially during the summer months. Mosses, wood sorrels, and ferns soften the tilted, wafer-thin layers of phyllite, while yellow birches clutch the rim. It feels a bit as though you're walking into a giant cave-like terrarium. Even on the hottest days, you may find snow and ice here.

When ready to continue the hike, walk back the way you came in or follow the short loop; both lead back to Taconic Crest Trail. Be sure to turn left when you rejoin the main trail, and watch for easy-to-miss Birch Brook Trail on the left to retrace your steps downhill to the junction with Upper Loop Trail. Turn right to cross a wooden bridge over the brook. This section of woodland contains all four common birch species—white, gray, black, and yellow, all separable by unique bark true to their names. Soon reach the Middle Branch of Birch Brook, lumpy with mossy stones, and cross it via another wooden span. Descend easily on a wide path.

Bear left in an arc to drop down close to the South Branch of Birch Brook. Shade-casting hemlocks—some sizable—populate the slope. In summer, shade-tolerant woodland butterflies, such as the northern pearly eye, may make an appearance, although they can be difficult to see when they alight because their coloring blends in with forest vegetation. This eye-spotted species rarely visits flowers, preferring to sip tree sap and other fluids. Soon meet the Middle Branch again, and cross a wooden bridge. The old roadway continues along Birch Brook under oaks, beeches, birches, and maples.

Gaze into the depths of clear pools to potentially spot native brook trout. A significant number of monumental oaks dominate this woodland—a 3.5-foot-diameter specimen stands on the right. Cross over the North Branch on a bridge built to accommodate vehicles, and climb easily back to the four-way intersection with the stone bench. After 1.7 miles on Upper Loop Trail, turn right at a marked junction to walk back on the south side of Lower Loop Trail along the dividing line between two watersheds—Ford Glen Brook and Birch Brook.

Pass through more fern glades, where an interpretive panel describes the possible chemical warfare waged by hay-scented fern against its competitors. Another informs readers that club mosses are more common in formerly pastured earth. All four local species—prince's pine, shining club moss, cedar club moss, and staghorn club moss—can be seen on this hike. Although capable of reproducing via spores, slow-growing club mosses rely mostly on cloning themselves.

Stride past a dark stand of Norway spruces planted by the U.S. Forest Service, which operated the forest from 1935 to 1968. Pass an ancient oak with rotting heartwood as you amble downhill. Exotic plants along the margins presage your return to the Rosenburg Visitor Center.

DID YOU KNOW?

The Taconic Mountains, a narrow, 150-mile-long range, and one of North America's oldest at 440 million years, runs from Brandon, Vermont, to the Hudson Highlands of New York. Taconic Crest Trail follows this ridgeline for 35 miles from Hancock, Massachusetts, to Petersburg, New York. Many historians believe *Taconic* is a derivation of an American Indian word meaning "in the trees."

MORE INFORMATION

Open dawn to dusk, year-round. Access is free. Public restrooms and drinking water are available at the Rosenburg Visitor Center, open 7 A.M. to 6 P.M. All pets must be leashed. Hunting is prohibited, except deer hunting by special permit in the Massachusetts portion of the property. Skiing is allowed. All vehicles, including mountain bikes, are prohibited. Collecting fauna and flora is prohibited; do not disturb research sites. Visit hmf.williams.edu for more information.

NEARBY

The fine Williams College Museum of Art, not as well known as the larger Clark Art Institute, is on the college campus and houses 13,000 objects that span the history of art. It is a teaching museum, open to the public, free of charge (hours: 10 A.M. to 5 P.M. Friday through Tuesday; 10 A.M. to 8 P.M. Thursdays; closed Wednesdays and major holidays). The museum is at 15 Lawrence Hall Drive, Suite 2, Williamstown, MA 01267 (413-597-2429; wcma.williams.edu).

3

PINE COBBLE AND EAST MOUNTAIN

A partial loop hike up East Mountain, the southern terminus of the Green Mountains, on sunny slopes covered with oaks and sheep laurel, leads to a summit studded with quartzite and pitch pines, offering some of the most stunning views in the region.

DIRECTIONS

From the Williamstown rotary (at the junction of MA 2 and US 7), follow MA 2 east for 0.6 mile to Cole Avenue on the left. Follow Cole Avenue for 0.75 mile (crossing the Hoosic River en route) and turn right onto North Hoosac Road. Drive for 0.4 mile to Pine Cobble Road on the left, and follow Pine Cobble Road for 0.1 mile to a gravel parking area on the left (space for six or seven vehicles). *GPS coordinates*: 42° 42.963′ N, 73° 11.116′ W.

TRAIL DESCRIPTION

From the parking area, cross Pine Cobble Road diagonally, walking uphill for about 100 feet to the signed trailhead on the right. The path initially parallels the road and passes a wooden sign on the left erected by the Williams Outing Club. The sign indicates that this blue-blazed trail leads 1.6 miles to Pine Cobble summit, 2.1 miles to the Appalachian Trail (AT) junction, and 3.4 miles to the Vermont border. Turn left at this sign to enter an oak woodland. White and red oak predominate, but black cherry, red maple, American beech, black birch, ironwood, tulip tree, and hop hornbeam add variety. Distinguish white oak by its flaky, light-gray bark. Rounded quartzite boulders litter the trail.

Striped maple appears as the trail gently climbs, along with chestnut oak, smooth-skinned black birch, and multitrunked witch hazel. The trail steepens, and lowbush

LOCATION
Williamstown and Clarksburg, MA

RATING
Moderate

DISTANCE
4.8 miles round trip

ELEVATION GAIN
1,340 feet

ESTIMATED TIME
3 hours

MAPS
AMC Massachusetts Trail Map 1: B3; USGS Williamstown; Williamstown Rural Lands Foundation map: wrlf.org/the-pine-cobble-trail

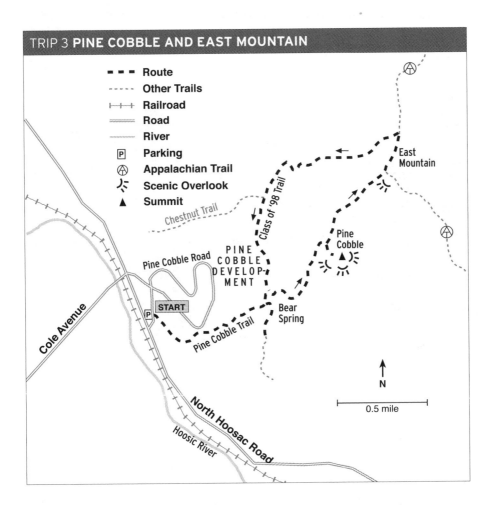

Legend:
- - - Route
----- Other Trails
+-+-+ Railroad
═════ Road
───── River
P Parking
Ⓐ Appalachian Trail
Ⲑⲓ Scenic Overlook
▲ Summit

Chestnut Trail

Class of '98 Trail

East Mountain

PINE
COBBLE
DEVELOP-
MENT

Pine Cobble Road

Pine
Cobble

START

Bear
Spring

Pine Cobble Trail

Cole Avenue

North Hoosac Road

Hoosic River

N

0.5 mile

blueberry thrives in the acidic soil under the tannin-rich oak. This section of the route is thought to be the ancient shoreline of Lake Bascom, a glacial lake that once extended along the Hoosic River Valley from southern Vermont to Pittsfield. To the north, its waters were once 500 feet deep. Sheep laurel, another indicator of acidic soil, first shows up near here and grows about 2 feet high, becoming abundant later. It is said to be poisonous to livestock. After another 0.25 mile, near a gray boulder, watch for an unmarked side path on the right that leads about 300 feet toward a dark-green wall of eastern hemlocks and Bear Spring.

Bear Spring, at the base of a resistant quartzite cliff, is the only surface water on this south-facing slope. The cooler microclimate here fosters sapling yellow birch and striped maple, both northern hardwood species. Ferns are more noticeable too, including common polypody on quartzite boulders. Rejoin the main trail, continue uphill past luxuriant growths of shiny-leafed wintergreen,

Nestled in the Hoosic River valley to the east, North Adams is visible from the quartzite summit of Pine Cobble.

and soon reach a signpost at the 0.8-mile mark, where the Class of '98 Trail heads left. You'll return by this route, but for now continue straight. The nutrient-poor soils here host a variety of heath family species, including blueberry, huckleberry, and the Massachusetts state flower: trailing arbutus, or mayflower. Its leaves have a sandy texture, and its delicate spring flowers are pale pink.

As you gain elevation, the oaks and other hardwoods decrease in height while the shrub layer thickens. Chestnut oaks, with wavy-margined leaves and deeply furrowed trunks, are now far more prevalent. The trail steepens again as you reach a sign, surrounded by a mat of moss, proclaiming, "Welcome to Pine Cobble, a unique natural area owned by the Williams Rural Lands Foundation and maintained for hiking and enjoyment of nature." As you pass through a small boulder field of gray, angular hunks of quartzite, notice low sheep laurel shrubs.

Sassafras trees, which do well in sandy soils, become common. Their leaves have one, two, or three lobes and emit a spicy aroma when crushed. Continue the steady climb amid white birches, young red maples, and chestnut oaks. Marvel at the wooden bowl formed by a triple-stemmed oak—the result of cutting long ago—that collects and holds rainwater.

After a rocky climb, look for a signpost indicating that Pine Cobble summit is to the right, and the AT and Class of '98 Trail are to the left. Follow the side path right to excellent vista points at the Pine Cobble summit (elevation 1,893 feet). The Williams College campus is visible from a perch atop rounded quartzite cobbles on the right of the summit. Beyond the campus lies the spine of the northern Taconics, with Berlin Mountain (Trip 4) as its most prominent feature. A bit farther, on the other side of the ridge, are views to the east of the nestled town of North Adams. Roughly 6 miles due south is the summit of Mount Greylock, complete with the Massachusetts Veterans War Memorial Tower.

The smooth, gray stone is Cheshire quartzite. Six hundred million years ago, it was beach sand. The pure silica of this rock type was once the raw ingredient in Sandwich glass. Some broken rock faces show a rusty tinge of iron.

When ready, return to the main trail and turn right to continue another 0.5 mile to the AT junction. After mostly level walking through oak, gray birch, red maple, witch hazel, lowbush blueberry, sheep laurel, and wintergreen, climb moderately over schist, a metamorphic rock that glistens due to its high mica content. Watch for a metal anchor point in the rock that once helped support a fire tower. The route levels out through a shrubby growth of birches and leaves the forest for an open, rocky promontory. The trail is marked with rock cairns and blue blazes on stones.

The views improve as you climb higher (especially after leaf fall). This boulder field is the perfect place to enjoy the Taconic panorama. The surrounding pitch pines are mostly 12 feet tall. Taller, longer-needled white pines are also present, and a few red spruces stand among the light-gray quartzite slabs. Follow the rock-strewn treadway to its junction with the AT at 2.1 miles (elevation 2,050 feet), marked by a signpost on the summit of East Mountain. A mountain azalea shrub stands to the left. Turn left onto the white-blazed AT and continue to the intersection with Class of '98 Trail, marked with blue blazes. Turn left and follow Class of '98 Trail downhill through deciduous woodland. Dense understory and stumps indicate fairly recent logging. A Caution sign marks a tricky descent over talus, but after a set of stone steps there are fewer rocks. Now parallel angular quartzite boulders—some capped by ferns—until you reach the three-way junction with Chestnut Trail. Turn left to remain on Class of '98 Trail. Before long, a dramatic 40-foot cliff catches your eye. Be sure to follow the blue blazes past side trails until you reach Pine Cobble Trail. Turn right to return to your vehicle.

DID YOU KNOW?

Glacial Lake Bascom—which covered the Hoosic River valley from present-day Cheshire, Massachusetts, to the Vermont border for 800 years—and Bascom Lodge on Mount Greylock are both named for John Bascom (1827–1911). The Williams College alumnus and faculty member was one of the first Greylock Reservation commissioners, appointed in 1898.

MORE INFORMATION

Open daily, year-round; no fee. The site has no restroom facilities. Pine Cobble Trail traverses lands owned by Williams College, Williamstown Rural Lands Foundation, 671 Cold Spring Road, Williamstown, MA 01267 (413-458-2494; wrlf.org/pine-cobble); the Massachusetts Department of Conservation and Recreation (West Regional Office, 740 South Street, Pittsfield, MA 01202, 413-442-8928); and private owners. The trail is maintained by members of the Williams Outing Club, 39 Chapin Hall Drive, Williamstown, MA 01267 (413-597-2317; woc.williams.edu) and the Williamstown Rural Lands Foundation.

NEARBY

The highly acclaimed Sterling and Francine Clark Art Institute is set on a 140-acre campus of expansive lawns, meadows, and walking trails. The museum is best known for its extraordinary collection of French impressionist paintings. Open Tuesday through Saturday (daily in July and August), 10 A.M. to 5 P.M. Closed Mondays and major holidays. The walking trails are open daily year-round. A museum admission fee is charged from June through September. The Clark Art Institute is at 225 South Street, Williamstown, MA 01267 (413-458-2303; clarkart.edu).

CAT O' TALL TALES

At the peril of leaping, figuratively at least, from the tangible to the mysterious, consider the controversy surrounding the presence, real or imagined, of mountain lions in the Berkshires. Sighting reports surface regularly, though hard proof—a body or bona fide photograph—is still lacking. But the possibility exists that these big cats, long absent from this region, once again roam here. Although not having the good fortune to see one myself, I know folks who are convinced they have done so. Some reports may be hoaxes, and others are doubtless simple cases of mistaken identity. Yet as someone who has observed more than a few bobcats, I can't imagine anybody mistaking one for a mountain lion.

A colleague of mine who takes a no-nonsense, scientific approach to nature reported spotting a mountain lion crossing a road in front of him as he rounded a corner on his bicycle while coasting down a hill at Quabbin Reservoir, just 40 miles east of the Berkshires. And scat found in 1997 at a predator-beaver kill at the reservoir tested positive for mountain lion DNA.

Mountain lion, cougar, puma, panther, or catamount—many terms describe this fabled creature. Local place names (such as the Catamount Ski Area) hark back to a time when these large felines did indeed inhabit western Massachusetts. The last one shot in the wild in the commonwealth (in Hampshire County) was way back in 1858, when the amount of forested landscape was significantly less than it is today. The mounted body of that mountain lion now resides at Mass Audubon's Arcadia Wildlife Sanctuary in Easthampton.

Scanning published distribution maps reveals the nearest population of this predator to be no closer than the Florida Everglades, although verified reports of sightings do exist from elsewhere in the eastern states. For example, a young male mountain lion was killed on a Connecticut highway in 2011. (DNA detective work traced the cat's origin all the way to South Dakota's Black Hills!)

If indeed a wild population exists—and that is yet unproven—the question of origin remains. Some claim that escaped pets are the genesis of local cougar sightings. That may indeed be correct, but could there be more to it? The catamount's chief prey are deer. Southern New England's large and thriving deer population would provide ample sustenance to support at least a few mountain lions. And black bear and moose have reclaimed much of their former range in southern New England.

4

BERLIN MOUNTAIN

A challenging loop route heads straight up the east face of the Taconic Range to its highest peak in Massachusetts. Views of Mount Greylock from Berlin Mountain's flat summit are particularly pleasing, and an enchanting little waterfall adds enjoyment at the end of the hike.

DIRECTIONS

From the intersection of MA 2 and US 7 in Williamstown, take MA 2 west for 0.3 mile to Torrey Woods Road on the left. Follow Torrey Woods Road (which becomes Berlin Mountain Road where the pavement ends after approximately 0.5 mile) for 2.1 miles to a small gravel parking area on the left (space for three or four vehicles). *GPS coordinates*: 42° 42.153′ N, 73° 16.231′ W.

TRAIL DESCRIPTION

Signs at the parking area read "Class of '33 Trail" (Williams Outing Club students cut the trail that year) and "WRLF Loop Trail." Walk back down the gravel road that you just drove on for approximately 300 feet and look for the signed trailhead on a white birch tree to the right. Enter a forest of mostly young white and yellow birches, red spruces, and red and striped maples; follow blue blazes as you descend easily. Oaks and American beeches soon appear.

As the downhill walking becomes steeper, you'll hear Haley Brook, a clear, fast-flowing stream that, according to an interpretive sign, is home to native brook trout and the rare Appalachian brook crayfish.

After crossing the brook, advance uphill under northern hardwoods and soon arrive at a signed intersection. Turn left to remain on blue-blazed Class of '33 Trail (the Williamstown Rural Lands Foundation [WRLF] Loop Trail

LOCATION
Williamstown, MA; Berlin, NY

RATING
Strenuous

DISTANCE
4.7-mile loop

ELEVATION GAIN
1,545 feet

ESTIMATED TIME
2.5–3.5 hours

MAPS
AMC Massachusetts Trail Map 1: C1; USGS Berlin, USGS Williamstown

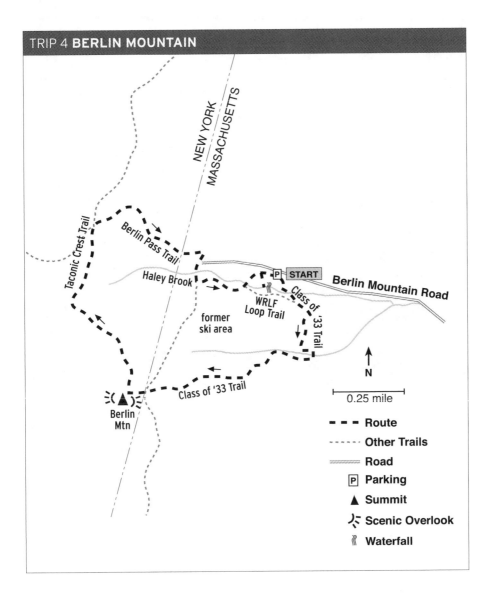

turns right). The abundance of young trees indicates fairly recent harvesting, and the remnants of former logging roads are still visible. The grade, initially level, soon increases and follows a trench-like former skid road with scattered hemlocks and spruces. Some of the hemlocks are considerably older than the hardwoods—beech, birch, and oak. Most of the beeches suffer from the beech bark disease that is prevalent throughout the region.

The path bears left away from the road, winds down rather abruptly, and then levels out among mature yellow birches and hemlocks. Pass the former Williams Outing Club Berlin Cabin site on the left (there were plans to rebuild the campsite

Hikers pass through a lush hay-scented fern glade just below the flat summit of Berlin Mountain.

in 2020). An intertwined hemlock and yellow birch provide a curiosity on the right. Turn sharply right and follow the contour under hemlocks for a short, sloping descent to a nameless brook that has exposed phyllite bedrock. Use caution when crossing on the slick, wet stones, and give the stinging nettles a wide berth.

This section of the trail starts on an old road. The next mile or so represents one of the most challenging ascents of any hike covered in this guide. A nearly relentless series of steep climbs is moderated only by an occasional less exhausting grade, permitting you to catch your breath. When you stop, note that the slope up to your left has more mature timber than that below you to the right. (Many neotropical migrant birds feel at home on this eastern face of the Taconics, including the black-and-yellow Canada warbler, black-throated green warbler, ovenbird, and rose-breasted grosbeak.)

At one point, pass a fallen hemlock. Once you see the root ball, it's easy to envision how heavy rain and high winds might have separated the tree's shallow root network from the bedrock. The sunny gap created has enabled shade-intolerant species to gain a foothold. Hay-scented ferns have colonized other light-filled gaps.

The trail continues to be challengingly steep, but well blazed with blue, through dense northern hardwoods and finally reaches an unmarked junction on the right with the old Williams College Ski Trail at the Massachusetts–New York border. The ski trail is not maintained and is even steeper than the one you just ascended, so it is not recommended for a return. Bear left to gain the mostly flat open summit of Berlin Mountain (elevation 2,818 feet), 2.0 miles from the trailhead.

The views of the Greylock Range, about 7 miles to the southeast, are splendid, but summit trees are growing taller, and vistas are limited. Red spruces ring the circular open area where a fire tower once stood. Crumbling concrete footings are all that remain. Sunshine has encouraged raspberry, bilberry, and lowbush blueberry to proliferate.

The return route follows a portion of the long-distance Taconic Crest Trail (TCT), blazed by a white diamond in a blue square (the section in New York also has blue disks), to Berlin Pass. Tire tracks make it obvious that ATVs frequently use this trail, so be on the lookout for them. Follow the wide, rocky track downhill to the right, passing through numerous fern glades. White birch trees, also known as paper birch, look especially attractive in this setting of yellow-green ferns. The broad path, steep at times and filled with lots of loose stones, is eroded to phyllite bedrock. As a result, side trails have been created. Juneberry (shadbush) trees are among the members of the low-stature ridgeline forest, producing white flowers in April before their leaves emerge.

After experiencing moderately steep descents alternating with level stretches along the wooded crest for 1.2 miles, arrive at a four-way intersection in a shrubby depression, or saddle, called Berlin Pass. The TCT continues straight, toward Petersburg Pass, but you will turn right onto pink-blazed Berlin Pass Trail. Opposite this trail, the old Boston to Albany Post Road descends to Berlin, New York. The treadway is wide, rutted, and damp in spots but easy to follow. Note the excellent examples of wafer-thin, layered phyllite bedrock in the trail. This rock began as clay deposits, rich in mica, in a shallow sea, and was then metamorphosed by great heat and pressure to produce a rock with grain size between shale and schist.

After you hike downhill for a while, the dry south-facing slope to your left sports lowbush blueberries, mountain azaleas, and a little member of the snapdragon family with the intriguing name of cow-wheat, which bears modest yellow trumpet-like flowers in summer. It draws its nourishment from the roots of oaks. And as you proceed rather steeply down the rocky trail, oaks indeed become more common. Haircap moss, meanwhile, softens the margins. Finally, bear right in an arc and emerge into a large gravel parking lot, where the trail meets Berlin Mountain Road. You could turn left and walk down the road 0.4 mile to your vehicle, but more fun awaits.

If you decide to extend your hike here, turn right. Still visible on the left slope are the runs of the old Williams College Ski Area, built in 1960. At the end of the gravel lot, turn left to head down a grassy track toward the base of the ski slope.

Yellow-blazed Bullock Trail is on your right, but turn left onto red-blazed WRLF Loop Trail. Haley Brook tumbles out of a large culvert and down a ravine on your left. A canopy of maples, ashes, birches, and beeches shades striped maples and patches of delicate maidenhair fern. Spring wildflowers called blue cohosh—forming solid stands—and wild leeks are profligate on this moist, nutrient-rich slope. Wild leek's twin leaves have an unmistakable onion fragrance; they wither completely away by the time the leek's globes of white flowers emerge in summer.

At the intersection, turn left onto Haley Brook Cutoff (also blazed red), and amble down to cross the stream. Briefly ascend a steep slope through deciduous woodland and bear right. At a wooden bridge outfitted with a wire mesh tread-way, turn right onto a side path that leads steadily and then more steeply down, past a beech snag on the right pitted with big pileated woodpecker excavations, to a small viewing platform. The enchanting waterfall consists of cascades and a horsetail for a total drop of at least 30 feet. The auditory aspect of this experience is to be appreciated as well. In late spring and early summer, listen for the exuberant song of the winter wren. After returning to the main trail, turn right and cross the wooden bridge. Berlin Mountain Road and your vehicle are a short distance ahead.

DID YOU KNOW?

To obtain use of a 41-acre site at the end of Berlin Road for a ski run, Williams College exchanged portions of a farm between MA 2 and Berlin Road with Williamstown, which wanted the farm acreage for campsites. The college ski team now trains at Jiminy Peak in Hancock.

MORE INFORMATION

This route has no restroom facilities or potable water sources. It crosses property owned by Williamstown Rural Lands Foundation, the town of Williamstown, Williams College, the New York Department of Environmental Conservation, and private owners. The Taconic Crest Trail is maintained by the Taconic Hiking Club (taconichikingclub.org). Class of '33 and Berlin Pass trails are maintained by the Williams Outing Club, 39 Chapin Hall Drive, Williamstown, MA 01267 (413-597-2317; woc.williams.edu). The WRLF Loop Trail is maintained by the Williamstown Rural Lands Foundation, 671 Cold Spring Road, Williamstown, MA 01267 (413-458-2494; wrlf.org/the-berlin-road-trail-system) and the New York Department of Environmental Conservation (dec.ny.gov).

NEARBY

Sheep Hill, a 50-acre former dairy farm and ski area now owned and managed by the Williamstown Rural Lands Foundation, features hillside trails offering expansive views of Mount Greylock and surrounding features. The entrance is approximately 1.2 miles south of Williamstown Center at 671 Cold Spring Road (US 7/MA 2). The property is open year-round for passive recreation and public programs on natural history and rural heritage (413-458-2494; wrlf.org/sheep-hill).

5

FIELD FARM RESERVATION

Lying in the valley between the Greylock Range and the Taconics, this Trustees property has an agricultural legacy dating back more than 250 years. Today it beckons hiker, cross-country skier, and snowshoer alike with a fine trail network in a truly bucolic setting offering delightful mountain vistas.

LOCATION
Williamstown, MA

RATING
Easy

DISTANCE
2.9-mile loop

ELEVATION GAIN
120 feet

ESTIMATED TIME
1.5-2 hours

MAPS
USGS Berlin; The Trustees of Reservations map: thetrustees.org/assets/documents/places-to-visit/trailmaps/Field-Farm-Trail-Map.pdf

DIRECTIONS

From the intersection of US 7 and MA 9 in Pittsfield (at the Berkshire Athenaeum), follow US 7 north for 16.3 miles to its intersection with MA 43 in Williamstown (also called the Five Corners). Turn left onto MA 43 and drive for less than 100 feet before turning right onto Sloan Road. Follow Sloan Road for slightly more than 1 mile to the signed entrance drive for Field Farm on the right. Drive 0.1 mile to the small gravel parking lot adjacent to the trailhead and maintenance garage/Discovery Room. *GPS coordinates:* 42° 39.931′ N, 73° 15.620′ W.

TRAIL DESCRIPTION

After stopping at the kiosk, where trail maps are available, turn onto Pond Trail and follow the mowed path through shrubby growth, which includes invasive exotic multiflora rose, Morrow's honeysuckle, and buckthorn.

When you reach a spring-fed pond adjacent to the former guesthouse, which is called The Folly, turn right to follow the pond shore past a cattail marsh where muskrats—smaller cousins of the beaver—reside. (*Note:* When the water level is high, you may have to tread gently over the waterlogged beaver dam and outflow before finding firmer footing beyond.)

At the intersection of Pond Trail and South Trail, bear right onto South Trail and walk among young woody growth draped with vines, including wild grape. Then

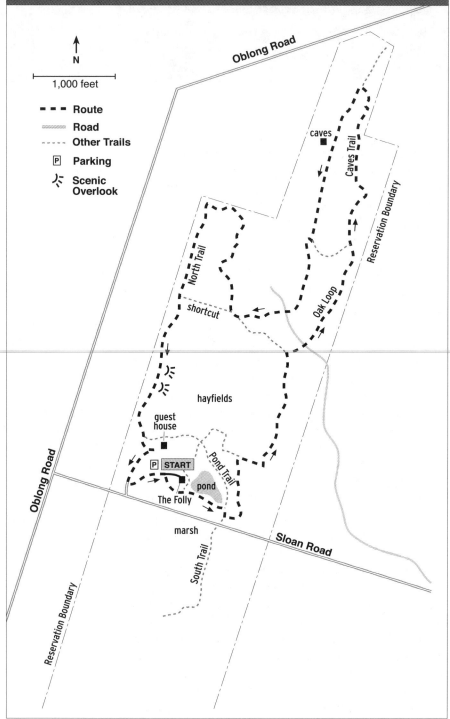

N

1,000 feet

- - - Route

Road

Other Trails

P Parking

Scenic Overlook

Oblong Road

caves

Caves Trail

Reservation Boundary

North Trail

shortcut

Oak Loop

hayfields

guest house

P START

Pond Trail

pond

The Folly

marsh

Sloan Road

South Trail

Oblong Road

Reservation Boundary

A tiny brook flows through a deciduous woodland of birch, beech, ash, and oak on its way to join the Green River.

turn left onto the connector to North Trail before meeting Sloan Road. Bigtooth aspen, black cherry, white ash, and white pine stand tall in this section. You'll see a large hayfield at the junction with North Trail; turn right and skirt the field's edge. In late spring and early summer, bobolinks nest in the grass, as do red-winged blackbirds. Pass through a hedgerow gap on the right; turn left and continue due north, paralleling the hedgerow.

Gaze left to admire the Taconic Range (especially after leaf fall), including Berlin Mountain (Trip 4). Pass through a gap in barbed wire fencing and enter an apple orchard. At the field's far end, follow orange-blazed Oak Loop as it jogs off to the right into a forest of cherry, white birch, ash, and sugar maple. Smaller, sinewy ironwood and flaky hop hornbeam trees comprise the understory. After crossing a couple of rivulets—one on a wooden span—and passing through another wire fence gap, the path enters a stand of lanky hardwoods. Pileated woodpeckers frequent these trees, so make sure to look for their big rectangular excavations in carpenter ant–infested trees and listen for their wild laughing call.

Soon you descend wooden steps and cross a bridge over a larger stream. Here, where the trail is rather level, watch for a massive, columnar black oak, 4 feet in diameter, on the left. Its lower section bears what appears to be a lightning strike scar. In season, on private property to the right, you may see hundreds of yards of plastic tubing linking taps placed on sugar maple trees. Leafy clumps of blue cohosh dot the forest floor.

After 0.3 mile on Oak Loop, reach a Y intersection; go right to follow Caves Trail and begin a gradual climb among numerous white birches and hop horn-beams, 5 to 10 inches in diameter. One of the first indications of marble bedrock pokes up on the left in the form of a layered boulder capped with mosses and evergreen wood fern. Other indicators of rich woods here are wild ginger and lacy maidenhair fern. When you reach the height-of-land, follow the contour over rolling topography where a steep dropoff looms to the left. In winter, homes along Oblong Road are visible from this high point as you begin your descent through younger woods.

You'll see a livestock barn on private property to the right as the trail bears left, and you may hear traffic noise from Oblong Road as you reach an intersection; bear left to continue on Caves Trail—now an old woods road.

The woods are dominated by bigtooth aspen (named for its leaves, which sport large "teeth" around the edges). Before long, reach a flowing brook on the right that mysteriously disappears beneath the marble bedrock that the trail crosses. To your left rises the rocky spine that you recently walked over. Belowground—out of sight—the brook's water, aided by acidic precipitation, dissolves the marble, carving out caves within the rock. Several examples of these so-called caves appear as you continue south.

After leaving the caves area, the trail bears left and rejoins Oak Loop after 0.7 mile. Turn right and pass an uptilted marble outcropping on the left. The outcroppings are excellent den sites for porcupines, a favorite prey species for fishers, members of the weasel family. Mosses, ferns, and bishop's cap—a spring wildflower with blossoms that resemble snowflakes and seed capsules that look like a bishop's headgear—adorn the rock. Continue over gently rolling terrain to a brook babbling through woodland of black and gray birch, beech, ash, and oak. Watch for a patch of primitive horsetails, resembling jointed green soda straws, before and after you cross the wooden bridge.

Beware the stout thorns of multiflora rose that fringe the pasture. Both it and the prickly Japanese barberry shrub are sure signs of soil disturbance. A few eastern junipers (red cedars) also indicate former pasture. Stay right and follow the orange blazes. This area may be damp, because water flows off the slightly higher pasture ahead during wet seasons. When you reach the T intersection, turn right on North Trail, and then right again at a trail sign. (Alternately, you can continue straight on a 0.1-mile short cut knocking 0.5 mile off the trip distance. This mowed path leads among more apple trees, multiflora rose, Japanese barberry, and other invasive exotic shrubs.)

If you follow North Trail, continue to a sharp left at the preserve boundary, where large ash trees, now threatened by the recent arrival of emerald ash borer, display their characteristic crosshatched bark. After bearing right, start a gradual climb and switchback up an easy slope. On the right are a few healthy American beeches, their smooth gray trunks unblemished by the Nectria fungus. Another large oak—this one red and forked low to the ground—rises as two trunks in a victory sign on the left. Gigantic sugar maples with wire embedded in them stand on the right. A large hickory has barbed wire protruding from a depth of 9 inches.

Continue to follow North Trail south along a wide, mowed path along the western edge of the hayfields. Panoramic views of the Greylock Range and the Hopper (Trip 7) on the mountain's west face become ever more splendid as you walk on. A lone nest box placed for the declining American kestrel stands like a sentinel out in the field. The Guest House at Field Farm, a bed-and-breakfast, is visible ahead. Continue through a sculpture garden to a paved drive, turn right, and follow it 150 yards to the roadway that leads left to the parking area, 0.9 mile from the Oak Loop junction.

DID YOU KNOW?

Bobolinks winter on the Argentine Pampas and arrive back in the Berkshires in May. Males sing their bubbly notes while on the wing above the meadows where the smaller, streaky-brown females nest. To ensure their nesting success, mowing after July 15 is recommended—a management practice followed at Field Farm Reservation.

MORE INFORMATION

Open year-round sunrise to sunset. Free admission, but a donation is suggested for nonmembers of The Trustees older than age 12. A portable toilet sits opposite the map kiosk. Dogs must be leashed at all times. Mountain biking is not permitted. The Trustees of Reservations, Berkshires Regional Office, 1 Sergeant Street, Stockbridge, MA 01262 (413-298-3239; thetrustees.org/places-to-visit/berkshires/field-farm.html).

NEARBY

The midcentury modern Guest House at Field Farm, built in 1948, offers bed-and-breakfast accommodations from early April through December. For reservation information, call 413-458-3135 or visit thetrustees.org/field-farm/accommodations.html. Guided tours of The Folly, a midcentury modern building designed by Ulrich Franzen in the mid-1960s, are conducted from June through October upon request.

6

GREYLOCK RANGE TRAVERSE

This long, strenuous day hike spans four summits, including the state's highest peak, and features arguably the most sensational panoramic vista in the entire commonwealth—one of six spectacular viewpoints along the route. It's the most exhilarating hiking the Berkshires has to offer!

DIRECTIONS

From the Five Corners area of South Williamstown, where US 7, MA 43, Sloan Road, and Green River Road intersect, turn right onto Green River Road and follow it 2.3 miles to Hopper Road and Mount Hope Park on the right. Turn right, cross Green River, and drive for 2.1 miles (bearing left at Potter Road) to a large gravel parking area on the right at Haley Farm. *GPS coordinates*: 42° 39.323′ N, 73° 12.325′ W.

TRAIL DESCRIPTION

From the parking area (elevation 1,100 feet), follow the cobbled road past a farm gate and a state forest gate, between stone walls overhung by sugar maples, to Haley Farm Trail (the return route for this hike) on the right. A panoramic view of the Hopper, a large cirque, or ravine, scoured by glaciers on Mount Greylock's western slopes, is laid out beyond a hayfield. For now, continue past the Hopper Trail intersection on your right and descend gently on blue-blazed Money Brook Trail, where a dense stand of pale touch-me-not blooms in midsummer. Unlike the predominant orange species in this area, though, these flowers are yellow. Amble through a grassy stretch on a mowed path that skirts Hopper Brook at the boundary of Hopper Natural Area. Bear left to cross a wooden footbridge over the clear brook and begin an easy uphill walk along the opposite bank.

LOCATION
Williamstown, Adams, and North Adams, MA

RATING
Strenuous

DISTANCE
12.1-mile loop

ELEVATION GAIN
2,390 feet

ESTIMATED TIME
6.5-8 hours

MAPS
AMC Massachusetts Trail Map 1; USGS Williamstown; Massachusetts Department of Conservation and Recreation map: mass.gov/files/2017-08/Trail%20map.pdf

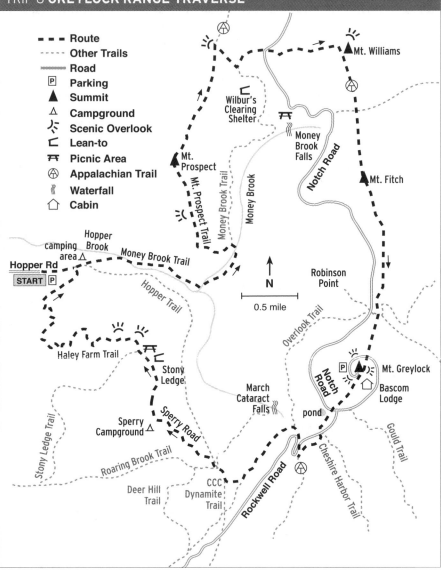

At a short reroute, where the raging brook has undercut the trail, bear left up stone steps and along the hillside to rejoin the fast-flowing brook. You are walking along the southern flank of Mount Prospect. Sugar maple, white ash, black birch, yellow birch, beech, and oak shield the path. The eroding force of water is evident at another bend in the brook.

Soon after a stone-lined cellar hole on the right, cross another wooden footbridge over cascading Hopper Brook. At a Y intersection, turn left to remain on spacious Money Brook Trail. At this point, the trail parallels Money Brook, a tributary of Hopper Brook, upstream. Magnificent eastern hemlocks rise from the steep slopes as you cross a stream. A wider feeder brook flowing down through the Hopper must be crossed on rocks; use caution. This is practice for a final crossing on Money Brook via stones a short distance beyond.

After 1.4 miles on Money Brook Trail, begin to ascend the rocky Mount Prospect Trail, when the path turns left at a signed T intersection and narrows. The grade soon becomes more challenging and winds along a virtual talus slope of schist that requires some use of hands to negotiate. Caution is called for, especially when the rocks are wet. Soon you bear right, under oaks, to climb the prominent spine of Mount Prospect, a subordinate peak of Mount Greylock once known locally as "the Hog's Back." Blueberries and huckleberries both offer sweet morsels in midsummer. Know huckleberry by its rough leaves. The challenging climb is interrupted now and again by more moderate sections, but the overall trek is relentlessly upward. Red maples, shad trees, and mountain azaleas join the oaks on this dry, south-facing slope. At a viewpoint on the left, you'll be treated to wonderful panorama of the Taconic Range and Haley Farm. Some moderate uphill stretches remain until the wooded high point, where a rock cairn marks the 2,690-foot summit of Mount Prospect at 2.7 miles.

An easy-to-moderate descent leads through ferns, under yellow birches, maples, beeches, and a few red spruces, and over gneiss (pronounced "nice") bedrock, alternately leveling out and dropping. One mile beyond the cairn, after passing dark stands of young spruces, emerge onto bedrock and enjoy fabulous vistas of the northern Taconics and Vermont's Green Mountains beyond. Turn sharply right here to follow the white-blazed Appalachian Trail (AT) south over a needle-cushioned treadway down a spruce-covered east slope to the intersection with Money Brook Trail. (A sign notes that Wilbur's Clearing Lean-To is 0.3 mile down the trail to the right.) Continue straight on the AT and traipse over bog bridges through a damp spruce stand.

Bear right to cross Notch Road and begin your ascent of Mount Williams, still following the white-blazed AT. Mature spruces are reproducing well here. Later, hobblebush and beech form a dense understory. The hike becomes more challenging as you climb rocky "steps," but switchbacks make ascending the west slope of Williams manageable. After leveling off in a low-stature woodland, the AT bears left to reach the 2,951-foot summit of Mount Williams—named for Ephraim Williams Jr., the founder of nearby Williams College—at 4.8 miles. Limited views to the northeast are a welcome respite from climbing. When you are ready to continue, be sure to turn left. The contorted bedrock along the initially level path shows the effects of the tremendous heat and pressure created by continental collision hundreds of millions of years ago.

A steeper and rockier downhill path (opposite a trail to Notch Road) leads to the Bernard Farm Trail junction on the left. Remain on the AT to begin an easy climb to Mount Fitch, where you may detect the aroma of balsam firs. You will

Beyond the summit of Mount Prospect, hikers emerge onto bedrock offering fabulous vistas of the northern Taconics and Vermont's Green Mountains beyond.

most likely have crested the 3,110-foot summit of Mount Fitch and dropped slightly in elevation again before you realize that you passed over it. The roughly 3 miles of trail between Mount Williams and Bellows Pipe Trail wend through pleasant woodland. More than a mile beyond Mount Fitch, Bellows Pipe Trail (Trip 9) goes left. It's only another 100 yards to steep Thunderbolt Trail—one of the Northeast's pioneering downhill ski runs—on the left. Just beyond Thunderbolt Trail, a side path leads right, to Notch Road and Robinson Point, but continue up on the AT, which in May is festive with wildflowers.

Blackberry canes fill a linear gap through which the trail passes on its somewhat rocky ascent past low beech, birch, and cherry trees. You'll have your first glimpse of the globe atop the Massachusetts Veterans War Memorial Tower here, if not obscured by clouds or fog. Tread up railroad ties and then flagstone steps to paved Notch Road. Look back to admire a spectacular panorama that includes the rocky spine of Ragged Mountain and the Hoosic River valley. Cross the paved auto road and climb over bony outcroppings to arrive shortly at the renovated Thunderbolt Shelter. The summit, topped by the iconic granite memorial tower, rises just a short distance ahead at 7.2 miles. A unique relief map near the tower depicts the Greylock Range. A web of trails encircles the summit, which is enlivened by the clear plaintive whistles (*Old-Sam-Peabody-Peabody-Peabody*) of white-throated sparrows in summer.

For fabulous scenery eastward, bear left at the Y split. A universally accessible path leads to an overlook where all promontories are identified on a granite tableau. Restrooms and drinking water are available at Bascom Lodge, a real gem, built in 1938 by the Civilian Conservation Corps. When you're ready to depart, pick up the AT beyond the tower. Stroll through bluish conical firs and cross the paved road again near the lofty radio antenna. Descend steeply over rock amid red spruce and firs to the next auto road crossing. Turn right and follow the AT along the road for 100 feet then reenter the woods on the right, remaining on the white-blazed AT. After a brief descent, bog bridges bring you to a scenic human-built pond—once the lodge's water supply and headwater for Hopper Brook. At 0.7 mile from the summit, leave the AT and stay right, heading downhill on blue-blazed Hopper Trail toward Sperry Road. Bear right at paved Rockwell Road and descend on a wide, rocky path, following Hopper Trail left at the junction with Overlook Trail on the right.

The grade is moderate as you continue down the slope under a canopy of beech and birch trees with red spruces mixing in. After leveling out and passing a shielded spring on the right, turn right at a T intersection to follow Hopper Trail down more steeply along an unnamed brook to gravel Sperry Road. Turn right and stroll down through the campground, passing junctions for several other trails, including Hopper Trail on the right. But remain on Sperry Road, passing toilet facilities. The road begins to climb, easily at first, then moderately, through mixed forest. After 1.1 miles (roughly the hike's 10-mile mark) the route loops and ends at Stony Ledge (elevation 2,560 feet), where some of the state's most breathtaking scenery awaits.

Directly across the 1,500-foot-deep chasm of the Hopper glacial cirque is Mount Greylock's summit, roughly 1,000 feet higher. From left to right, an impressive panorama encompasses all the peaks you scaled today—Prospect, Williams, Fitch, and Greylock. Picnic tables invite a long pause. Hopper Brook is audible, and the flutelike voices of thrushes spiral up from the extensive forest below in late spring and summer. When you're ready to continue, find the "Stony Ledge Group Site" sign at the trailhead on the far end of the gravel turnaround. At the Y split, follow the sign left for Stony Ledge and Haley Farm trails. The drop is fairly steep amid hardwoods and spruce to the junction with blue-blazed Haley Farm Trail; turn right onto that trail to begin a 2.1-mile descent to the trailhead.

A final splendid vista, this one north toward Williamstown and Vermont's Green Mountains, is yours at the end of a short path on the right. Haley Farm Trail descends among beech, maple, cherry, and yellow birch, and then through an oak-covered slope showing signs of selective logging decades back. Switchbacks lead down quite steeply through two small bowls and continue through a forest of well-spaced large sugar maples, beneath which new growth seeks the sun. (Sugar maples thrive in such nutrient-rich soils.) Reach level ground at last among birches and arrive at the hayfield you gazed across hours ago at the start of your trek. Mount Prospect looms ahead. Stroll through the meadow and turn left on the old road toward the parking area to end a rewarding day.

DID YOU KNOW?

After Captain Ephraim Williams Jr. died in battle during the French and Indian War in 1755, his estate provided funds for a free school in West Township—later Williamstown. The school would eventually become world-renowned Williams College.

MORE INFORMATION

Open daily, year-round. No admission fee. A parking fee ($5 MA resident, $10 out of state) is charged only on the summit from May to October. Biking, skiing, and leashed dogs are allowed. Hunting is prohibited from May 20 to Columbus Day and is never permitted within War Memorial Park. Toilet facilities are at the trailhead, the summit, Bascom Lodge, the campground on Sperry Road, and Stony Ledge. Carry in, carry out rules apply. Mount Greylock State Reservation is managed by the Massachusetts Department of Conservation and Recreation. Visitor center/park headquarters, 30 Rockwell Road, Lanesborough, MA 01237 (413-499-4262; mass.gov/locations/mount-greylock-state-reservation).

NEARBY

According to the Williams College archives, Captain Ephraim Williams Jr. supervised the completion of Fort Massachusetts in 1745, which was strategically situated by the Hoosic River. Today it would lie between the towns of North Adams and Williamstown. A plaque in the parking lot of a former supermarket along MA 2 in North Adams marks the site.

7

HOPPER TRAIL TO MOUNT GREYLOCK SUMMIT

Arguably the most scenic route to the summit of the state's highest peak, and among those requiring the greatest elevation gain, Hopper Trail leads from Haley Farm through lush woodland to a campground on Sperry Road, the Appalachian Trail (AT), the state's only true boreal forest, and the summit. The descent on Overlook Trail and Money Brook Trail adds variety.

DIRECTIONS

From the Five Corners area of South Williamstown, where US 7, MA 43, Sloan Road, and Green River Road intersect, turn right onto Green River Road and follow it 2.3 miles to Hopper Road and Mount Hope Park on the right. Turn right, cross Green River, and drive for 2.1 miles (bearing left at Potter Road) to a large gravel parking area on the right at Haley Farm. *GPS coordinates*: 42° 39.323′ N, 73° 12.325′ W.

TRAIL DESCRIPTION

A trail map is posted at the kiosk; paper copies may be available as well. A view of the Hopper, which is a cirque, or ravine, scoured by glaciers—so named because of its resemblance to a grain hopper—greets you from the very beginning. Follow the farm road past machinery, livestock, hayfields, and pastures of the functioning Haley Farm—a bucolic setting for a trailhead to be sure. The angular mound of Mount Prospect rises to your left. Pass a sign with park regulations and a brown metal barway. The cobbled road is lined by stone walls and overarching sugar maples. Blue blazes mark the route.

When you reach Haley Farm Trail on the right, step out into the hay meadow for a fabulous vista of the Hopper,

LOCATION
Williamstown and Adams, MA

RATING
Strenuous

DISTANCE
9 miles round trip

ELEVATION GAIN
2,390 feet

ESTIMATED TIME
5-6 hours

MAPS
AMC Massachusetts Trail Map 1; USGS Williamstown; Massachusetts Department of Conservation and Recreation map: mass.gov/files/2017-08/Trail%20map.pdf

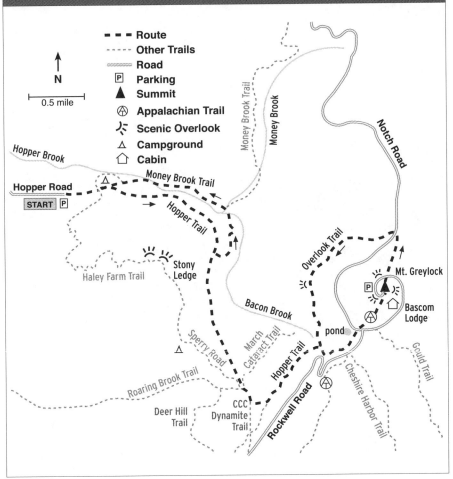

but then continue straight on Hopper Trail. A bit farther, Hopper Brook Loop Trail leads off to the left.

Continue straight to the Hopper Trail intersection and bear right on a narrow path up through prickly Japanese barberry, multiflora rose (which blooms in June), and honeysuckle shrubs—all invasive exotics characteristic of human disturbance. Before long, enter a maple and white birch woodland and traverse bog bridges across seepages. Hopper Brook is audible. If you're wearing shorts, give a wide berth to stinging nettles lining the path. A steeper climb over a rocky path begins soon after you enter the Hopper—a 1,600-acre National Natural Landmark.

After 1.0 mile on Hopper Trail, reach the cutoff to signed Money Brook Trail on the left. You'll take this trail upon your return, but continue uphill for now.

At the Haley Farm Trail intersection near the beginning of this hike, step out into the hay meadow for a fabulous view of the Hopper, a National Natural Landmark.

Shiny schist with high mica content litters the route through sugar maple, white ash, and American beech woodland. Work your way up a grade that exceeds 25 degrees in places. Yellow birch, another northern hardwood forest indicator, becomes numerous. Take a moment to appreciate the abundant birdlife. From late spring to midsummer, male black-throated blue warblers, black-throated green warblers, ovenbirds, American redstarts, red-eyed vireos, and hermit thrushes sound off to attract mates and announce their claims to nesting territories.

Pass sugar maples with an understory of sapling beech, striped maple, and hobblebush. Sharp-needled red spruce becomes dominant as you approach the campground on gravel Sperry Road (elevation 2,400 feet), 2.4 miles from the trailhead. The road was named for William H. Sperry, the longest-serving Grey-lock Reservation commissioner (1900–1938). Turn left to follow Hopper Trail along Sperry Road and pass another gravel road on the right that leads to both Roaring Brook Trail and Deer Hill Trail and Shelter. Opposite the campground entrance is the path to March Cataract Trail. A wayside panel relates the history of the Civilian Conservation Corps (CCC), which at its zenith employed workers throughout the United States, including 100,000 men in 68 Massachusetts camps. Based here from 1933 to 1942, crews of 200 men rotated every six months. The region continues to benefit from their fine work.

Continue past two gushing high-gradient streams—the first bounces over schist steps. About 100 yards past the entrance station, turn left to continue on Hopper Trail. Native stone steps indicate the route up through mixed woods of beech, birch, and spruce to a T intersection with an old carriage road—Deer Hill Trail. Turn left to remain on Hopper Trail, which continues on a gentle grade, past the source of a spring below. Striped maple and hobblebush, with paired, heart-shaped leaves, are abundant. Black-throated blue warblers construct cup nests among the latter's pliable branches. Cross a few small flowages and maneuver over bedrock outcroppings that are often slick underfoot. The evocative aroma of balsam may soon be apparent.

In some spots, the layered bedrock serves as a handy staircase. At 0.7 mile from Sperry Road, turn sharply right at the junction with Overlook Trail and continue uphill on Hopper Trail, which becomes rocky. Follow the path left when it nears paved Rockwell Road, part of the Mount Greylock Scenic Byway. Turn left to follow the signed path to the Appalachian Trail (AT). The narrow walkway climbs into the balsam fir zone—part of the circumspect boreal forest in Massachusetts. Here, at 3,000 feet above sea level, among the stunted yellow birches and firs, blackpoll warblers breed. These small, black-capped, black-and-white birds are abundant in the vast boreal forests of Canada, but in the United States are virtually unseen outside upper Greylock in Massachusetts. Their sibilant, vibrating notes are insect-like.

At the intersection with the white-blazed AT, continue straight ahead on the AT, following a line of bog bridges to a serene pond that once supplied drinking water to Bascom Lodge. If clouds do not obscure the summit, the 200-foot radio tower with a 70-foot TV antenna will be visible across the pond—the summit is but a few hundred vertical feet away. The trail follows the shoreline briefly, leads up over a staircase ledge, and meets Rockwell Road near its junction with Notch Road (leading to North Adams and MA 2) on the left. Turn left and walk about 100 feet (past the intersection) to pick up the AT again on the left.

Your final ascent is through low-stature beech, yellow birch, mountain ash, and young balsam. The soil is thin at this elevation, and the growing season is short. Some trees show signs of stress, from both the harsh climate and acidic deposition. Cloud droplets contain an elevated level of atmospheric pollutants, sulphuric acid among them. Although the terrain is mostly exposed bedrock, *Clintonia* manages to thrive in pockets of soil. Its yellow flowers transform into dark blue berries that confer its other moniker—blue-bead lily.

Finally, step out onto pavement near the summit garage and radio tower, 4.1 miles from the trailhead. (*Note*: In winter, chunks of windblown ice from the structure can be hazardous to anyone below.) Rustic Bascom Lodge, constructed mostly by the CCC in the 1930s and named for John Bascom, an original member of the Greylock Commission, stands a short distance to the right. The lodge offers restroom facilities, meals, and accommodations. A water spigot at the back of the building is for hikers' use. Walk straight ahead, cross the access road, and continue on the AT through clumps of firs to the Massachusetts Veterans War Memorial Tower, erected in 1932. A bronze relief model of the Greylock Range invites examination just after you cross the roadway again at the entrance to the summit parking area. Ahead, the 93-foot granite tower may be ascended via a spiral staircase. From a paved path on the other side of the tower, enjoy excellent views north, east, and south, including the bare summit of Mount Monadnock in New Hampshire. Porcelain plaques interpret key landmarks. In summer, listen for the signature plaintive whistle of the white-throated sparrow—*Old-Sam-Peabody-Peabody-Peabody*—at these heights.

From the summit, retrace your steps and bear right, around the end of the radio tower, to blue-blazed 1.6-mile Overlook Trail. Descend under the dense shade of low spruce and fir. Listen for Swainson's thrushes and golden-crowned kinglets in early summer. The trail becomes rutted and passes shrubby mountain maples before crossing paved Notch Road; then it leads easily down past gnarled and diseased beech trees. Many mature yellow birches hug the trail, which is also lined by the hobblebush that covers the slope. The melodious flute-like calls of hermit thrushes may be heard here. At a wide spot in the trail, a spur leads right 80 feet to a view west to the Hoosic Valley and the Taconics beyond, and north to nearby Mount Prospect and ridgelines in Vermont. Back on the mostly level Overlook Trail, tread bog bridges until you hear the sound of flowing water.

Cross narrow Hopper Brook above March Cataract Falls and ascend fairly steeply for a short distance to the familiar junction with Hopper Trail. Turn right and retrace your steps through the campground and down Hopper Trail 0.9 mile back to the connecting path to Money Brook Trail (which you passed on your ascent) on the right. Turn right and amble downhill under a canopy of sugar maples and ashes. Sharp-lobed *Hepatica* (one of the earliest bloomers in April), red trillium, baneberry, jack-in-the-pulpit, mitrewort, and foamflower make this a fine wildflower trail in spring. Maidenhair fern adds to its charms in summer. Red oaks appear as you descend toward rushing Bacon Brook; the trail turns left at a flat spot under hemlocks. Pass large oaks and descend to Bacon Brook after crossing a shallow feeder stream on stones.

Bear left, walk 90 feet, and turn right to cross a wooden bridge over Bacon Brook. Bear left again on a short, level section, and then cross another wooden span. At the T intersection on the far side, turn left on Money Brook Trail (notice the large white ash on the bank), following energetic Money Brook and blue blazes briefly downstream to its confluence on the left with Bacon Brook. The merged streams flow west together as Hopper Brook. An old cellar hole on the left is all that remains of a former farmstead. Red-flowering raspberry thrives in a seepage area and blooms in late June. This old woods road, adjacent to Hopper

Brook (on Money Brook Trail), winds downhill easily over stones—a pleasing finale to this mountain excursion.

The erosive force of flowing water is evident where the stream has cut deeply into the bank. Cross a wooden bridge over the brook and then pass through a couple of small, grassy clearings. Reenter woods and ascend gradually, soon rejoining Hopper Trail on the left; continue straight ahead to return to your vehicle.

DID YOU KNOW?

A small population of Bicknell's thrush once bred on Mount Greylock, wintering on the Caribbean island of Hispaniola. Never exceeding two dozen, they had dwindled to only a handful by the 1960s. The last one was spotted in 1972. Degradation of their wintering habitat, climate change, and a catastrophic storm may have played a role in their disappearance from Greylock.

MORE INFORMATION

Open dawn to dusk, year-round. Access for hikers is free. A parking fee ($5 MA resident, $10 out of state) is charged at the summit from May to October. The Massachusetts Veterans War Memorial Tower is open 9 A.M. to 5 P.M. daily from Memorial Day to Columbus Day; from middle to late May it is open only on weekends. Bascom Lodge is open mid-May to mid-October (see bascomlodge.net for more information). Biking, skiing, and leashed dogs are allowed. Hunting is prohibited from May 20 to Columbus Day and is never permitted within War Memorial Park. Visitor center/park headquarters, 30 Rockwell Road, Lanesborough, MA 01237 (413-499-4262; mass.gov/locations/mount-greylock-state-reservation).

NEARBY

The Williamstown Historical Museum, founded in 1941 and located in the South Center School building at 32 New Ashford Road in Williamstown, offers an interesting glimpse into local history. The museum is open Wednesday to Friday, 10 A.M. to 2 P.M., and Saturday and Sunday, noon to 4 P.M. Admission is free (413-458-2160; williamstownhistoricalmuseum.org).

OLD-GROWTH CHAMPIONS

The recognized guru of old-growth forest in Massachusetts is an amiable, soft-spoken native North Carolinian named Robert Leverett. Leverett has, more than once, bushwhacked up and down just about every rugged hillside that could possibly hide ancient trees. To be sure, almost all old-growth stands occur on steep, virtually inaccessible slopes that defy logging. Finding them has been a career-long challenge and a labor of love for Leverett, who is executive director of the Eastern Native Tree Society and president and cofounder of Friends of Mohawk Trail State Forest, where many of the ancient trees reside.

In Massachusetts, approximately 2,700 acres of old-growth forest remain out of a statewide forested expanse of 3 million acres. The two largest stands are only 200 acres each, and most are far smaller. To be considered old growth, a stand must cover at least 5 acres and hold at least eight trees per acre that are a minimum 150 years old. One would think this is not a high threshold to meet, but in Massachusetts, which was 75 percent deforested by the mid-1800s, meeting even those standards is not an easy proposition.

The largest Berkshire stand is in the Hopper, a federally designated 1,600-acre National Natural Landmark on the western flanks of the Greylock Range. Those 115 acres and another 60 in Mount Greylock State Reservation still hold 200-year-old red spruce. Six parcels totaling almost 100 acres remain in southwestern Berkshire County, in Mount Washington State Forest and Mount Everett State Reservation, including Bash Bish Falls (Trip 43), Mount Race (Trip 44), Mount Everett (Trip 45), Alander Mountain (Trip 46), and Sages Ravine and Bear Mountain (Trip 49). Additionally, several stands of 20 acres or more exist in Monroe State Forest, including Dunbar Brook (Trip 14).

But old-growth forest is much more than aged trees sporting eye-popping statistics. Old growth is a climax forest type; by definition, that means it is self-perpetuating. For that to occur, the old trees must regenerate, or the entire stand would eventually succumb to old age. Trees have natural life spans; for example, the eastern hemlock can live about 600 years, and the red spruce about 400.

In addition to trees of every age class, old-growth forests host a myriad of other species. Nothing can compare with standing in the dim light beneath 150-foot-high old-growth giants and listening to the ascending flutelike notes of a Swainson's thrush.

8
STONY LEDGE VIA HALEY FARM TRAIL

This short but fairly steep hike in Mount Greylock State Reservation leads to one of the most scenic panoramas in the entire commonwealth. The return is by way of one of the reservation's most popular trails along the southern slope of the bowl-shaped Hopper.

LOCATION
Williamstown, MA

RATING
Moderate to Strenuous

DISTANCE
5.6-mile loop

ELEVATION GAIN
1,460 feet

ESTIMATED TIME
2.5-3 hours

MAPS
AMC Massachusetts Trail Map 1; USGS Williamstown; Massachusetts Department of Conservation and Recreation map: mass.gov/files/2017-08/Trail%20map.pdf

DIRECTIONS
From the Five Corners area of South Williamstown, where US 7, MA 43, Sloan Road, and Green River Road intersect, turn right onto Green River Road and follow it 2.3 miles to Hopper Road and Mount Hope Park on the right. Turn right, cross Green River, and drive for 2.1 miles (bearing left at Potter Road) to a large gravel parking area on the right at Haley Farm. *GPS coordinates: 42° 39.323′ N, 73° 12.325′ W.*

TRAIL DESCRIPTION
Walk past the barn and a farm gate bordered on both sides by hayfields and then around a state forest gate. Continue along an old cobbled lane under a canopy of sugar maples for a couple hundred yards to the signed Haley Farm Trail intersection, where there's a fine easterly view to the Hopper. Turn right and follow blue-blazed Haley Farm Trail through a hayfield and up into the forest. The path, initially level as it passes through the shade of maple, birch, and white ash, steepens before bearing left on the first of a series of four major switchbacks that take you up the slope. As you ascend, the terrain becomes steeper and rougher.

The first of numerous patches of maidenhair fern graces the verge after a right turn. Proceed on quite an incline; diagonal trenches (water bars) shunt water off the treadway. Under sugar maples—characteristic of rich woods—a profusion of ferns flourish, including spinulose wood, Christmas, glade, and maidenhair. Climb a series of stone

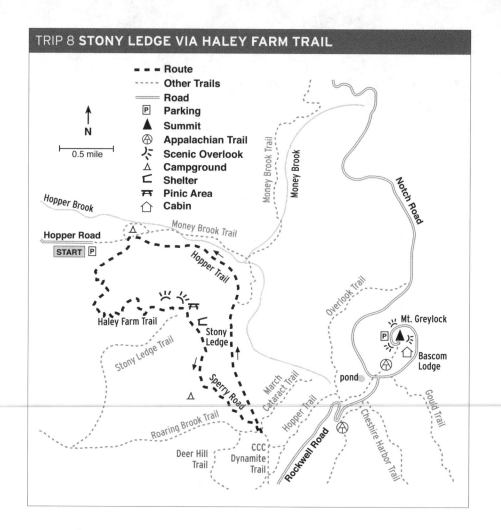

Route
Other Trails
Road
P Parking
▲ Summit
⊕ Appalachian Trail
☆ Scenic Overlook
△ Campground
⊏ Shelter
⊤⊤ Pinic Area
⌂ Cabin

N
0.5 mile

Hopper Brook

Hopper Road

START P

Money Brook Trail

Money Brook

Notch Road

Hopper Trail

Haley Farm Trail

Stony Ledge Trail

Stony Ledge

Sperry Road

Overlook Trail

Mt. Greylock

P

Bascom Lodge

pond

March Cataract Trail

Hopper Trail

Gould Trail

Roaring Brook Trail

Cheshire Harbor Trail

Deer Hill Trail

CCC Dynamite Trail

Rockwell Road

steps at the steepest section to arrive at a small saddle; turn left here and continue the ascent. Younger forest here is a clue to past logging, as are the rotting stumps you'll encounter farther on. Oak and American beech now join the deciduous woodland mix, and a few hemlocks make an appearance amid rockier ground. Oaks predominate as the grade eases, but gone are the lush ferneries in this drier environment. Instead, wild sarsaparilla and prince's pine enliven the forest floor. Pass through a small cleft in a low ledge and enter northern hardwoods again—sugar maple and yellow birch, joined by hop hornbeam, a small understory tree. At the end of a narrow gap, turn right and continue ascending over rocks and a network of surface roots. Easy switchbacks lead through woodland with abundant undergrowth to a fine viewpoint on the left; enjoy the vista of farm fields and the buildings of Williams College, all against the backdrop of southern Vermont's verdant ridges. The Dome, a rounded quartzite peak that serves as a local landmark, is clearly visible at the Vermont state line. Note the deep green patch of conifers ringing its summit.

Stony Ledge, once called Bald Mountain, offers arguably the most spectacular vista in Massachusetts.

Continue on a relatively easy grade up through dense fern growth. Note the outcropping on the right, cushioned by a thick mat of yellow-green sphagnum moss. Just beyond, the first short red spruces appear. The path levels out under deciduous trees and arrives at a signed T intersection with Stony Ledge Trail, a former ski trail built by the Civilian Conservation Corps in the 1930s. Turn left onto this trail and proceed up a steep section toward Stony Ledge Shelter and Stony Ledge. The wooden lean-to group shelter stands on the left just before you emerge from the shade of the forest at a brown metal bear box into the open at Stony Ledge (elevation 2,560 feet) at 2.1 miles, where a spectacular panorama of the Greylock Range and the Hopper awaits. From left to right, Mounts Prospect, Williams, Fitch, Greylock, and a portion of Saddle Ball Mountain are all visible. From a nearby bench or picnic table, you can hear the distant roar of March Cataract Falls and Money Brook flowing wildly some 1,000 feet below.

To continue, follow gravel Sperry Road through the picnic area to the primitive campground under spruces and native hardwoods for about 1 mile—an easy downhill jaunt. Pass two composting toilets opposite a wooden picnic shelter just before reaching Hopper Trail at the signed intersection on the left. This is your return route, descending 2.3 miles to the Haley Farm trailhead. The level, blue-blazed path leads through young spruce growth, but the woods are mostly deciduous, with an abundance of hobblebush, common in moist deciduous forests. In late summer, this plant's paired, palm-sized, heart-shaped leaves morph from green to maroon, and its coral-red berry clusters ripen to blue-black. The grade increases as you drop down along the southern flank of the Hopper, and the sound of flowing water is much more evident than it was from Stony Ledge. Many wildflowers, including red and painted trilliums and white violets, bloom in the ravine's rich soils in late May.

The angle of descent becomes more acute and rockier. Eastern hemlocks are more numerous on this north-facing slope, which, in turn, lowers the temperature. After leaf fall, a fine view through the trees on the east side of the Hopper is possible as the flowing water gains volume. When you reach the first of three large, fallen trunks across the trail, the descent eases, and soon you'll see Money Brook Trail on the right. Remain on Hopper Trail as it leads under a canopy dominated by sugar maple, with some white ash. Copses of stinging nettle and yellow jewelweed alternately impinge on the path; avoid contact with the nettle.

The route crosses a few intermittent drainages, levels out, and soon traverses a series of bog bridges. After the last set, invasive Japanese barberry—a sign of human disturbance—makes an unwelcome appearance. Walk through a small clearing and reach the cobbled roadway where you began your hike. Turn left to return to your vehicle, passing the Haley Farm Trail junction along the way.

DID YOU KNOW?

The Haley and Greene families sold their farmland to the commonwealth in 1990, protecting the access and approach to the scenic and biologically significant Hopper. The Massachusetts Department of Conservation and Recreation and the Williamstown Rural Lands Foundation together created the Haley Farm Trail as a shorter route to Stony Ledge in 1997.

MORE INFORMATION

Open dawn to dusk, year-round. Access for hikers is free. Biking and skiing are allowed. Dogs are permitted but must be on a 10-foot-maximum leash, and owners must have a current rabies vaccination certificate in their possession. Hunting is not allowed from May 20 to Columbus Day. Visitor center/park headquarters, 30 Rockwell Road, Lanesborough, MA 01237 (413-499-4262; mass.gov/locations/mount-greylock-state-reservation).

NEARBY

Mount Hope Park in Williamstown—located at the intersection of Green River Road and Hopper Road (see trip directions above)—is a scenic and pleasant place to have a picnic after your hike or to do some fishing (license required). The high-gradient and coldwater Green River is a trout stream that tumbles and gushes over rocks as it flows through the small, well-kept park.

9

MOUNT GREYLOCK AND RAGGED MOUNTAIN VIA BELLOWS PIPE TRAIL

Spring wildflowers grace the mixed woodlands along this historic route followed by Henry David Thoreau in 1844. A side path leads to Ragged Mountain and a magnificent view of Mount Greylock's east face.

LOCATION
North Adams and Adams, MA

RATING
Strenuous

DISTANCE
8.8 miles round trip

ELEVATION GAIN
2,140 feet

ESTIMATED TIME
5 hours

MAPS
AMC Massachusetts Trail Map 1: D5; USGS Williamstown; Massachusetts Department of Conservation and Recreation map: mass.gov/files/2017-08/Trail%20map.pdf

DIRECTIONS

From MA 8 (State Street) and MA 2 in downtown North Adams, follow MA 2 (West Main Street) west 1.1 miles and turn left onto Notch Road at the brown-and-white Mount Greylock State Reservation sign. Follow Notch Road for 1.2 miles to where it turns sharply left near the Mount Williams Reservoir. Take that sharp left and continue straight ahead into a small gravel parking area with room for about six vehicles. *GPS coordinates*: 42° 40.404′ N, 73° 08.325′ W.

TRAIL DESCRIPTION

Begin by following the blue blazes of Bellows Pipe Trail south along an old gravel road under an inviting canopy of sugar maples. This initial portion of the route passes through the North Adams watershed. Planted Norway spruces, impressive red oaks, and white ashes border the raised path that likely follows a road built by pioneering farmer Jeremiah Wilbur in the late 1700s. Notch Reservoir is visible down to your left. The gravel road soon crosses a feeder stream confined to a culvert. In all, there are about twenty water crossings (some merely a trickle) in the first 2 miles, but none pose a problem for hikers. Wildflowers, such as wild ginger, foamflower, false Solomon's seal, and jack-in-the-pulpit, grace the verge here.

Three mills once operated along Notch Brook, down to the left. Old trees now border the roadway's left flank. Iconoclastic naturalist and transcendental thinker Henry

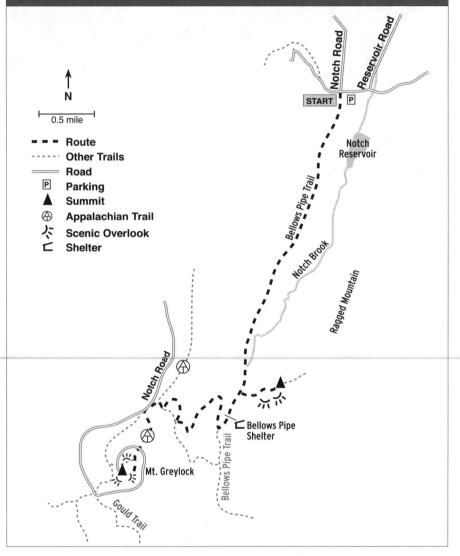

David Thoreau tramped this route toward the summit just days after his 37th birthday. Of it he wrote, "My route lay up a long and spacious valley called the Bellows, because the winds rush up or down it with violence in storms, sloping up to the very clouds between the principal range and a lower mountain." That lower mountain is Ragged Mountain. Trees now hem in Thoreau's "spacious valley." In his day, the landscape was virtually devoid of trees and the half-pipe shape of the Bellows would have been much more discernible.

The path steepens and becomes rockier, leading past small ravines carved by feeder streams; in spring some sections of the trail may be wet. Also during

The scar produced by the 1990 landslide on Greylock's eastern face seems relatively close at hand from a perch on Ragged Mountain.

spring, the lacy leaves and white, heart-shaped flowers of squirrel corn are common. (Squirrel corn is the original version of bleeding heart, a cultivated plant.) False Solomon's seal is also numerous among the ashes, maples, and birches. As you continue your ascent, trees of a typical northern hardwood forest soon appear—American beech and yellow birch, with striped maple in the understory. Wildflowers grow lush in these rich woods, blooming in spring—among them are mitrewort, named for the traditional bishop's headdress; *Clintonia* (blue-bead lily); and wild sarsaparilla. Trout lily (also called adder's tongue because of its tongue-shaped leaves) blankets the steep slopes. Solomon's seal, rose twisted stalk, Indian cucumber-root, violets of various hues, and Canada mayflower delight the eye as well. You may notice that wildflowers that have begun to set seed in the valley, such as red trillium, are in full bloom at this elevation. You're literally following spring up the mountain.

The path soon becomes narrower and more eroded. The trail splits briefly, immediately after you cross a flowing brook, and turns sharply left (avoid an eroded path here). A mill once stood at the head of the brook. (Watch out for the stinging nettle that borders the route.)

The trees are of shorter stature here due to the harsher growing conditions and less fertile soils. Watch for another temporary trail split and stay left. Spring beauty, with five delicate, pink-veined, whitish petals, blooms in profusion here. As the slope moderates, young deciduous growth is common, along with planted spruces and red pines. After a brief, steep climb, reach the 0.5-mile side trail to Ragged Mountain South Peak on the left at 2.2 miles—just before the remnant of a stone wall. (*Note*: Pay close attention here; this intersection can be easily missed.) Turn left to follow a narrow woodland path under Norway spruces. The undulating trail reaches a stone wall that once bordered sheep pasture and turns left to parallel it for a short stretch. Bear left and commence climbing quite steeply through semi-open birch, beech, and maple woods.

Reach a schist ledge on the right, perhaps 15 to 20 feet high. Stunted trees, mountain ash, and azalea convey the effects of elevation. At the upper end of the ledge, watch for the sharp turn to the right that takes you up the steep and rocky trail via switchbacks—it's easy to miss. Shiny fragments of schist dot the path. After a second hard right, an attention-getting view of Mount Greylock's east face presents itself—especially after leaf fall. Notice the flaky brown rock tripes (lichens) attached to the outcropping a bit farther on the right. Watch for a side path on the right that leads 40 feet to an open ledge fringed with lowbush blueberry, where a truly stunning vista of the Greylock Range awaits. Ahead lies the Hoosic River valley.

From the vista, retrace your steps along the out-and-back trail back to blue-blazed Bellows Pipe Trail and turn left on the mostly level old road. Jewelweed carpets the forest floor in late spring. Yellow birch with brassy and peeling bark dominates, along with sugar maple and gray birch. Reach a signed intersection and turn right to leave Bellows Pipe Trail and ascend moderately. From here, it is 1.0 mile to the Appalachian Trail (AT) and 2.0 miles to the summit on a rockier path via the lean-to shelter on the right. Continue past the shelter. In spring, watch for native small white butterflies—West Virginia white and mustard white. The trail alternately rises and levels out and then becomes steeper. In May, white-blooming hobblebush brightens this slope.

Among the stunted gray beeches and rocky outcroppings, the golden stars and glossy leaves of trout lilies glorify the hillside in spring, along with abundant spring beauties and red trilliums. At the three-way trail intersection with the AT, bear left (more or less straight ahead) on the white-blazed AT. To the left is a shed for Thunderbolt Ski Trail first-aid supplies. You'll soon arrive at intersections with Thunderbolt Trail (the pioneering downhill ski trail) on the left and a short trail leading to Notch Road on the right, but continue straight ahead and ever uphill on the AT. The treadway is firm, and the sweet, spicy aroma of balsam fir permeates the mountain air. The plaintive *Old-Sam-Peabody-Peabody-Peabody* tune of white-throated sparrows is emblematic of this bit of boreal forest. Yellow-rumped warblers and dark-eyed juncos (sparrows that are slate-gray above and snowy white below) also breed at these heights.

The beacon on the top of the Massachusetts Veterans War Memorial Tower comes into view ahead, appearing as a huge crystal sphere. Stone steps lead you up to Rockwell Road. Cross it and climb the last angular section over a ledge to the restored Thunderbolt Shelter on the right. Follow the paved path to skirt the summit parking area and find yourself among 15- to 20-foot-tall pyramidal balsams before arriving at the granite tower on the commonwealth's highest summit at 3,491 feet. The tower is at the center of a web of summit paths leading to various lookout points that offer views northeast to New Hampshire's Mount Monadnock and many other points 60 miles or more distant. Water, restrooms, meals, and trail merchandise are available at nearby Bascom Lodge, constructed by the Civilian Conservation Corps (CCC) in the 1930s. (*Note*: Hikers are asked to fill water bottles from a spigot around the back of the building rather than from the drinking fountain inside.)

When you're ready to return, walk back to the Thunderbolt Shelter and the AT to begin the 3.9-mile descent to the trailhead along the same route. Enjoy the lofty view of Ragged Mountain after you cross the road.

DID YOU KNOW?

The Thunderbolt Ski Trail, built in 1934 by the CCC, was one of America's premier expert downhill ski runs. Its 2,175-foot vertical drop served as the site of numerous sanctioned races until the mid-1950s. A proposed ski area was never built, and the trail gradually became overgrown. A few years ago, a group of Thunderbolt aficionados reinstated an annual ski race.

MORE INFORMATION

Open dawn to dusk, year-round. Access is free. The memorial tower is open 9 A.M. to 5 P.M. daily from Memorial Day to Columbus Day; from middle to late May, it is open only on weekends. Biking, skiing, and leashed dogs are allowed. Hunting is prohibited from May 20 to Columbus Day and is never permitted within War Memorial Park. Bascom Lodge is open mid-May to mid-October. Visitor center/park headquarters, 30 Rockwell Road, Lanesborough, MA 01237 (413-499-4262; mass.gov/locations/mount-greylock-state-reservation).

NEARBY

The Massachusetts Museum of Contemporary Art (Mass MoCA), housed in a sprawling nineteenth-century mill complex on 13 acres, is one of the world's premier centers for making and showing modern art. With an annual attendance of 120,000, it ranks among the most visited institutions in the United States dedicated to cutting-edge art. The admission fee, good for two days, is $20 for adults, $8 for children ages 6 to 16, and free for children younger than 6. Mass MoCA is at 1040 MASS MoCA Way, North Adams, MA 01247 (413-662-2111; massmoca.org).

PINECONE JOHNNIES

As you hike Berkshire trails, you can't help but be impressed by the work of the Civilian Conservation Corps (CCC). The Corps is one of President Franklin Delano Roosevelt's enduring legacies. Created during the Great Depression, a time of national economic calamity, the CCC provided meaningful employment for thousands of young men. They built roads; countless trails, ponds, and dams; various park facilities; and even such noteworthy structures as Bascom Lodge atop Mount Greylock (constructed between 1933 and 1937). Much of their handiwork is still serviceable today. Certainly our public lands had never before seen such an infusion of manpower directed at creating and improving recreational facilities and have not seen it since.

At the height of the CCC's involvement in Massachusetts, approximately 100,000 men worked in camps statewide. Of these camps, fourteen operated in the Berkshires. Monuments to the CCC's work are everywhere, which is especially amazing because it has been more than 75 years since the workers left the woods. At Sperry Road Campground in Mount Greylock State Reservation and at the Benedict Pond dam in Beartown State Forest, wayside exhibits relate some of the fascinating history made by the recruits. We owe these "Pinecone Johnnies," as they were known, a debt of gratitude.

In his gripping book *Berkshire Forests Shade the Past*, local historian Bernard A. Drew relates the tale of two CCC companies that operated in Beartown State Forest on one site from June 1937 until October 1941. According to Drew, each camp was assigned some 200 men, most in their early 20s and all hailing from Massachusetts. Fort Devens, northeast of Worcester, served as their boot camp. The U.S. Army was responsible for the operation of the camps, while the U.S. Forest Service was charged with overseeing the work. Local men were hired as foremen. At Beartown, the workers' accomplishments included building and fortifying roads, adding 6 miles of trails, and constructing two dams—one of which expanded the size of Benedict Pond to 35 acres. In fact, the Beartown companies were among the most active in all of New England.

10
CLARKSBURG STATE PARK

This scenic artificial pond, nestled between mountains and ridges at the Vermont state line, features a loop trail with fine views, prime wildlife habitats, and colorful fall foliage.

DIRECTIONS

From the junction of MA 2 and MA 8, on the east side of downtown North Adams, follow MA 8 north for 3.0 miles to the four-way intersection with Middle Road and Henderson Road in Clarksburg. Turn left on Middle Road and drive 0.1 mile to the park entrance; then continue another 0.8 mile to Horrigan Road on the right. Follow Horrigan Road 0.9 mile to the Vermont Line Trail parking area on the right. *GPS coordinates*: 42 44.531' N, 73 05.386' W.

TRAIL DESCRIPTION

Clarksburg State Park, not to be confused with nearby Clarksburg State Forest on the Appalachian Trail corridor, protects 368 acres of wetlands and forests along the Vermont state line. Scenic Mauserts Pond, a 45-acre artificial pond with fine views of the surrounding Berkshire Hills and southern Green Mountains, is its main attraction. This trip begins at the Horrigan Road trailhead (the hike's height-of-land at 1,285 feet) at the state line, where quiet woodland paths connect to the scenic 3-mile loop trail around Mauserts Pond and its surrounding habitats. The trails are marked with blue blazes. For a shorter outing, walk only the circuit, starting from the main entrance on Middle Road.

Begin by following Vermont Line Trail into the woods at a trail sign, passing behind the adjacent private residence. False Solomon's seal, a lily with tiny white flowers, blooms in late spring and early summer. Cross a footbridge over a cascading stream, one of Mauserts Pond's sources. Canada mayflowers and various ferns cap a large boulder at the crossing. The presence of oak trees, which favor milder

LOCATION
Clarksburg, MA

RATING
Easy to Moderate

DISTANCE
4.1 miles round trip

ELEVATION GAIN
340 feet

ESTIMATED TIME
2-2.5 hours

MAPS
AMC Massachusetts Trail Map 1; USGS North Adams; Massachusetts Department of Conservation and Recreation map: mass.gov/files/documents/2016/12/rv/clarksbrg.pdf

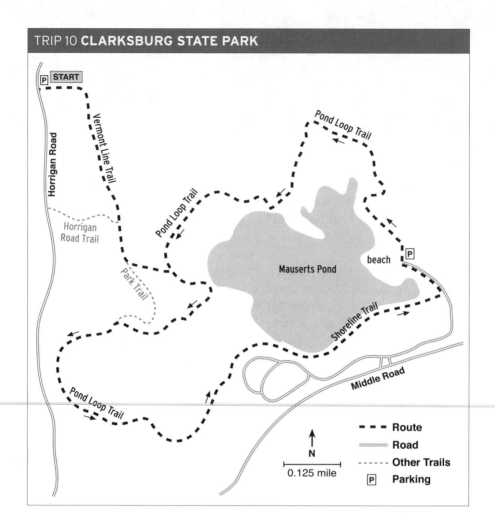

START

Horrigan Road

Vermont Line Trail

Pond Loop Trail

Horrigan Road Trail

Pond Loop Trail

Park Trail

Pond Loop Trail

Mauserts Pond

beach

Shoreline Trail

Middle Road

N

0.125 mile

- - - Route
═══ Road
----- Other Trails
P Parking

lowland environments, indicates a transition forest, also including a mix of northern hardwoods (characteristic of high elevations), and coniferous hemlocks and white pines. A stone wall, evidence of past land clearing for agriculture, runs through the woods to the left. After the pastures and farms were abandoned, white pines colonized the old fields. Some of the pines have multiple spreading trunks caused by white pine weevil infestation.

Enter a hemlock grove and cross the stream again on another footbridge. Red trilliums bloom on the banks in midspring. Familiar migratory songbirds, benefiting from the region's undeveloped woodlands, include scarlet tanagers, Blackburnian warblers, and black-throated green warblers. Their melodious calls are most evident from midspring into early summer as they establish territories. Diminutive spring azures, just an inch long, the tops of their wings pale blue, are among the first butterflies to appear in April. Holes in dead trees are evidence of woodpecker feeding activity.

The loop trail around Mauserts Pond offers scenic views of the Hoosac Range and surrounding mountains and hills in the northern Berkshires and Vermont.

Pass the junction with Horrigan Road Trail (which leads to Horrigan Road south of the parking area) on the right.

At a marked intersection at 0.5 mile, turn left on Park Trail and descend for 0.1 mile to join Pond Loop Trail, which enters from the left. Begin a counterclockwise circuit by continuing straight on Pond Loop Trail, heading down the valley slope. After another 0.1 mile, reach a scenic view from the pond's western shores at an elevation of 1,070 feet. The Hoosac Range ridge rises steeply above the water to the east, capped by wind turbines. The Hoosac Wind Power Project, encompassing 19 turbines on Bakke Mountain in Florida and Crum Hill in Monroe, was completed in 2012.

Follow Pond Loop Trail as it bears right (west), away from the shore, along the north side of Beaver Creek, Mauserts Pond's main source. Pass another stone wall and skirt the wetland edge.

Goldthread, which thrives in cool woods, swampy areas, and mountains, blooms here in May and June. (*Note*: While not overly difficult, this section of trail is more rugged than the rest, traversing rolling terrain and a few rocky areas.)

Pass a twin-trunked birch at a wet area, and bear left at a trail sign, where more tall pines grow along the slope. Descend to a dark hemlock grove along the swampy wetland edge. Carefully cross a boardwalk bridge and step over rocks in a wet area with a large colony of false hellebore, which grows along stream banks and in open woods. The trail curves back to the east at the park boundary near Horrigan Road, passing below private residences at the top of the slope.

Descend to cross Beaver Creek on a footbridge, about a half-mile upstream from the pond inlet. Another large false hellebore colony thrives along the wetland edge. After passing posted private land, continue through another wet area, shaded with hemlocks and pines. A red squirrel may scold you with a long, chattering call for entering its territory. Watch for red admiral butterflies, which frequent moist woods and floodplain forests, where many of their favored host plants grow. They are one of the last butterflies on the wing in Massachusetts each year, lingering along the coast as late as early December. Follow blue-blazed Pond Loop Trail left at a Do Not Enter sign near the park campground, and pass through an area of trees uprooted by a storm.

At 1.9 miles arrive at Lookout Point on the pond's southern shore, where a picnic table is an ideal spot to take a break and enjoy sweeping views across the water, including another perspective of the Hoosac Range. To the west are the rolling wooded hills on the Appalachian Trail corridor; Clarksburg State Park's swimming beach and pavilion are visible along the shore to the right. The shallow pond has an average depth of just 5 to 8 feet. Fish species include chain pickerel, yellow perch, pumpkinseed, brown bullhead, golden shiner, and white sucker.

Enjoy outstanding fall foliage starting in late September and early October, when red maples and highbush blueberry shrubs on the pond's shore and the wetland edges turn bright crimson. Color on the surrounding ridges usually peaks around Columbus Day to mid-October. In spring, trees don't usually leaf out until middle to late May, due to the northerly location and high elevation.

Resume the loop on Shoreline Trail to the right of the picnic table, following the blue-blazed path past mossy boulders and a hemlock grove, where painted trillium and goldthread bloom in May. The loud *conk-la-ree* call of red-winged blackbirds is another early sign of spring. Cross boardwalk bridges and enjoy fine open views from the pond's southeastern corner. A few paper birches grow amid the hemlocks.

Pass junctions with Bullhead Trail, Headquarters Trail, and Timberline Trail and reach the park's day-use area at 2.5 miles. Turn left and follow the paved access road past planted paper birch trees and a picnic area. An interpretive sign details a shoreline restoration project, implemented after Canada geese fouled the area to the extent that the swimming beach had to be closed. At the pavilion, a short path leads to more fine westerly views from the beach. Bluet and violet wildflowers carpet the lawn in spring.

Pass the restroom building and rejoin signed Pond Loop Trail, following a dirt road to another viewpoint near the dam. Look for migratory waterfowl, such as common and hooded mergansers and ringed-necked ducks, in early spring after ice melts and in late autumn. Walk to the right, past the dam, and then turn left and cross a footbridge over Beaver Creek at Mauserts Pond's outlet. Beaver Creek empties into North Branch Hoosic River, part of the Hudson River watershed, just east of the park.

Pond Loop Trail now traverses swampy wetland, where another source stream empties into Mausert Pond's northern tip. Many boardwalk bridges and footbridges provide a safe and dry passage. In winter, look for tracks of snowshoe hares, discernably larger than those of eastern cottontail rabbits, around brushy growth. Beavers have altered the ecology of the area, and the wetland is now transitioning to meadows. This is prime moose habitat; signs include heart-shaped tracks and piles of large, ball-shaped droppings. Many dragonfly and damselfly species, including rare ski-tailed emeralds, have been recorded here.

After glimpsing the Hoosac Range and the swimming beach through the trees, come out to a last open view from the north shore. Watch for resident mallard ducks and Canada geese with their chicks in late spring and summer. Cross a boardwalk and a stream and reenter boulder-strewn woods on the pond's western side. Pink lady's slippers emerge in mid-May.

At 3.6 miles, complete the circuit at the signed junction with Park Trail. Turn right on Park Trail, and retrace your steps uphill to Vermont Line Trail and Horrigan Road, ascending at mostly gentle grades to the trailhead.

DID YOU KNOW?

According to one legend (detailed in the park's interpretive brochure), Colonial farmers once used Beaver Creek's meadows for horse racing. The town built a dam to flood the meadows and end the racing, creating Mauserts Pond.

MORE INFORMATION

Open sunrise to a half hour after sunset year-round. No fee at this hike's trailhead; a seasonal parking fee ($5 MA residents, $10 out of state) is charged at the main entrance from late May to September. Skiing, biking, dogs, and hunting in season are allowed. Restrooms, a swimming beach, and a boat launch are available at the day-use area. The campground offers 45 sites ($17 MA residents, $27 out of state). Download an interpretive brochure at mass.gov/files/documents/2016/08/vx/clarksburgmauserts.pdf. Clarksburg State Park, 1199 Middle Road, Clarksburg, MA 01247 (413-664-8345; mass.gov/locations/clarksburg-state-park).

NEARBY

Natural Bridge State Park is home to a true natural phenomenon—the only white marble bridge arch in North America formed by water erosion. Open weekends 9 A.M. to 4:30 P.M. Memorial Day to Columbus Day. Parking fee: $5 MA residents, $10 out of state. The entrance is on MA 8, 0.5 mile north of the intersection with MA 2 (413-663-6392; mass.gov/locations/natural-bridge-state-park).

11

HOOSAC RANGE TRAIL TO SPRUCE HILL

A largely out-and-back hike on a portion of fabled Mahican-Mohawk Trail follows the spine of the Hoosac Range to a stunning vista atop Spruce Hill. This is a longer but less traveled option to Spruce Hill than via Busby Trail (Trip 12).

LOCATION
North Adams, MA

RATING
Moderate

DISTANCE
5.4 miles round trip

DIRECTIONS

From the intersection of MA 8 and MA 2 (Mohawk Trail) in downtown North Adams, follow MA 2 east past the Hairpin Turn for a total of 4.7 miles to an ample gravel parking area on the right (0.9 mile beyond the Hairpin Turn). *GPS coordinates*: 42° 41.789′ N, 73° 03.886′ W.

ELEVATION GAIN
540 feet

ESTIMATED TIME
2.5-3.5 hours

TRAIL DESCRIPTION

The route, marked by red-on-white blazes on trees, begins at an elevation of more than 2,000 feet at a wooden kiosk complete with a large trail map. Walk up into the fern-rich forest of northern hardwoods—American beech, red maple, birch, and oak. Hobblebush (viburnum) is abundant in the understory along the mostly level trail, though oaks soon become abundant. It's an interesting mix of forest types: northern hardwoods versus oaks with southern affinities. Goldthread, lowbush blueberry, and other northern forbs (herbaceous flowering plants) grace the forest floor. Notice also the small spruces; oddly, they are the only ones along the entire route.

Begin a gradual ascent over a treadway with a few protruding quartzite rocks. Virtually all the beech trees (many appear young) show signs of disease—a fungus has disfigured their normally smooth, gray trunks. The 4-inch-tall, bottle brush-like stalks of shining club moss form soft mats beneath. This trail is well constructed, as evidenced by the stone steps that lead to the first

MAPS
USGS North Adams;
Berkshire Natural Resources
Council map: bnrc.org/
wp-content/uploads/
2019/05/Hoosac_Range_
trailmap.pdf

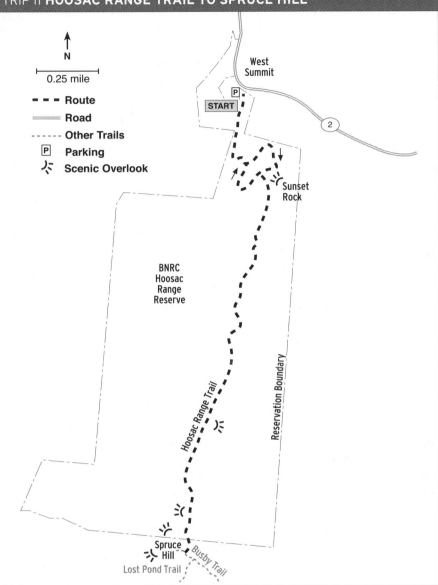

switchback. After 0.5 mile, reach a signed intersection where the trail splits to form a loop to the Sunset Rock outlook. Stay straight for the most direct route to the view. You'll return via the other fork later; both are 0.3 mile.

Yellow birch joins the beech and red maple. The path is littered with chunks of glistening, mica-rich schist. As you near the ridge top, the trees become shorter.

Hedge bindweeds (with white and pink morning glory–like flowers in summer) and raspberry canes blanket the forest floor under breaks in the canopy. In shady spots, some tree trunks are cushioned with mosses. More stone steps and easy switchbacks bring you to Sunset Rock (elevation 2,253 feet) and a nearly 180-degree view—from west to northeast—of the Hoosic River valley, downtown North Adams, and the rolling hills beyond. A stone bench offers a nice place for a snack. When you're ready, continue about 100 feet to a signed intersection, and turn left on Hoosac Range Trail toward Spruce Hill, 1.9 miles away.

Amble up through woodland marked by open patches nearly smothered in hedge bindweeds and raspberries. Through gaps in the foliage, catch a glimpse of wind turbines along a ridgeline to the left. Ascend the modest slope under more hardwoods, including black cherry, with beech sprouts forming a fairly dense understory. Parasitic flowering plants called beechdrops draw nourishment from beech roots and produce inconspicuous purple-brown, orchid-like blossoms in early fall. For nearly the rest of the route, the path undulates, using stone steps, through a low-stature forest with occasional canopy breaks. A notable old yellow birch—hollow at the base—fronts a moss-adorned ledge more than 100 feet long that walls in the treadway. In midspring, enjoy profuse blooms of trout lilies, spring beauties, and other wildflowers.

Bear left away from the ledge, but know you'll encounter more yellow birches later on. These trees are adept at gaining a foothold, and mosses cushion the hard stone, helping them along. In fact, there is another one on the left here, flecked with rock tripes, leafy lichens.

A short wooden span leads over an intermittent brook, the only one along this ridgeline route. The walking is easy as you stroll past expansive patches of shining club moss and hobblebush. The paired, heart-shaped leaves of hobblebush turn shades of maroon in late summer, and its berry clusters turn from red to blue-black. Reach a signed intersection with a 250-foot side path to a viewpoint on the left. The vista of rolling hills to the east is worth a look. Return to the main trail and continue past more ledge outcroppings.

Emerge into a narrow, linear clearing—a power-line cut. You are standing directly above the Hoosac Tunnel, the 4.75-mile railroad tunnel bored through the heart of the range in the late nineteenth century, a quarter-mile beneath your feet! The tunnel opened up a crucial rail line to markets in New York and beyond, but nearly 200 people died during its construction. Reenter forest, walk past more ledge outcroppings, and pass an unmarked trail on the left. Arrive at a short path on the right leading to an expansive vista—bordered by blueberries and hay-scented fern and rimmed with mountain ash—across bedrock westward over the valley to the Greylock Range. Mountain ash glows with coral-red berry clusters in late summer. Return to the main trail and turn right to hike the last 0.2 mile to Spruce Hill.

After walking through two more small clearings, past more ledges, arrive at a point where a couple of well-worn paths on the right lead steeply up over bedrock

Just before reaching the Spruce Hill summit, hikers enjoy an expansive vista westward beyond the Hoosic River valley to the Greylock Range.

to the summit; take the wider second path. From here, the route (now Busby Trail in Savoy Mountain State Forest) is blazed blue. Look back for a view of two sets of wind turbines on a ridgeline several miles away. Bear left to follow a narrow path a short way to the open summit of Spruce Hill, marked by two USGS benchmarks. Atop this cliff, enjoy views in virtually all directions—especially south and west—but be sure to watch your footing as you maneuver for that perfect photo. The southern Green Mountains of Vermont are visible to the north, and the Mount Greylock range rises high above the valley to the west. The quarry at the foot of Mount Greylock is distinguished by its brilliant white color. When you're ready, scramble down the short, steep bedrock to the main trail, and retrace your steps all the way to the T junction near Sunset Rock. Turn left for a slight variation (both routes are 0.3 mile) back to the start of the loop. Descend to the lower junction, and turn left to walk 0.5 mile back to your vehicle.

DID YOU KNOW?

The Hoosac Range is a southward extension of Vermont's Green Mountains. Hoosac (also spelled Hoosic, Hoosick, and Hoosuck) is an Algonkin word that means "place of stones."

MORE INFORMATION

Hoosac Range Trail is open during daylight hours and is free of charge. The route traverses lands owned and managed by the nonprofit Berkshire Natural Resources Council, a regional land trust. Motorized vehicles, fires, camping, littering, and cutting or removing plant material are prohibited. Open to hunting in season. Berkshire Natural Resources Council, 20 Bank Row, Pittsfield, MA 01201 (413-499-0596; bnrc.org). Spruce Hill summit is in Savoy Mountain State Forest, 260 Central Shaft Road, Florida, MA 01247 (413-663-8469; mass.gov/locations/savoy-mountain-state-forest).

NEARBY

Savoy Mountain State Forest offers camping (mid-May through mid-October) and many miles of recreational trails. From the BNRC trailhead, follow MA 2 east less than 0.5 mile and turn right on Central Shaft Road. Travel 2.8 miles to the park headquarters, 3.3 miles to the North Pond day-use area, and 3.7 miles to the campground.

The famous Hairpin Turn on the Mohawk Trail Highway (MA 2), renowned for sweeping views of the Taconic Mountains and Hoosic Valley, is just 1.0 mile west of the BNRC trailhead. The road's highest point, 2,275-foot Whitcomb Summit, is 2.5 miles to the east.

12
SPRUCE HILL VIA BUSBY TRAIL

Perhaps the best views after a short hike in the entire region. An old road leads past an early-nineteenth-century cellar hole to a rocky perch with stunning vistas of the eastern face of the Greylock Range and the Taconic Range beyond, as well as points north and south.

DIRECTIONS

From the intersection of MA 8, MA 2, and MA 8A in downtown North Adams, follow MA 2 (Mohawk Trail) east for approximately 5.1 miles (via the Hairpin Turn). Turn right onto Central Shaft Road just after the Florida town line. Stay to the right at each of the next two forks and drive an additional 1.0 miles (passing the Savoy Mountain State Forest headquarters on the right) to a roadside parking area at the Busby Trail trailhead on the right. *GPS coordinates*: 42° 39.477′ N, 73° 03.351′ W.

TRAIL DESCRIPTION

From the kiosk, where trail maps may be available, walk up into a young forest of birch, maple, and beech, with a few red spruce. After about 150 feet, reach blue-blazed Busby Trail, a dirt road that suffers from off-road vehicle traffic in spite of it being prohibited. Turn right onto the level path bordered and shaded by sugar and striped maples, white and gray birches, and hobblebush shrubs. Cross a power-line clearing filled with raspberry canes, gray birches, and red maple saplings. Chestnut-sided warblers whistle their *pleased, pleased, pleased to meetcha* breeding refrain and nest in shrubs here from May through July.

Back in the forest, Busby Trail bypasses the rutted and often wet road to the left for a couple hundred yards and continues through a northern hardwood forest of birch, beech, maple, and hemlock. Patches of the Massachusetts state flower, trailing arbutus (more commonly known as

LOCATION
Florida and North Adams, MA

RATING
Moderate

DISTANCE
2.6 miles round trip

ELEVATION GAIN
670 feet

ESTIMATED TIME
1.5-2 hours

MAPS
USGS North Adams; Massachusetts Department of Conservation and Recreation map: mass.gov/doc/savoy-mountain-state-forest-trail-map

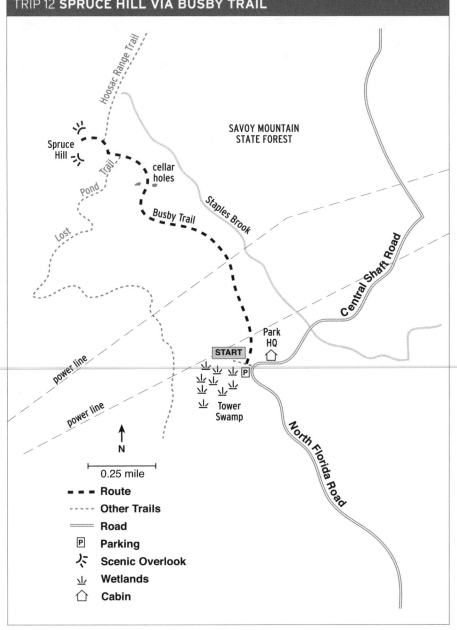

Hoosac Range Trail

Spruce Hill

Pond Trail

Lost

cellar holes

Busby Trail

Staples Brook

SAVOY MOUNTAIN STATE FOREST

Central Shaft Road

Park HQ

START

P

Tower Swamp

power line

power line

↑ N

|—— 0.25 mile ——|

- - - **Route**

⸺⸺⸺ **Other Trails**

═══ **Road**

P **Parking**

⅄ **Scenic Overlook**

⅄ **Wetlands**

⌂ **Cabin**

North Florida Road

mayflower), grace both sides at one point, their pale pink blossoms emerging for a short time in early May. More common are the little paired leaves of partridge-berry and the heart-shaped leaves and spike of tiny white blossoms of Canada mayflower. Soon the road rises a bit and becomes drier and more pleasant.

Traverse another power-line cut filled with arrowwood (note the straight branches), bilberry, raspberry, and birch. The cut—devoid of trees—reveals the

This farmstead cellar hole along Busby Trail creates an opportunity for reflection on farm life here two centuries ago.

lay of the land as it dips and then rises to a ridgeline on the right. Ignore the narrow roadway that joins Busby Trail from the right a bit farther along, and begin a gradual ascent. So far, you've had to expend little effort.

During the 1930s, the renowned Civilian Conservation Corps planted groves of Norway spruce here and at many other locations. These trees are now maturing and provide habitat for birds and mammals that prefer conifer stands, such as black, white, and fiery orange Blackburnian warblers, and impish red squirrels that feast on bird eggs as well as spruce seeds and fungi. Spruce Hill itself has virtually no spruces, and nearly all that you encounter along the trail have been planted.

Listen for the sound of flowing water to your right and soon gaze upon a small brook. The stone remnants of former bridge abutments are visible along the far bank, as is a stone wall. White ash trees here are identifiable by their crosshatched bark; they do well in moister ground. In fact, other than the spruce plantations, deciduous trees predominate. The clean white trunks of paper birch here are most attractive. Continue an easy climb, bear right, and cross a narrow drainage (wet in spring). At one point, flowing water has eroded a gully, exposing rock and forming a modest falls during wet seasons. Watch your step.

A bit farther, tread up and over bedrock steps; the remains of an unmortared wall stand on your left. The old road becomes rockier before you arrive at a jumble of rectangular cut blocks of schist on the left at the site of a former foundation at 1.0 mile. A few feet farther and on the opposite side gapes a well-preserved cellar hole. A yellow birch threatens to cleave the stones of the right wall. (It's interesting to contemplate what farm life would have been like here some 200 years ago.)

Busby Trail now turns sharply left, where the shiny, pointed leaves of trout lily carpet the ground profusely in late spring, and begins to climb. The terrain becomes briefly sandy under a canopy of black cherry, ash, birch, and beech and sparkles with flecks of the mineral mica. Here is where you'll finally have to exert yourself. Cross a stone wall built of good-sized schist blocks—moving them into place would have been no easy chore. A bench sits on the right. Continue straight up the slope. A luxuriant growth of skunk currant about 18 inches high fills the sunny forest floor where you turn left, and shining club moss forms a patch of green "bottle brushes" on the right.

The path winds up through attractive woodland. Listen for the *beer, beer, bee* songs of tiny black-throated blue warblers in late spring and early summer as you approach ledge outcroppings. These birds nest low among the wiry branches of hobblebush, which in spring are lovely with bunches of white flowers resembling doilies. At the trail split (note the arrow carved into the bark of a small beech), turn right through a swale, or gap between the rocks.

Climb a steep but well-built stone staircase that leads up the ledge. A bouquet of exquisite painted trillium—three petals, three leaves—clamors for attention partway up in May. Bear left and continue a more moderate climb under stunted beech trees into a wonderful spring wildflower garden. *Clintonia* (blue-bead lily), bunchberry (a tiny, ground-hugging dogwood), wild oat, and lowbush blueberry have turned this into a fairyland forest. The paired, heart-shaped leaves and flat, white flower clusters of hobblebush are abundant. The tiny, fertile flowers produce red berries, and in late summer and fall, the leaves turn lovely shades of maroon.

After a few short switchbacks, reach the junction with the southern end of the Hoosac Range Trail (Trip 11), which leads 2.7 miles to MA 2. Turn left for one last ascent over a ledge outcropping and emerge into the open. Follow the blue blazes left over bedrock and through a hobblebush thicket for the best views from exposed, slanted schist bedrock at an elevation of 2,566 feet. What a fantastic vista from this perch on the Hoosac Range! The Greylock Range sprawls to the west, with Ragged Mountain lying below, and the Taconics loom beyond Greylock. North Adams lies in the Hoosac Valley to your right, with Pine Cobble poking up beyond. To the left is the town of Adams. At your feet, lowbush blueberry crowds the perimeter and shows creamy, bell-shaped blossoms in spring, while a few wind-trimmed mountain ashes hold forth to the right.

Linger here and soak in all the stunning scenery. (The spectacular fall foliage is a great reason to visit in October.) When you're ready to leave, retrace your steps 1.3 miles back to your vehicle.

DID YOU KNOW?

If you have planned your hike for mid-September to early November, be on the lookout for southbound migrant hawks heading for wintering grounds in Central America. You are most likely to observe broad-winged hawks (sometimes in "kettles" of dozens of birds in September), sharp-shinned and Cooper's hawks, turkey vultures, and ospreys.

MORE INFORMATION

Open sunrise to sunset, year-round. Busby Trail access is free. Biking, skiing, and hunting are allowed. Pets must be on a 10-foot-maximum leash and attended at all times. Pet owners must have proof of current rabies vaccination. Motorized off-road vehicles and alcoholic beverages are prohibited. Savoy Mountain State Forest, 260 Central Shaft Road, Florida, MA 01247 (413-663-8469; mass.gov/locations/savoy-mountain-state-forest).

NEARBY

Mass Audubon's West Mountain Wildlife Sanctuary, in Plainfield, near the boundary of Berkshire, Hampshire, and Franklin counties, protects 1,835 acres on the slopes of West Mountain. A 1.3-mile loop trail leads to a beaver pond, cascading streams, and northern hardwood and spruce-fir forests. The roadside entrance is on Prospect Street off MA 116, west of the town center (massaudubon.org/get-outdoors/wildlife-sanctuaries/west-mountain).

PATHWAY TO HISTORY: THE MAHICAN-MOHAWK RECREATION TRAIL

For thousands of years, travelers have followed a route that links the Connecticut and Hudson rivers via the Deerfield, Cold, and Hoosic rivers, as well as the imposing Hoosac Range. American Indian tribes, Colonial armies, industrial traders, and well-known figures, including Benedict Arnold and Henry David Thoreau, all trod this highly scenic and historically significant route, which evolved over time to accommodate modern transportation. The Mahican-Mohawk Trail is now being developed as a long-distance recreational trail along the corridor, connecting a wealth of natural and cultural features.

The region's American Indian tribes, including the Pocumtuck of the Pioneer Valley, the Mohawk of upstate New York, and the Mahican of New York and western Massachusetts, created and used the original trail for trade, hunting, fishing, and war. After the Mohawk defeated the Pocumtuck in a 1664 battle, the passage eventually became known as the "Mohawk Trail," a term coined in the twentieth century to market the region for tourism.

European settlers relocated and widened the narrow footpaths to facilitate travel by horses and wagons. After serving as a key military route during the French and Indian War and the American Revolution, the corridor became a vital commercial link between Massachusetts and New York during the nineteenth century.

The Mohawk Trail Highway, one of New England's iconic scenic roads, opened to automobiles in 1914. The region quickly became a popular tourist destination, thanks to the sweeping views from outlooks such as the fabled Hairpin Turn and 2,275-foot Whitcomb Summit. The highway roughly parallels the original American Indian path, but there is likely little overlap.

The Mahican-Mohawk Trail began to take shape in 1992, when Williams College students researched the historical route and opportunities to develop the trail. Thanks to the efforts of the Massachusetts Department of Conservation and Recreation, Berkshire Natural Resources Council, Deerfield River Watershed Association, and many other regional organizations, landowners, and volunteers, approximately 40 miles of the proposed 100-mile route are open, including 30 miles of foot trails and a 10-mile paddling segment on the Deerfield River.

Heading east from North Adams, the Mahican-Mohawk Trail follows a portion of a historical turnpike up to Western Summit and then continues on Hoosac Range Trail (Trip 11) along the ridge to Spruce Hill (Trip 12). After traversing several existing trails in Savoy Mountain State Forest, the route crosses steep-banked Cold River and MA 2 in Drury. On the north side of the Cold River valley, it joins the original American Indian footpath over Clark and Todd mountains, passing by and through old-growth forest, groves of 150-foot white pines, and meadows at the confluence of the Cold and Deerfield rivers.

East of the Hoosac Range, the Deerfield River offers a scenic paddling route from Charlemont to Buckland. The foot trail resumes near Shelburne Falls, paralleling the river through portions of South River State Forest to a historical truss bridge at Bardwell's Ferry (a short section on private land was closed as of this writing). The trail's eastern end follows the abandoned New Haven and Northampton Railroad grade past the stone remains of a giant railroad trestle at the South River crossing, now spanned by a fiberglass hikers' bridge. Three side paths loop along the Deerfield River's wooded banks, offering opportunities to see barred owls and other wildlife. From the Hoosac Road trailhead in Deerfield, lightly traveled country roads lead to the official eastern terminus at Historic Deerfield, an outdoor museum set up as an eighteenth-century village.

Future plans include developing the route's western segments from North Adams and Williamstown to the Hudson River. For more information and updates, visit mass.gov/location-details/mahican-mohawk-trail.

13

TANNERY FALLS AND PARKER BROOK FALLS

The twin cascades of Tannery Falls and Parker Brook Falls share the same enchanting ravine in Savoy Mountain State Forest. Several trails and roads loop to Balance Rock and hemlock-lined Ross Brook, upstream from the falls.

DIRECTIONS

From the junction of MA 2 and Black Brook Road in Savoy (1.7 miles west of the Florida town line), follow Black Brook Road uphill for 2.6 miles, bearing right at a fork after 1.3 miles. Turn right and follow dirt Tannery Road for 0.2 mile to the state forest boundary, and then continue downhill 0.5 mile to the parking area on the right, opposite Tannery Pond. Tannery Road is unmaintained in winter beyond the last residence. (*Note*: It is possible to reach the trailhead from the Savoy Mountain State Forest main entrance on Central Shaft Road, but the dirt roads are often rutted and potentially difficult for low-clearance vehicles. *GPS coordinates*: 42 37.328′ N, 73 00.304′ W.

TRAIL DESCRIPTION

This hike combines the popular out-and-back walk to Tannery Falls and Parker Brook Falls with a 4.5-mile circuit on Tannery Trail, Tannery Road, and Ross Brook Trail. To reach the falls, start from the back of the parking area and follow the unnamed blue-blazed trail north into the woods between Parker Brook (Tannery Pond's outflow) and Ross Brook. Eastern hemlock, a fire-intolerant species, thrives in wetlands and sheltered ravines. After a few hundred feet, continue along a fence above Ross Brook, which cascades through a narrow gorge scoured through the bedrock.

At 0.2 mile, the trail bends right, opposite the crest of Tannery Falls (also known as Ross Brook Falls). Wood and

LOCATION
Savoy, MA

RATING
Easy to Moderate

DISTANCE
0.6 mile round trip (waterfalls), 4.5 miles loop (circuit)

ELEVATION GAIN
200 feet (waterfalls), 615 feet (circuit)

ESTIMATED TIME
30 minutes (waterfalls), 2.5 hours (circuit)

MAPS
USGS Windsor; Massachusetts Department of Conservation and Recreation map: mass.gov/ files/documents/2016/12/ns/ savoy.pdf

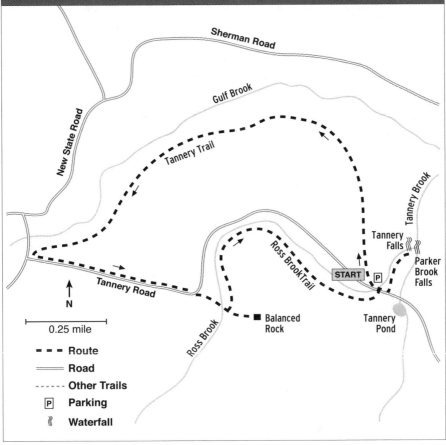

rock steps provide a steep but safe passage to the bottom of the ravine. At the base of the descent, Parker Brook Falls is on your right. Distinctive, jagged mossy walls line the 60-foot cascade in a gorge of angular bedrock, with several smaller drops along its base.

Tannery Falls is a quick 100-foot walk from the steps. Pass water gliding over smooth rock at the top of the falls on the left before reaching a dead-on view of the 80-foot waterfall at the trail's end. Roughly dividing the two main drops is a small, shelflike pool. Ross Brook and Parker Brook merge at the base of the falls, forming Tannery Brook, which empties into Cold River about a mile downstream. All of these waterways are part of the Deerfield River watershed. The steep slope below the falls shelters a 120-acre grove of old-growth hemlock, spruce, sugar maple, and birch. In May, look for a patch of flowering hobblebush, Canada mayflower, and painted trillium on the bedrock between the two waterfalls. After enjoying the views and the sound of the rushing water, retrace your steps to the parking area.

Now that you've seen the falls, begin hiking the loop on the north side of Tannery Pond, which was originally created in the nineteenth century by damming Parker Brook. As the place and trail names suggest, this was once the site of a tannery, where animal hides were converted to leather. Workers immersed the skins in tannic acid to add durability and color. Eastern hemlock was the primary source of tannin in the Northeast, and many of the region's hemlock groves were harvested for use at tanneries in the mid-nineteenth century, when the industry peaked. Civilian Conservation Corps workers rebuilt the dam during the 1930s as part of improvements to the property (the Bog Pond and Burnett Pond dams were also upgraded). A beaver dam and lodge are visible at the pond outlet on the left.

Walk right (when facing the pond) on Tannery Road and cross the bridge over Ross Brook. Turn right on Tannery Trail, a multiuse trail on an old woods road, marked with periodic orange triangle blazes. Portions of the path may be seasonally wet or muddy (partly due to erosion by off-road vehicles), but the edges are usually passable. After briefly paralleling Tannery Road, the trail bends north through northern hardwoods interspersed with hemlocks and a few white pines, a forest community characteristic of high elevations, such as the Hoosac Range. In autumn, the birches, maples, and beeches are alive with colorful foliage. In spite of the remote location and rocky terrain, these woods were mostly cleared for agriculture in Colonial times. Savoy Mountain State Forest was originally formed by purchases of abandoned farmland in the early twentieth century.

Hobblebush, a common shrub of northern hardwood forests, thrives in the cool, moist environment. The white flowers bloom in May, and the broad leaves offer colorful, sometimes multihued maroon foliage in autumn. Abundant trout lilies, with narrow, mottled leaves and yellow flowers, line the trail edges in midspring.

Arrive at a shady hemlock grove that indicates a wet area. Note the lack of understory vegetation relative to broadleaf forests. Cross a seasonal stream draining into a wetland on the right. Chestnut-sided warblers frequent the shrubby growths here in spring and summer.

Continue an easy walk on Tannery Trail along the slope high above Gulf Brook, which cascades through a deep valley, out of view to the right. A few yellow violets bloom along sunlit trail openings in May and June. Wooded ravines are an ideal habitat for winter wrens, easily identified by their distinctive long, melodious, warbling call. Dark-eyed juncos, which favor mountain settings, are familiar year-round residents. During spring and summer listen for the loud and frequent *teacher-teacher-teacher* call of ovenbirds, which build nests on the ground in mixed broadleaf forests.

Facing page: The picturesque cascades of Tannery Falls (shown) and Parker Brook Falls share the same ravine in Savoy Mountain State Forest.

The trail narrows in a seasonal wet area, where flexible water bars have been installed to mitigate erosion. Sadly, the ash trees, identified by crosshatched bark, are threatened by the emerald ash borer, which was confirmed in the northern Berkshires in 2018. Enter another hemlock grove, where intermittent brooks drain the steep slope. Red trilliums bloom along the embankments in April and May. Juvenile red-spotted newts (or red efts) roam the forest floor before returning to ponds and streams as mature adults.

At 2.3 miles, reach Tannery Trail's western end at the junction with Tannery Road, adjacent to New State Road on the right. Make a sharp left on Tannery Road, heading uphill along the north side of 2,177-foot Lewis Hill, one of seven prominent Hoosac Range summits within the state forest. Look for more red trilliums along the road edges in midspring.

Reach an interpretive sign at a large forest management area, where trees were cut to promote age diversity, slow the spread of diseases, and create wildlife habitat. Mixed-aged forests enhance resilience to storms, forest pests, and other disturbances. Moose, white-tailed deer, black bears, and other wildlife often feed on regenerating vegetation at harvest sites, and prairie warblers and common yellowthroats nest in young growth. Thanks to its expansive size and remote location, Savoy Mountain State Forest is an ideal habitat for large mammals, including a healthy bear population.

Continue through the timber harvest, past the junction with Lewis Hill Trail on the right. After 0.7 mile on Tannery Road, reach an unmarked but obvious intersection at the edge of the clearing. Turn right (leaving Tannery Road, which bends left at the junction) and descend a woods road to Ross Brook, about 1.4 miles upstream from Tannery Falls. False hellebore, with photogenic green leaves, unfurls along the banks in midspring. Step across the brook and ascend past the unmarked junction with Ross Brook Trail (your return route) on the left. In another 150 feet, reach the intersection with Balance Rock Trail, marked by a sign on the right. Turn left and make a quick 0.1-mile climb to Balanced Rock, 3.2 miles from the trailhead. Rock tripes (lichens) coat this large, angular glacial boulder, perched atop a ledge at an elevation of 1,890 feet.

Return to the junction with blue-blazed Ross Brook Trail and turn right (north) onto it to begin the final 1.1-mile segment, a pleasant descent along the hemlock-lined brook. The narrow footpath is open to hiking and skiing (though maps may show crossings, the trail stays entirely on the brook's southern banks until reaching a footbridge near the trailhead). Eroded portions of the channel are evidence of torrential flooding associated with the remnants of Hurricane Irene in August 2011.

After about 0.3 mile, the trail briefly bends away from Ross Brook, descending the moderately steep ravine to a dense hobblebush growth. Wild oats (also known as sessile bellwort) display cream or pale-yellow bell-shaped flowers in middle to late spring. A few winterberries dot the forest floor. Return to the brook edge at a small cascade, and cross a low knoll where the path levels. Pass a large, old yellow birch and follow the blue markers along the winding banks.

The trail's lower segment leads through another rich wildflower area. Blue-bead lilies, sometimes mistaken for much rarer yellow lady's slippers because of their similar elongated leaves and yellow flowers, thrive in cool, acidic woodlands. Look for, but don't eat, the lilies' rather foul-tasting (and potentially poisonous) blue berries during the summer. Cross a footbridge near Tannery Pond's northwestern corner and complete the circuit at Tannery Road and the parking area.

DID YOU KNOW?

Tropical Storm Irene's torrential rains caused several landslides on the Cold River valley's steep slopes in 2011. A 6-mile segment of the Mohawk Trail Highway washed out, and Black Brook Road wasn't repaired until 2017.

MORE INFORMATION

Open dawn to dusk, year-round. Access is free. Biking, skiing, and dogs are permitted; hunting is allowed in season. The state forest campground has 45 sites in an old orchard and four log cabins at South Pond. From the intersection of MA 2 and Central Shaft Road, follow Central Shaft Road 2.8 miles to the park headquarters, 3.3 miles to the North Pond day-use area, and 3.7 miles to the campground. Savoy Mountain State Forest, 260 Central Shaft Road, Florida, MA 01247 (413-663-8469; mass.gov/locations/savoy-mountain-state-forest).

NEARBY

The 7,882-acre Kenneth Dubuque Memorial State Forest, part of a large conservation corridor in the Deerfield River watershed, offers 35 miles of trails. An easy loop around Hallockville Pond leads to an old mill site and dam, and the woods roads are ideal for skiing and mountain biking. The main entrance is on MA 8A (West Hawley Road) at Hallockville Pond (413-339-5504; mass.gov/locations/kenneth-dubuque-memorial-state-forest).

14

DUNBAR BROOK

Old-growth trees, massive boulders, and roaring waters make Dunbar Brook Trail a path of superlatives. A steep slope leads to gravel woodland roads that enable a great loop through wild uplands at the northeastern edge of the Berkshires. Fording the brook when the water level is high can be difficult.

LOCATION
Florida and Monroe, MA

RATING
Moderate to Strenuous

DISTANCE
6.8 miles round trip

ELEVATION GAIN
1,010 feet

ESTIMATED TIME
4 hours

MAPS
USGS Rowe; Massachusetts Department of Conservation and Recreation map: mass.gov/files/documents/2016/12/rw/monroe.pdf

DIRECTIONS
From the intersection of MA 2 and MA 8 (opposite the Massachusetts Museum of Contemporary Art) in North Adams, follow MA 2 east past the Hairpin Turn, Western Summit, and Whitcomb Summit to the intersection with Whitcomb Hill Road on the left at 7.5 miles. Follow Whitcomb Hill Road (staying right at the intersection with Monroe Road) for 2.5 miles to the junction with River Road. Turn left and drive on River Road to the railroad crossing at the Hoosac Tunnel and continue another 4.0 miles to a gravel parking area (day use only) on the left, across from the Dunbar Brook Picnic Area. *GPS coordinates*: 42° 42.275' N, 72° 57.161' W.

TRAIL DESCRIPTION
From the parking area, where a stylized map and recreation area rules are posted, follow the rough track up the inclined power-line corridor for about 150 feet to a footpath on the right, and enter a dark hemlock wood. Blue blazes mark the trail. Do not follow the wooden staircase fitted with railings down to the small concrete dam that spans the brook.

Amble along the hill's contour beneath shade-casting hemlocks along a rocky slope. Yellow birches rise from the gneiss boulders they firmly grasp. As you descend, the sound of water cascading over rocks captures your

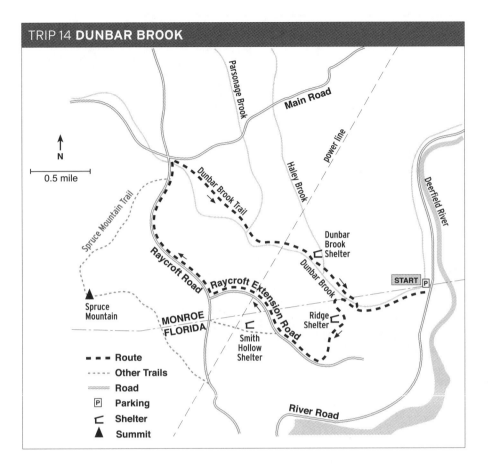

N

0.5 mile

Route

Other Trails

Road

P Parking

Shelter

▲ Summit

attention. Dunbar Brook, an evocative tributary of the nearby Deerfield River, flows below. The brook, as well as the forest, has a wild, untamed appearance. You'll be struck by the sheer size of some of the boulders in the streambed.

A bordering outcropping drips moisture from its mossy sphagnum coat. More boulders—some the size of trucks—protrude from the slope; others, rounded by flowing water, litter the brook. Yellow birches soon become more numerous. Along the path, foamflowers, with leaves that resemble those of geraniums, send up frothy white heads of modest blossoms in late spring. Hobblebush also grows here, with paired, heart-shaped leaves and white blossoms earlier in spring.

Bear left and climb rock steps, gradually moving higher above the brook and into a mixed forest. A towering white ash, with crosshatched bark, stands like a sentinel on the right. Big-tooth aspen, red maple, and beech join the deciduous mix along the banks of Dunbar Brook. Early yellow violet, red trillium, baneberry, jack-in-the-pulpit, starflower, and wild ginger are among the woodland wildflowers you may spot in spring.

Dunbar Brook pours over gneiss boulders polished to a fine patina by the abrasive actions of the swift current.

At 0.8 mile, reach an intersection where stone steps lead down to the brook bank. Turn left to ascend the steep slope (you'll cross the brook on stepping stones in this vicinity to close the loop later—if water levels are high, you may want to check conditions before completing the loop). Blue blazes lead in both directions. The path undulates, then slants up the steep incline, and finally bears right toward the height-of-land. Nearly two-thirds of the hike's total elevation gain occurs here. Some impressive trees—sugar maples, yellow birches, and white ashes—that escaped the ax thanks to the slope's acute angle dot the slope.

Reach Ridge Shelter on the right, bearing left just before it. A privy is 100 yards farther along this old woods road on the right. Blazes are a bit spotty here, but the path is easy to locate on this somewhat-level stretch. A pond on the left, transitioning to a bog, has been virtually filled in with fallen leaves and branches. At the end of the blazed trail at 1.5 miles, turn right on gravel Raycroft Extension Road (a snowmobile corridor). Although technically a road, it is more of a wide, nearly level path through pleasant deciduous woodland that now includes oak and American beech. Because you're far from the roaring waters of Dunbar Brook, the voices of neotropical songbirds, such as the scarlet tanager, American redstart, ovenbird, red-eyed vireo, and rose-breasted grosbeak, are audible in late spring and early summer.

White birch—one of the most attractive of the northern trees—abounds along the road, and red spruce soon becomes common at this elevation. In late spring and early summer, when you reach the unsigned intersection with a woods road bearing left down to Smith Hollow Shelter, listen carefully for the ascending flutelike song of Swainson's thrush, a species found in Massachusetts only at high elevation. Continue on Raycroft Extension Road through mixed woods dotted with big gneiss boulders, and then traverse a bright power line right-of-way. Back in the forest, plantations of Norway spruce and red pine were established in the 1930s. The 6-inch-long cones of this exotic spruce litter the ground. Some trees have been harvested, allowing deciduous growth—cherry, birch, and raspberry—to fill the sunny void. Canada mayflower and *Clintonia* (blue-bead lily) both bloom in spring along the roadway.

Arrive at a T intersection with unsigned gravel Raycroft Road at 2.6 miles, and turn right onto this route—more traveled by motor vehicles. Potential ATV traffic on summer weekends (despite being illegal here) is a good reason to plan your hike for a weekday. Sugar maples and light-green hay-scented ferns line the mostly level road, while gneiss boulders protrude from the forest floor. The road begins an easy descent and then becomes rougher. Large, platy-barked yellow birches bear little resemblance to youthful, brassy-skinned individuals of the same species. Two brooks flow through culverts under the roadway. Cabin-sized boulders—one characteristically serving as an anchor for a yellow birch on the left—are astonishing. After a short rise, continue the descent, sometimes steeper and in the dense shade of hemlocks, and follow the road as it bends right. On the left, pass the northern end of blue-blazed Spruce Mountain Trail, which leads up to the wooded summit of Spruce Mountain.

As you continue downward on Raycroft Road, the sound of flowing water becomes apparent. More monumental boulders appear—one with a sheer face toward the road. Reach a flat pull-out area on the right adjacent to Dunbar Brook and soon cross the brook on a modular wooden bridge at 4.0 miles. Turn right on blue-blazed Dunbar Brook Trail immediately after the crossing, and enter a mixed forest of hemlock, beech, and yellow birch. The roaring, cascading water gushes through tight squeezes between and over rocks, creating an evocative scene. (*Caution*: Be careful if you move closer for a better view, as the rocks are slippery and the current unforgiving!) Note how eons of flow have abraded and sculpted the bedrock. Between here and where you parked, the brook drops some 700 vertical feet.

The northern end of Dunbar Brook Trail may be a bit difficult to follow initially, but the route soon becomes clearer. Look for the stone ruins of a millrace on the left, where diverted water once turned a mill wheel. Watch for blue blazes that lead across a feeder stream's rocky tumble where foot-tall American yew bushes (a favorite of deer) thrive. Their needles resemble those of hemlock but are longer and a lighter shade of green. Climb up under a canopy of large hemlocks and northern hardwoods away from Dunbar Brook on a needle-cushioned path. Bear right when you reach a narrow woods road that traverses mature woodland dotted with more boulders. One on the right where the path narrows further is the size of a cottage. Little undergrowth exists except where big trees have fallen to admit light. Look for the cloverlike leaves of wood sorrel. In June, its five-petaled, pink-veined blossoms resemble those of spring beauty.

Now temporarily out of sight of the brook, the trail climbs under hemlocks, undulates, and then follows the grade downward, sometimes with moderate steepness. Glimpse Spruce Mountain through a screen of trees to your right. Watch for the large pink slippers of the moccasin flower in the acidic soil during early June. Red spruce is regenerating very well here, as evidenced by the abundant seedlings and small trees. No doubt the most imposing boulder along the route—verdant with moss and capped by polypody ferns—lies where the trail turns sharply right and skirts its overarching face. Other boulders are a veritable nursery for hemlocks and spruces. Tiny, orange-throated Blackburnian warblers sing their lisping refrains from high in the evergreens during the breeding season.

As you continue a steady and sometimes rather steep descent, the sound of rushing water becomes evident again. The trail levels out just above the brook and bears left to parallel it. The rocky streambed, cascades, and crystalline pools beckon the photographer. Walk over level ground where red-backed salamanders hide under logs by day and search for tiny morsels by night, while poisonous (to eat) red efts wander blissfully in broad daylight. Watch for piles of moose droppings. After you cross Parsonage Brook on a log bridge, the delightful trail widens under a leafy canopy on the far bank and turns right. Watch for a boulder with a thick milky quartz intrusion on the right just before the power-line cut.

Raspberry, bush honeysuckle, meadowsweet, interrupted fern, birch, and red maple fill the linear light gap. Back in mixed woodland, you'll be awed by a pair of massive white pines—one twin-trunked—on the right. Tiny prince's pine, a club moss, and lots of ground-hugging partridgeberry, with coral-red berries, create a miniature woodland beneath.

Descend the slope toward Haley Brook, a tributary of Dunbar Brook that enters from the left, near a mammoth split white ash. Indian cucumber-root (which has an edible tuber), false Solomon's seal, and red trillium thrive in the rich soil as you reach Dunbar Brook Shelter. Turn left and walk about 100 feet to cross a wooden bridge over Haley Brook. Native stone abutments indicate that a bridge of higher capacity once spanned the water. Continue to parallel the brook's course.

Watch for an old millstone in Dunbar Brook just before you arrive at another pair of giant, straight-boled white pines, more than 100 feet tall. Not surprisingly, Monroe State Forest is known for its old-growth pines. Soon bear right to cross Dunbar Brook on rocks (as mentioned earlier in these directions). Use caution, as the stones may be slippery. A shallow water crossing may be available about 175 feet downstream. After crossing, gain the trail above the brook and turn left on the path that you took earlier, back to the parking area. Near the end, where the trail splits, be sure to take the right fork uphill.

DID YOU KNOW?

Old-growth forest in Massachusetts is limited to approximately 2,700 acres state-wide. To qualify as old growth, a forest must not have been significantly disturbed for at least the last 150 years. In Monroe State Forest, some 270 acres meet those criteria, including pockets of old-growth hemlock, white pine, red spruce, and associated hardwoods—yellow birch, American beech, and white ash.

MORE INFORMATION

Open sunrise to sunset year-round. Free access. Skiing, biking, leashed dogs, and hunting are allowed. Portable toilets are available at Dunbar Brook Picnic Area across River Road. Privies are available at shelters along the route. Carry in, carry out rules apply to all trash. Snowmobiling is permitted when conditions allow. All-terrain vehicles and alcoholic beverages are not permitted. Monroe State Forest, Tilda Hill Road, Monroe, MA 01247 (413-339-5504 [Mohawk Trail State Forest]; mass.gov/locations/monroe-state-forest). Trailhead parking area and restroom facilities at Dunbar Brook Picnic Area are owned and managed by Great River Hydro (greatriverhydro-relicensing.com).

NEARBY

The Hoosac Tunnel was an engineering marvel when it was completed in 1875. At 4.75 miles long, it remains the longest active transport tunnel east of the Rockies. It was built at considerable cost in dollars and human lives (193 people died during its construction, which began in 1848). The eastern portal in the town of Florida can be viewed from the railroad crossing on River Road, 4.0 miles south of the Dunbar Brook trailhead. This freight line is still active—do not linger near the tunnel entrance or tracks!

15

SADDLE BALL MOUNTAIN

While it terminates short of the Mount Greylock summit, this challenging hike has its own delights—a flower-filled hillside meadow offering incredible views and a damp boreal forest atop Saddle Ball Mountain, where sphagnum moss carpets the ground.

LOCATION
Adams, Cheshire, New Ashford, and Williamstown, MA

RATING
Strenuous

DIRECTIONS

From the south: From MA 8 in Pittsfield at Allendale Center, drive north on MA 8 for 9.1 miles into Cheshire, and turn left onto Fred Mason Road. Follow it north for 2.9 miles (it becomes West Road after approximately 1 mile) to West Mountain Road on the left. Turn left and follow West Mountain Road 1.6 miles, past parking for Gould Trail, to the Cheshire Harbor trailhead.

From the north: Take MA 8 south to Adams and turn right at the President William McKinley monument onto Maple Street. Follow Maple Street 0.9 mile, and turn right onto West Mountain Road. Follow it for 1.6 miles to the trailhead. *GPS coordinates*: 42° 36.635′ N, 73° 9.399′ W.

DISTANCE
10.4 miles round trip

ELEVATION GAIN
1,675 feet

ESTIMATED TIME
6-7 hours

MAPS
AMC Massachusetts Trail Map 1: D4; USGS Williamstown, USGS Cheshire; Massachusetts Department of Conservation and Recreation map: mass.gov/files/2017-08/Trail%20map.pdf

TRAIL DESCRIPTION

All Mount Greylock State Reservation trails, except for the white-blazed Appalachian Trail, are blue-blazed. Park in the gravel lot at road's end (elevation 1,560 feet). Follow the gravel roadway to your right (northwest) that leads into a meadow. Except in summer, when it is blocked by leaves, Greylock's summit looms above a gap in the treeline as you make your way past a small sign: "Old Adams Rd. to Cheshire Harbor Tr. to Summit 3.5 mi." Reach a map board at the woodland's edge. Just before a metal forest gate, a sign on the right reads "To Cheshire Harbor Trail." A short path cuts the corner off the rutted road. Bear right and follow the lower portion of blue-blazed

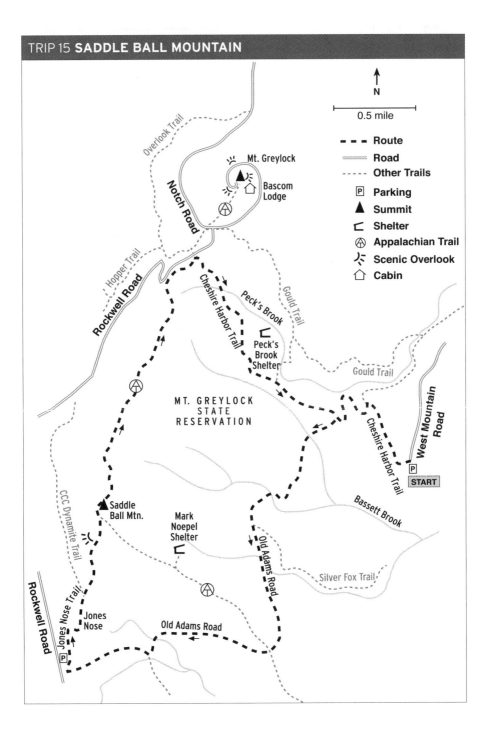

N

0.5 mile

- - - Route
═══ Road
· · · · Other Trails
Ⓟ Parking
▲ Summit
⊏ Shelter
Ⓐ Appalachian Trail
⅄⅃ Scenic Overlook
⌂ Cabin

Overlook Trail

Mt. Greylock

Bascom Lodge

Notch Road

Hopper Trail

Rockwell Road

Cheshire Harbor Trail

Peck's Brook

Gould Trail

Peck's Brook Shelter

Gould Trail

West Mountain Road

MT. GREYLOCK STATE RESERVATION

Cheshire Harbor Trail

Ⓟ START

Bassett Brook

CCC Dynamite Trail

▲ Saddle Ball Mtn.

Mark Noepel Shelter

Old Adams Road

Silver Fox Trail

Rockwell Road

Jones Nose Trail

Jones Nose

Old Adams Road

Ⓟ

A small ledge outcrop on Saddle Ball ridge offers panoramic views south to the Central Berkshire Lakes, Lenox Mountain, and New York's distant Catskills.

Cheshire Harbor Trail along a rocky roadbed past stone walls in a forest of sugar and red maples, black and gray birches, young red spruce, and hemlock. Green-trunked striped maple and American beech fill the understory. Hay-scented fern, New York fern, and spinulose wood fern border the road. Bits of rusty barbed wire embedded in trees hint that livestock grazed on what was once a grassy hill.

Parallel the slope's contour lines uphill; you will soon cross intermittent brook beds. Watch for old steel culverts held together with rivets—artifacts of a bygone age of engineering. As the route curves sharply left, it passes the junction with a blue-blazed path connecting to Gould Trail on the right. Several switchbacks lead up the slope, where you'll find the first balsam firs. At 1.0 mile, reach the intersection with Old Adams Road, where the loop begins. Turn left onto this predominantly level route as it contours along the lower slopes of Saddle Ball Mountain. These rich woods are fertile ground for wildflowers, including Indian cucumber-root, sessile-leaved bellwort, Canada mayflower, red trillium, and *Clintonia* (blue-bead lily).

Stream crossings are an enjoyable feature of this trail. In short order, the route crosses a wide wooden bridge over an unnamed tributary of Bassett Brook. The brook wends through a rocky ravine, producing small cascades en route. Mixed woodland has reclaimed these slopes. Hobblebush and spindly moosewood (striped maple) and beech saplings dominate the understory, while hay-scented ferns soften the road shoulders. Arcing through a deeply cut bank brings you to a hemlock ravine offering a glimpse of a staircase of gushing cataracts—another Bassett Brook tributary. On the right, a small vernal pool hosts wood frogs and salamanders that play out age-old breeding rituals in early spring. Cross another wide vehicle bridge and relish a small cataract and horsetail falls a few feet upstream.

Enjoy the easy grade on wide Old Adams Road and soon pass the junction with Silver Fox Trail on the left. Remain on Old Adams Road. Trees with multiple trunks, as well as young regenerating trees, indicate former logging. A third brook crossing, the final Bassett Brook feeder stream, lacks the drama of the previous two. Vehicles have gouged muddy swales in the road, which winds through forest dominated by beeches and other hardwoods.

Near the signed intersection with Red Gate Trail on the left, red spruces become more numerous—first 6- to 15-foot-tall trees, then mature ones with boles 2 feet across. Continue straight ahead 150 more feet to cross the Appalachian Trail (AT). Remain on Old Adams Road and head easily downhill through mixed woods and past plush, green schist boulders. Note the remnants of a stone wall that once bounded a sheep pasture. After you pass a multitrunked yellow birch, the trail bends left, and the descent soon steepens on a rougher track. Cross the modest headwater of Kitchen Brook on another wooden bridge and arrive at a signed T intersection. Turn right to stay on Old Adams Road and head upward over protruding, thinly layered phyllite rock toward Jones Nose.

Here, the roadway is cut deeply into the earth, and the ascent soon becomes gradual. A few oaks, the first of the day, mingle with beeches, birches, maples, and spruces. Lush undergrowth characterizes this young, spacious forest, which soon gives way to a shrubby clearing of chokecherry, meadowsweet, steeplebush, raspberry, and birch. A grassy path runs through this early growth, where indigo buntings and common yellowthroats reside in summer. The trail splits where a snowmobile route bears left. After 3.2 miles on Old Adams Road, walk around a metal gate and emerge into the open at the gravel parking lot for Jones Nose trailhead, along paved Rockwell Road.

Pick up Jones Nose Trail on the right before the kiosk, which has a map of Mount Greylock State Reservation. The blue-blazed route leads up a sharply sloping meadow, resplendent with blooming shrubs in midsummer. In late July and early August, fireweed, steeplebush, and meadowsweet all add splashes of pink to the angular hillside, which is said to resemble the profile of Seth Jones, who once farmed this area. Fireweed colonizes burned sites; the spikes of orchid-like flowers are candy for the eyes. Steeplebush (hardhack) is also well named because this shrub's tiny magenta blossoms form a spire. Meadowsweet, which is related to steeplebush, has pale pink, frothy flowers that attract both bees and beetles.

Chokecherry (with blood-red fruits), goldenrod, and yellow Saint-John's-wort enliven the slope. Scrumptious blueberries may be reason enough to make the climb in midsummer. As you tread the narrow, grassy path, glance over your shoulder to take in the expansive view to the south and west. The Taconic Range forms the border between Massachusetts and New York to the west. As the ascent becomes tougher, a switchback leads up over stone steps into sapling, mountain, and striped maples, and over bedrock outcroppings. A moist glade holds the odd white blossoms of turtlehead, whose leaves comprise the diet of the Baltimore checkerspot butterfly caterpillar. The big, coarse fern with bronzy-green fronds is Goldie's fern. Hobblebush is abundant here.

At a signed Y intersection with CCC Dynamite Trail, take the right fork toward the AT, 0.5 mile distant. The climb increases as you near the summit of Saddle Ball. Hermit thrushes can be heard in summer. An outcropping on the right is a veritable rock garden of mosses, ferns, tree seedlings, and flowers. Reach a small bedrock clearing, bounded by spruce, mountain ash, and birch. A bit farther, an obvious side path on the left beckons you to a panoramic view; you won't be disappointed. From the schist ledge, you can see the central Berkshire lakes, Lenox Mountain, and, on a clear day, the distant Catskills. Back on the main trail, bear right at the blue blaze for a detour. Watch your footing over rocks and roots under wet conditions. The fairly steep path grows serpentine and rocky, undulating as you enter the boreal zone of redolent balsam fir just before the signed AT junction.

Bear right on the white-blazed AT and follow it north for 1.6 miles, passing over the level wooded Saddle Ball summit at 3,247 feet, which is marked with a rock cairn. The most abundant wildflower along the trail is *Clintonia* (blue-bead lily); in midsummer, clusters of dark blue fruits top its flower stalks. The spongy ground forms a great seedbed for balsam fir. Milky quartz pops up here and there. The trail alternately rises and falls, crossing a small brook, its flow stained the color of tea by tannins. The erect stems of shining club moss poke up in luxuriant patches. At this elevation, fog, cloud droplets, and rain produce conditions similar to those of a temperate rainforest. The result: boulders covered with mossy mats. Sphagnum moss, containing dead cells that hold moisture, carpets low areas. Ghostly white Indian pipes rising from the mossy mats lack chlorophyll and must obtain nourishment from other plants. Thin bog bridges lead through this cool, acidic wetland, past ground-hugging bunchberries adorned with clusters of scarlet berries.

Continue on the AT to an S curve on Rockwell Road—a reliable site for nesting blackpolls, warblers found in the commonwealth only on upper Greylock. Turn right to continue on the AT and reenter woodland. This forest is predominately deciduous—featuring beech—and the trail alternates level spots with steep climbs and descents, soon arriving at the intersection with blue-blazed Cheshire Harbor Trail on the right at Rockwell Road. Watch for an intriguing view of Greylock's summit, Bascom Lodge, and the Massachusetts Veterans War Memorial Tower before the road crossing. Turn sharply right off the AT onto Cheshire Harbor Trail for the final 3-mile leg of the hike on this wide, cobbled path under a canopy of northern hardwoods. Begin a moderate-to-steep descent over a well-worn trail that is heavily used on good-weather weekends. Stay right at the split, and soon cross Peck's Brook on a wooden bridge.

Pass the signed intersection with Peck's Brook Loop Trail on the left approximately halfway down. Cheshire Harbor Trail levels out amid copious hobble-bush and then descends in earnest. At the familiar intersection with Old Adams Road on the right, continue straight on Cheshire Harbor Trail, retracing your steps 1.0 mile to the parking area at the end of West Mountain Road.

DID YOU KNOW?

Greylock Glen, a 1,000-acre state-owned parcel on the eastern flank of Mount Greylock, has been the site of a number of controversial commercial development proposals over the years. The town of Adams, in conjunction with environmental groups and the state, is developing a resort for outdoor recreation, ecotourism, and environmental education.

MORE INFORMATION

Open daily, year-round. No fee. Biking, skiing, and leashed dogs are allowed. Hunting is not allowed from May 20 to Columbus Day, and is never permitted within War Memorial Park. The route has no toilet facilities. Carry in, carry out rules apply. Mount Greylock State Reservation is managed by the Massachusetts Department of Conservation and Recreation. Visitor center/park headquarters, 30 Rockwell Road, Lanesborough, MA 01237 (413-499-4262; mass.gov/locations/mount-greylock-state-reservation).

NEARBY

The life of a prominent American civil rights leader of the nineteenth century is celebrated at the Susan B. Anthony Birthplace Museum, 67 East Road, Adams. Born here in 1820, Anthony was a social reformer, a pioneering feminist, and a suffragist. The museum is open year-round and has a small admission fee. Hours: Memorial Day to Columbus Day, Thursday to Monday, 10 A.M. to 4 P.M.; Columbus Day to Memorial Day, Monday, Friday, and Saturday, 10 A.M. to 4 P.M., and Sunday, 11:30 A.M. to 4 P.M. (413-743-7121; susanbanthonybirthplace.com).

16

MOUNT GREYLOCK STATE RESERVATION: EAST SIDE

This is one of the shortest routes to the summit of the state's highest peak. Despite the significant elevation gain, anyone in reasonably good physical condition should be able to complete the hike.

DIRECTIONS

From the south: From MA 8 in Pittsfield at Allendale Center, drive north on MA 8 for 9.1 miles into Cheshire and turn left onto Fred Mason Road. Follow it north for 2.9 miles (it becomes West Road after approximately 1 mile) to West Mountain Road on the left. Turn left and follow West Mountain Road 1.6 miles, past parking for Gould Trail, to a circular gravel parking area where the road ends. The trailhead is on the right.

From the north: Take MA 8 south to Adams and turn right onto Maple Street at the statue of President William McKinley. Follow Maple Street for 0.4 mile and turn left onto West Road. Follow West Road for 0.6 mile to West Mountain Road on the right. Drive on West Mountain Road for 1.6 miles to a circular gravel parking area where the road ends. The trailhead is on the right. *GPS coordinates*: 42° 36.635′ N, 73° 09.399′ W.

TRAIL DESCRIPTION

Begin at an elevation of 1,560 feet and follow the gravel road to your right (northwest) that leads through a field. Pass a small sign on the left that reads "Old Adams Rd. to Cheshire Harbor Tr. to Summit 3.5 mi." A map board sits at the woodland's edge. Walk past a metal gate and follow the lower portion of Cheshire Harbor Trail along an old, rocky roadbed.

Follow the slope's contour; the route curves sharply left. At this point, a narrow path leads down into the forest to Gould Trail, but stay on wide Cheshire Harbor Trail. It splits briefly here, but rejoins 50 yards farther up. As the

LOCATION
Adams, MA

RATING
Moderate to Strenuous

DISTANCE
6.6 miles round trip

ELEVATION GAIN
1,930 feet

ESTIMATED TIME
4-4.5 hours

MAPS
AMC Massachusetts Trail Map 1: D5; USGS Cheshire, USGS Williamstown; Massachusetts Department of Conservation and Recreation map: mass.gov/files/2017-08/Trail%20map.pdf

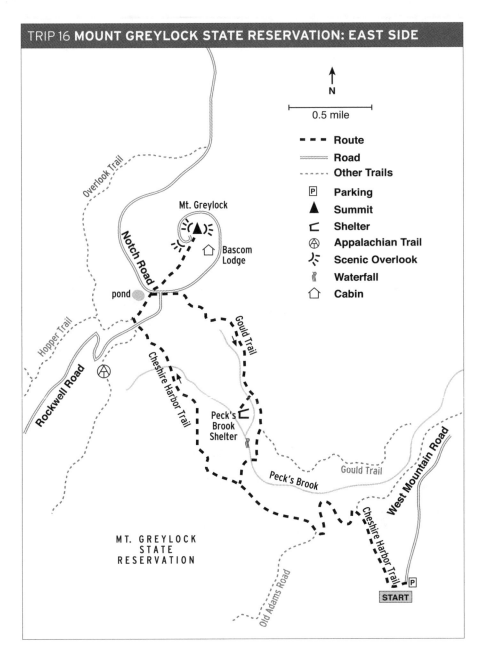

trail curves right, note the first red spruces of the hike. After some twists and turns, you will reach a signed intersection with Old Adams Road on the left at 1.0 mile, but continue straight on Cheshire Harbor Trail. The heart-shaped, paired leaves of chest-high hobblebushes provide nest sites low to the ground for black-throated blue warblers. The scoured treadway becomes even rockier; step over ledge outcroppings of metamorphic schist rock. Reach a sign for Peck's Brook Loop on the right (you will return via this way later), but continue

The 93-foot-tall granite Massachusetts War Veterans Memorial Tower, from which five states may be visible, was dedicated in 1933. The bronze relief map in the foreground shows topography of the Greylock Range.

straight uphill. The triangular seed capsules of a patch of sessile-leafed bellwort are notable on the right in autumn. A large, shaggy, three-trunked red maple stands on the left where the surface roots of beech lace the trail.

The path now leads up through woods of beech and yellow birch. Although some trees are sizable, this forest is generally young. Beeches sprout from roots and form clones of smooth, gray-barked trees. A 4-foot-long quartz boulder perched on schist to your left will catch your eye. Mountain maple saplings have taken root among the boulders. Distinguish their leaves, which porcupines are fond of, by the sawtooth edges. Hear the sound of flowing water and smell the sweet aroma of balsam fir as you reach Peck's Brook. Beware of possible loose and missing boards as you cross a wide wooden snowmobile bridge over the brook.

On the far side, the path splits but soon rejoins as it ascends, so you can follow either fork. Evergreens are now more numerous. When you reach Rockwell Road, the southbound Appalachian Trail (AT) is on the left, just before the pavement. Cross the road (note the sign on a tree indicating this is the way to the summit) and follow the white-blazed AT north over wooden stairs amid a heavenly balsam fragrance. The AT is narrow as it weaves through stunted spruce, yellow birch, and mountain ash and over bog bridges to reach a T intersection with blue-blazed Hopper Trail on the left. Turn right to continue on the AT over more bog bridges toward the summit.

Walk through a boreal forest zone in the company of spruce and fir trees that grow above 2,600 feet in elevation, a height reached in only a handful of locations in Massachusetts. The zone's climate is equivalent to that of interior Canada. Upper reaches of the mountain are often foggy, and the condensing moisture is acidic, which, when combined with shallow soil and harsh temperatures, negatively affects the growth of woody vegetation. When you arrive at a scenic spring-fed pond, which once supplied water to the summit lodge, the communication tower on the summit is easily visible, unless fog shrouded.

Briefly follow along the shore and soon reach Rockwell Road again. Turn left, walk about 100 feet, past the intersection with Notch Road, and catch the AT on the left side of Rockwell Road. Follow the signature white blazes over a rocky path and reach an asphalt parking area adjacent to the communication tower. Composting toilets are located here. From this point, the 93-foot tower on the summit is only a few hundred feet across the roadway. Attractively rustic Bascom Lodge—where drinking water, flush toilets, meals, and overnight accommodations are available May through October—stands to the right. Take time to explore the summit (3,491 feet) and, on a clear day, admire the expansive views. Look for the distinctive low pyramid-shaped profile of southern New Hampshire's Mount Monadnock, 60 miles to the northeast.

When you're ready to descend, retrace your steps past the composting toilets and continue south on the AT (beware of wet or loose rocks), soon reaching Rockwell Road. Now return via a more interesting and challenging route by using a portion of Gould Trail. Look for the trailhead on the left at a small gravel parking area opposite the intersection with Notch Road. Initially narrow and steep, blue-blazed Gould Trail soon levels out among maple, beech, striped maple, hobblebush, and dense jewelweed. Pass through a stand of yellow birch and fragrant balsam fir. Raspberry canes flourish in the light gaps. At a junction with an almost-unrecognizable overgrown trail, bear left to continue descending. Sugar maples predominate in the now-deciduous woodland. Cross a couple of intermittent streambeds, the first over a wooden span. The bedrock channel of the second one is virtually moss lined. The trail leads through much spruce regeneration on the fairly steep slope and then widens to become a rocky roadway.

At 1.4 miles from the summit, a short, signed trail on the right crosses the brook to Peck's Brook Shelter. The lean-to nestled on the hillside above the tumbling brook is well worth the short walk of less than five minutes, especially for the waterfall that flows there during wet seasons. Return to the main trail, which turns right and levels out under hardwoods. Bear right at a wide, overgrown path, as the sign directs, and reach a signed Y intersection. Turn right toward Cheshire Harbor Trail and Peck's Brook Ravine, leaving Gould Trail, which continues left down to West Mountain and Gould roads. The path descends gently past prince's pine, shining club moss, and wildflowers, such as *Clintonia* (blue-bead lily), Canada mayflower, and wild sarsaparilla. Bear right and proceed toward the sound of cascading water. A series of switchbacks down the steep slope deposits you at the exceedingly rocky Peck's Brook. Follow the brook downstream briefly, through a narrow ravine. Clear pools provide abodes for brook trout and spring salamanders in this idyllic spot.

Across the brook, watch for a blue blaze on a maple on the far side. Follow the blue-blazed trail, eroded in places, steeply up stone steps and short switchbacks. Continue through a hobblebush thicket to the intersection with Cheshire Harbor Trail at the end of the loop. Turn left to follow Cheshire Harbor Trail back to the intersection with Old Adams Road on the right. From here, it is 1.0 mile back to your vehicle. Continue straight, and after the series of switchbacks, reach the parking area.

DID YOU KNOW?

The name Cheshire Harbor Trail is an odd one because the trail does not originate at a body of water. Rather, it refers to a former settlement, midway between Adams and Cheshire, reputed to have served as a way station on the Underground Railroad, which assisted formerly enslaved people who had escaped.

MORE INFORMATION

Open year-round; no access fee. A parking fee ($5 MA resident, $10 out of state) is charged at the summit from May to October. Biking, skiing, and leashed dogs are allowed. Hunting is not allowed from May 20 to Columbus Day and is never permitted within War Memorial Park. Carry in, carry out rules apply.

Mount Greylock State Reservation is managed by the Massachusetts Department of Conservation and Recreation. Visitor center/park headquarters, 30 Rockwell Road, Lanesborough, MA 01237 (413-499-4262; mass.gov/locations/mount-greylock-state-reservation).

NEARBY

Berkshire Outfitters in Adams is a full-service outdoor sports store offering both sales and rentals. The store is open daily; call for hours (413-743-5900) or visit berkshireoutfitters.com. The store is on MA 8 (169 Grove Street), 1.2 miles north of the intersection of Fred Mason Road and MA 8.

17
MOUNT GREYLOCK STATE RESERVATION: JONES NOSE AND ROUNDS ROCK

A delightful ramble along Greylock's middle slopes features stunning vistas, prolific blueberry barrens, and a small plane crash site from the late 1940s—easily one of the most fascinating and enjoyable walks on the mountain.

LOCATION
Cheshire and New Ashford, MA

RATING
Easy to Moderate

DISTANCE
2.6-mile loop

ELEVATION GAIN
235 feet

ESTIMATED TIME
1.5-2 hours

MAPS
USGS Cheshire; Massachusetts Department of Conservation and Recreation map: mass.gov/files/2017-08/Trail%20map.pdf

DIRECTIONS

From Park Square in the center of Pittsfield, drive north on US 7 (North Street) for 6.6 miles to North Main Street in Lanesborough. Turn right onto North Main Street, bearing right at Scott Road at 0.7 mile. The reservation's visitor center is 1.0 mile farther along Rockwell Road on the right. Continue past the visitor center an additional 3.8 miles to a large gravel parking lot at Jones Nose on the right. *GPS coordinates*: 42° 36.102′ N, 73° 12.023′ W.

TRAIL DESCRIPTION

After examining the information regarding the history of Jones Nose at the kiosk (elevation 2,420 feet), cross Rockwell Road to blue-blazed Northrup Trail. The mowed path leads through a meadow filled with goldenrod, dewberry, meadowsweet, and steeplebush, which all bloom in summer. Clumps of cherry, mountain ash, and gray birch are surrounded by a luxuriant growth of hay-scented fern. Indigo buntings and chestnut-sided warblers sing in summer from treetops and shrubs. At the T junction, turn left to continue on Northrup Trail (Stage Trail is on the right), which descends easily into deciduous woods, dominated by sugar maple and white ash. The path undulates through fern glades, where you can hear the songs of red-eyed vireos, ovenbirds, and rose-breasted grosbeaks in spring and early summer.

Cross a small brook and continue through forest where American beech and yellow birch—two important

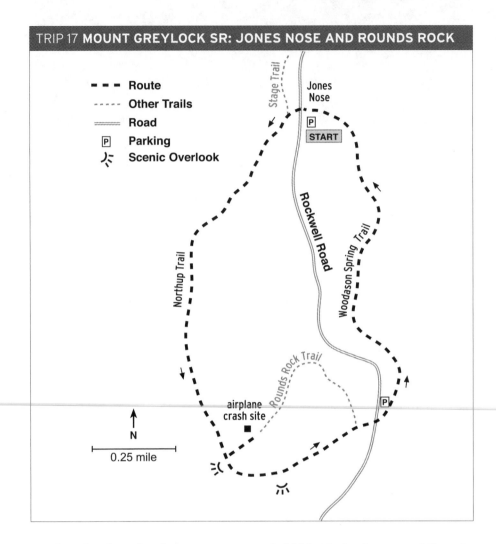

TRIP 17 MOUNT GREYLOCK SR: JONES NOSE AND ROUNDS ROCK

Route
Other Trails
Road
P Parking
人 Scenic Overlook

Stage Trail
Jones Nose
P
START
Rockwell Road
Woodason Spring Trail
Northup Trail
Rounds Rock Trail
airplane crash site
P
N
0.25 mile

northern hardwoods—form a canopy over hobblebush shrubs as you follow the contour of a hillside that drops off steeply to the right. Prickly raspberry canes fill light gaps as you pass a garden of wildflowers; red trillium, blue cohosh, and various violets bloom in spring before the forest canopy blocks out the sun. The mature woodland hosts summer breeders, including hermit thrushes and both black-throated green and black-throated blue warblers.

After about 0.5 mile, reach a ledge outcropping on the left and a series of angular boulders. One impressive slab is capped by mosses, polypody fern, and sapling yellow birches. The presence of wild ginger, wild leek, and maidenhair fern all indicate nutrient-rich soil. Turn left when you reach a signed side path that connects to Rounds Rock Trail. Climb easily under more hardwoods—especially beech, which fills the understory with sprouts and laces the footpath with its roots. Cross a series of springs and seeps along this slope and continue through a younger forest of numerous low, deformed trees to a

From the first vista point, a cliff-top perch, hikers enjoy a fine view of the Taconic Range and on clear days, New York's Catskill Mountains beyond.

blueberry-and-fern-filled barren, dotted with clumps of mountain holly, white (paper) birch, and mountain ash at the signed intersection with Rounds Rock Trail.

Turn left and follow Rounds Rock Trail about 250 yards to the site of an August 12, 1948, airplane crash. An interpretive sign, rusted wreckage, and a memorial to deceased pilot John Newcomb tell the tragic tale. Return to the intersection and continue to a short side path on the right at 1.1 miles that leads to an excellent scenic view of the Taconic Range, Jiminy Peak ski area, a ridgeline of white wind turbines, and New York's Catskill Mountains beyond.

Return to Rounds Rock Trail and turn right to continue through more blueberries (ripening late July through August), ferns, and pyramidal red spruces. Eastern towhees skulk in the brush. At a side path on the right, walk down some 200 feet to a fantastic view of Lenox Mountain and the central Berkshire Lakes from a clifftop perch. Retrace your steps to Rounds Rock Trail and turn right. Conical red spruces stand sentinel-like amid the blueberries and ferns—a scene reminiscent of Maine. Back in the deep woods, North Country wildflowers, such as goldthread, appear. Beech trees soon replace spruces, and Canada mayflower carpets the ground as you reach a gray granite marker, erected in 1912, indicating the boundary between New Ashford and Cheshire.

Continue to follow Rounds Rock Trail as it bends left through mixed woods and a grove of spruces, and under a canopy of yellow birch, black cherry, sugar maple, and spruce with lush undergrowth. At a junction at the northern end of the loop, continue straight (right) toward the Rockwell Road trailhead (an optional starting point for a shorter hike on Rounds Rock Trail). Cross Rockwell Road and turn left (north) on Woodason Spring Trail at 1.5 miles, toward Jones Nose. Creeping partridgeberry blooms here in early summer; its coral-red fruits are edible but virtually tasteless. Beeches sprout prolifically; the understory is predominantly beech, but hobblebush shrubs are numerous and head high. Many American beech trees in these woods are diseased, their normally smooth gray bark disfigured by the *Nectria* fungus. *Clintonia* (blue-bead lily), sessile-leafed bellwort, and Canada mayflower thrive beneath the trees.

The winding path parallels gurgling Kitchen Brook for a stretch, crosses it and several other small waterways in rapid succession, and then enters a forest that appears recently cut. The forest soon gives way to a savannah with a view of Jones Nose (the southern end of Saddle Ball Mountain). From early summer to midsummer, enjoy pink fireweed stands just before you return to the parking lot and your vehicle.

DID YOU KNOW?
Jones Nose took its name from local farmer Seth Jones, and Rounds Rock was named for Jabez Rounds. Both worked their mountain farms in the 1790s. Forty-two farmers once tended the land that is now Mount Greylock State Reservation. Sheep grazed at the Rounds farm, which was added to the reservation in 1915.

MORE INFORMATION
Open dawn to dusk, year-round. Access is free, but there is a summit parking fee ($5 MA resident, $10 out of state). Biking and skiing are allowed. Pets are permitted on a 10-foot-maximum leash. Pet owners must have proof of current rabies vaccination and must clean up after their pet. Alcoholic beverages are not permitted. Hunting is not allowed from May 20 to Columbus Day and is never permitted in War Memorial Park—a 0.75-mile radius around the Massachusetts Veterans War Memorial Tower (413-499-4262; mass.gov/locations/mount-greylock-state-reservation).

NEARBY
Before or after your hike, stop at the Mount Greylock State Reservation visitor center at the mountain's base (30 Rockwell Road, Lanesborough). Features include a 13-minute orientation film and exhibits on the cultural and natural history of the mountain. Open year-round; check website for hours. For more information, call 413-499-4262 or visit mass.gov/locations/mount-greylock-state-reservation.

A BEAR IN THE WOODS

Few local creatures engender more trepidation than black bears. I'll readily admit to an elevated pulse every time I see one of these magnificent mammals. You're more likely to come upon one while motoring toward the trailhead, but trail encounters do occur.

Black bears are formidable beings and, indeed, larger than life. An adult male—or boar—generally weighs in at 250 pounds in Massachusetts, but record-sized individuals have tipped the scales at 600 pounds or more. Although they may be brown or blond, I've never seen any shade other than black in these parts. The considerably larger grizzly bear does not dwell in the eastern United States.

Healthy black bears are rarely aggressive toward humans. They generally detect our scent or hear us coming and make a hasty exit. If you do meet one, remain calm, back off, and allow the bear to retreat. You can thrill about the encounter once the animal has departed. A mother bear with cubs or yearlings merits special concern, but do not panic. Giving the animals a wide berth is the best action.

Some bears, unfortunately, have learned to associate humans with food, and this is potentially dangerous—usually for the bear. Bears that are coaxed near human habitation by garbage, birdseed, or even deliberate handouts are far more apt to be struck by automobiles, shot, or otherwise treated poorly. And a diet of human food is certainly not a recipe for good bear health. Sadly, as more and more of us choose to live in proximity to bears, the odds that conflicts will result increase.

Black bears are now quite common in the state. While only 100 roamed area woodlands in 1978, the current population is estimated at more than 4,500, according to the Massachusetts Division of Fisheries and Wildlife. Several factors seem to be at work. The fact that our woodlands have come of age is probably foremost. In addition, a breeding nucleus was always present in northern New England, and as that population increased, competition forced animals south.

If you spend much time on the trail, you will find bear "sign"—a polite word for fecal matter. An ample pile of large-diameter, dark, blunt-end droppings is almost certainly of bear origin, especially if major constituents are seeds and berry pits. Coming upon bear scat is a tangible reminder that we share this land with some rather amazing creatures—what conservationists like to refer to as "charismatic megafauna."

18

CHESHIRE COBBLES AND GORE POND

A fantastic vista and the solitude of a scenic pond are the major rewards of this out-and-back hike along the Appalachian Trail.

DIRECTIONS

From the junction of MA 9 and MA 8 in the Allendale section of Pittsfield, travel north on MA 8 for 7.3 miles to a traffic signal at Church Street in Cheshire. Turn right onto Church Street and follow it 0.4 mile, just past the post office on the right to the expansive Ashuwillticook Rail Trail parking area on the right. *GPS coordinates*: 42° 33.745' N, 73° 09.399' W.

TRAIL DESCRIPTION

The first 0.4 mile or so of the route is on pavement. Walk left (north) on the Ashuwillticook Rail Trail to the Appalachian Trail (AT) at Church Street (note the white blazes on utility poles). Turn right at Church Street, following the AT south, and cross the Hoosic River. Reach the intersection of Main and East Main streets. Walk up East Main Street 150 feet to Furnace Hill Road on the right. Turn right onto Furnace Hill Road and head up, following white-blazed utility poles for almost 0.25 mile, at which point the AT turns left into the forest at a private drive.

Immediately begin the ascent following white, rectangular blazes under hemlocks and a few Norway spruces. Hardwood companions include black birch, red maple, and American beech. Cross a short wooden span and stride up railroad ties through a mixed hemlock and hardwood forest. Soon the hemlocks yield entirely to hardwoods, including flaky-barked black cherry. At a clearing, the AT turns sharply right, along an old tote road. Pass through a gap in a fallen stone wall built of tough

LOCATION
Cheshire and Dalton, MA

RATING
Moderate

DISTANCE
7.6 miles round trip

ELEVATION GAIN
1,250 feet

ESTIMATED TIME
4 hours

MAPS
AMC Massachusetts Trail Map 1; USGS Cheshire

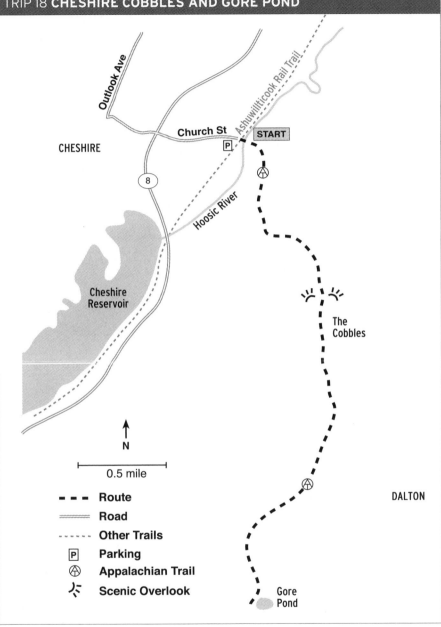

quartzite, and then turn left off the tote road. After leaf fall, the rounded hump of Mount Greylock is visible to the left from the undulating trail. After the AT turns left, white birches appear. Multitrunked hardwoods indicate former logging. The tiny evergreen shoots of primitive club mosses—prince's pine, shining, and cedar—soften the forest floor.

From the Cheshire Cobbles, panoramic views of Ragged Mountain and the 6-mile-long Greylock Range beyond reward the hiker.

The path now steepens a bit, crossing a number of old tote roads in the process; follow the white blazes at junctions. White ash, yellow birch, and, in the understory, striped maple join the woodland mix with the increasing elevation. Beneath the trees spreads a luxuriant cover of evergreen spinulose wood fern. At a junction with a well-traveled path, follow the AT as it turns right to wend up the slope.

Constructed water bars, edged with rock, shunt water off the trail; a jumble of quartzite boulders define the slope. Over eons, the rocks have eroded to sand that now whitens the path. Pass massive boulders on the left—some capped by polypody fern. Crevices between the boulders invite porcupines and other creatures to den. As you walk, look ahead to the looming, iron-stained Cobbles, which are hills formed of quartzite. Mountain laurel wreathes their base. The path roughens as you continue past the impressive cliff face and climb stone steps to the crest of the Cobbles at 1.3 miles. Bear left at a protruding rock on a short blue-blazed side path among laurel and hemlock, and pass through a sort of "secret passageway" hemmed in by evergreen laurel to emerge onto exposed bedrock that offers an expansive vista. (Watch your footing.)

From atop this rocky perch—composed of 500-million-year-old Cheshire quartzite—look southwest to Cheshire Reservoir, northwest to the hamlet of

Cheshire just below, and north to Mount Greylock and Ragged Mountain to its right—approximately 10 miles distant. The Hoosac Range lies farther right, studded with wind turbines. These fine views make the Cobbles a popular destination for hikers. When you're ready, return to the AT on the blue-blazed side path and continue straight (south) to begin a moderate ascent through mixed woodland to a USGS marker embedded in the bedrock. The AT follows the cliff edge for a distance, passing another USGS marker and screened views of the reservoir. The bony ridgeline is flanked by gray birches, blueberry shrubs, and a few mountain ashes.

Reach an attractive small, grassy clearing dotted with small red maples and reindeer lichen, and then begin an easy descent over glacially grooved bedrock and amble through more hardwoods—birch, beech, maple, and cherry. Clumps of hobblebush sport clusters of white flowers in May. The route undulates, crosses a grassy woods road, and uses stepping stones to span a brook. Climb moderately again and cross modest flows three more times in fairly short order. Then traverse an old logging road and bear left to remain on the AT. White ashes become numerous as the trail winds among stands of raspberries in light gaps— former pastures. The climb steepens somewhat and leads into a level landscape of young beech trees in an area damaged by a storm. Traverse a damp, hummocky area under hemlocks with some red spruces. Goldthread grows here—a low wildflower sporting shiny, rounded leaves, delicate white flowers, and telltale orange roots.

Climb steadily up the slope of North Mountain, passing a boulder reminiscent of an overstuffed couch. After cresting the wooded summit at 2,211 feet, begin a descent among numerous white ashes (note their crosshatched bark) and cross another woods road. The path leads into the shade of a hemlock grove alongside a beaver wetland and then turns right to cross Gore Brook over a series of split log bridges and stones. Beaver dams on the left hold back the flow, and another pond is visible to the right. Follow the AT over a few more split logs to the west shore of Gore Pond on the left at 3.8 miles. Under the shade of hemlocks, enjoy the pond's tranquil beauty, and look for a beaver lodge off to the left. This is the turnaround for the hike, so linger a bit before retracing your steps northward.

DID YOU KNOW?

The Cheshire quartzite of the Cobbles is almost pure quartz and was once used to make glass. A glass industry was established in the local area, but much of the quartzite was shipped east to Cape Cod for use in making the renowned Sandwich glass.

MORE INFORMATION

The National Park Service administers the Appalachian National Scenic Trail. Motorized vehicles, biking, and hunting are not permitted within the

1,000-foot-wide AT corridor, but hunting is allowed in season on some adjacent properties. Camping is permitted only at designated sites. Appalachian Mountain Club Berkshire Chapter volunteers maintain approximately 90 miles of the AT in Massachusetts. AMC Berkshire Chapter Appalachian Trail Management Committee, P.O. Box 2281, Pittsfield, MA 01202 (amcberkshire.org/at; at@amcberkshire.org).

NEARBY

A replica of the Cheshire Cheese Press stands at the intersection of Church and School streets, adjacent to the AT message board, just a short walk from the Ashuwillticook parking area. A bronze plaque from 1940 commemorates the Baptist elder John Leland, of Massachusetts and Virginia, who presented the Big Cheshire Cheese, weighing 1,235 pounds, to President Thomas Jefferson on January 1, 1802. The people of Cheshire had voted unanimously for Jefferson in the election of 1800.

SECTION 2
CENTRAL
BERKSHIRES

The central Berkshires are home not only to Berkshire County's most populous city (Pittsfield, with a population of around 45,000) but also to Massachusetts's most expansive state forest, October Mountain State Forest, which covers nearly 16,000 acres. The Taconic Range continues along the border with New York on the west; to the east, the high, undulating, and sparsely settled Berkshire Plateau stretches for mile after forested mile. Between the range and plateau, the Housatonic River carves a wide valley through relatively soft marble bedrock.

Fourteen of the hikes in this guide are in this region. For the most part, the high points are not as lofty as those in the northern or southern Berkshires, but there are fine vistas to be seen nonetheless. Several trips in this area are far from run-of-the-mill, such as the historical destinations of Old Mill Trail (Trip 22) and Shaker Mountain (Trip 23). A significant number have moving or still water as a major focal point. These include spectacular Schermerhorn Gorge (Trip 29) and tranquil, scenic Upper Goose Pond (Trip 32). Summit vistas are available too. Among the hikes with a long view are Pleasant Valley Wildlife Sanctuary: Fire Tower Loop (Trip 24) and Pittsfield State Forest (Trip 20). Stevens Glen (Trip 30) contains an enchanting waterfall, and Ashuwillticook Rail Trail (Trip 19) provides universal access to Cheshire Reservoir and adjacent wetlands teeming with life.

19

ASHUWILLTICOOK RAIL TRAIL: LANESBOROUGH TO CHESHIRE

The Ashuwillticook Rail Trail's southernmost section passes through biologically rich wetlands that host a panoply of birds and ends at picture-perfect Cheshire Reservoir. Though there is negligible elevation gain, the "moderate" rating is based on distance.

DIRECTIONS

From the south: From the intersection of MA 8 and MA 9 in Pittsfield (at Allendale Shopping Center), drive north on MA 8 for 2.5 miles to Berkshire Mall Road on the left. A large paved parking lot straddles the road. The trailhead is to the right.

From the north: From the intersection of MA 8 and Maple Street at the statue of President William McKinley in the center of Adams, take MA 8 south for 10.9 miles to Berkshire Mall Road on the right. *GPS coordinates*: 42° 29.331′ N, 73° 12.220′ W.

TRAIL DESCRIPTION

This 10-foot-wide, paved, universal-access trail is without doubt the most popular, if unconventional, trail in Berkshire County. Cyclists, inline skaters, walkers, joggers, and bird-watchers all share the path amicably. This portion of the rail trail is extremely popular, and the parking lot is often filled with vehicles by late morning. For the best chance of spotting wildlife, arrive early in the morning, when many species are most active. Basic rail trail etiquette mandates that users stay to the right. When you stop, be sure not to block the path. Cyclists and inline skaters approaching from behind will call out that they are passing on the left or ring a bell to alert you to their presence. Because courtesy is the rule, there is little conflict between user groups on Ashuwillticook.

LOCATION
Lanesborough and Cheshire, MA

RATING
Easy to Moderate

DISTANCE
7.4 miles round trip

ELEVATION GAIN
20 feet

ESTIMATED TIME
3 hours

MAPS
USGS Cheshire; Massachusetts Department of Conservation and Recreation map: mass.gov/files/documents/2016/12/rk/ashu.pdf

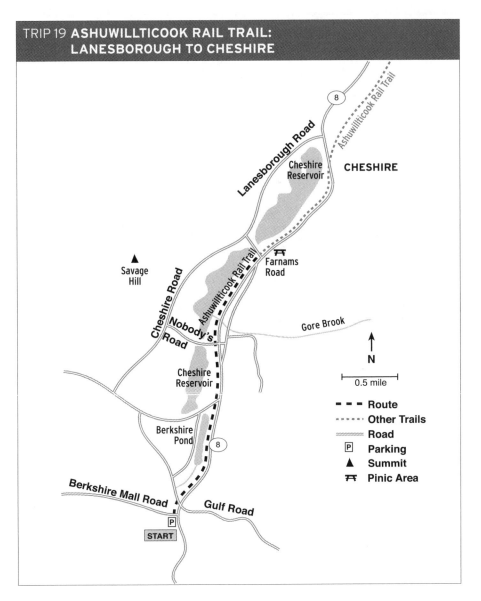

Begin by heading north toward a brick restroom building. Just beyond it on the left stands a kiosk where trail maps may be available. A donation pipe is nearby. Pass through a gap in a green metal gate and immediately peer into a wooded swamp with skeletal white pines and ribbon-leafed cattails on the left—just the sort of habitat favored by many aquatic and semiaquatic creatures. The swamp is the headwater of the Hoosic River, a northward-flowing tributary of New York's mighty Hudson.

Binoculars are recommended for this hike as the many open wetlands invite wildlife and thus wildlife viewing. During the warm months, you're apt to

Cole Mountain borders the northern basin of Cheshire Reservoir as seen from Farnams Road.

observe familiar mallards, elegant wood ducks, Canada geese, and perhaps a great blue heron. Spring and summer are prime times for seeing a wide range of species, including various waterfowl, wading birds, and migratory songbirds. Smaller birds include feisty eastern kingbirds, skulking gray catbirds, olive-drab warbling vireos, male red-winged blackbirds flashing their scarlet epaulets, and crested cedar waxwings. Look for painted turtles basking on logs and various species of camouflaged frogs, including bellowing bullfrogs and green frogs. Green frogs can be distinguished by their call, which sounds like the note of a plucked banjo.

Seek out smaller game as well. Butterflies are numerous in summer. Darting darners and skimmers—dragonflies—are hard to miss. Some to watch for are the common whitetail, ebony jewelwing, and widow skimmer. And don't worry; they are harmless. Extensive patches of bullhead lilies blanket sections of the wetlands, their stalks rooted in the muddy bottom 3 or 4 feet down. Their yellow flowers never seem to fully open

Continue along the paved trail, and soon stride beneath an overpass and enter a shaded section bounded by oaks, maples, black birches, ashes, and white pines. Shrub swamps and marshy sloughs continue on both sides of the asphalt. Trees felled by North America's largest rodent, the beaver, are in evidence in the red maple swamp. Red maples are among the most tolerant of trees. They thrive in poor, dry soils and in saturated ones, in bottomlands, and on mountaintops. Along a lengthy straightaway, a marshy pond on the left, known as Berkshire Pond, is filled shore to shore in late summer with both of Massachusetts's native lilies: the aforementioned bullhead and the exquisite fragrant white waterlily. Picnic tables and benches overlook the lily pond.

As you move out of sight of the water, shift your attention to nonflowering plants, including lush sensitive and interrupted ferns—and the green stalks of horsetails. Both these plant groups have existed virtually unchanged on Earth for hundreds of millions of years. Pass a few homes, and watch out for a patch of poison ivy on the right before the next crossing at Old State Road, where you'll walk around green metal gates. (Quite handily, trail distances are stenciled on the pavement.)

Perhaps the last remaining artifacts of the rail line, other than the railroad bed itself, are concrete whistle posts. A large white *W* adorns the top of each one. The posts let the engineer know when to sound his locomotive's whistle. They're situated at 0.25-mile intervals on either side of a road crossing. The first whistle post appears near the Cheshire town boundary marker on your right, roughly 2 miles from the Berkshire Mall Road trailhead.

At this point, it's obvious that you're walking along a former railroad track bed because it drops off steeply to either side. Pass under utility lines supported by tall, paired wooden poles that cut a swath over the hills to either side. The next road crossing, right after a miniature duck pond with domestic fowl, is the intriguingly named Nobody's Road. The origin of the name is anybody's guess. A panoramic vista of North Mountain lies to the east, beyond Route 8. After passing some willows, cross clear Gore Brook, which nourishes an alder and red maple swamp. Ahead and to the west, Savage Hill, at 1,924 feet above sea level, represents the height-of-land.

The view becomes expansive moments later as you gain the southern end of the Cheshire Reservoir basin. While cattails and lilies provide habitat and food for aquatic mammals and birds, to the north the surface is more open. Two series of benches and picnic tables face the lake at this especially scenic location. Check out a little pool on the right where bluegills are often visible. Camp Mohawk's beach lies on the opposite shore.

As you reenter refreshing woodland shade, note the young quaking (or trembling) aspens, the favorite food of beavers. They may all have sprouted from the same rootstock—clones, if you will—something aspens are apt to do. Their heart-shaped leaves are attached to twigs by means of long, laterally flattened stems, which makes them flex and rustle (quake) with the wind. Maples, ashes, and oaks are more dominant here, and some of the oaks are quite large. After another whistle post, young and middle-aged white ashes and giant cottonwoods dominate the scene. The latter are fast-growing relatives of aspens and produce truckloads of minute seeds, each seed attached to a mass of cottony fluff that enables it to fly on the air currents. Wind carries the seeds far from the parent trees, and in summer, they pile up in windrows.

Arrive at Farnams Road between the familiar green metal gates. A restroom building sits to your left along the shore of Cheshire Reservoir's upper basin. This is a favorite shore-fishing location. The benches and picnic tables here make it a nice spot for a relaxing break before you retrace your steps 3.7 miles to the parking area at Berkshire Mall Road.

DID YOU KNOW?

The name Ashuwillticook is derived from the American Indian word for the south branch of the Hoosic River. It means "at the in-between pleasant river," or "the pleasant river between the hills," those hills being the Greylock Range to the west and the Hoosac Range to the east.

MORE INFORMATION

Open dawn to dusk, year-round. No fee. Dogs must be leashed and under control; owners must clean up after their pets. Motorized vehicles (except electric-powered vehicles used by people with disabilities), horses, alcoholic beverages, fires, hunting, trapping, feeding of wildlife, and removal of park resources are prohibited. Accessible restrooms are available at Berkshire Mall Road parking area in Lanesborough and at Farnams Road at the turnaround point in Cheshire. Massachusetts Department of Conservation and Recreation, West Regional Office, P.O. Box 1433, 740 South Street, Pittsfield, MA 01202 (413-442-8928; mass.gov/locations/ashuwillticook-rail-trail). For information about the Department of Conservation and Recreation's Universal Access Program, call 413-545-5353.

NEARBY

If you're looking for a takeout meal, cold drink, or cider and doughnuts (in season) after your hike, try Whitney's Farm Market & Garden Center, a local favorite, at 1775 South State Road (MA 8) in Cheshire; open 9 A.M. to 6 P.M. (413-442-4749; whitneysfarm.com).

20

PITTSFIELD STATE FOREST: LULU CASCADE, BERRY POND, TILDEN SWAMP

This triangular loop boasts a trifecta of water attractions: lovely cascades along Lulu Brook and two of the state's highest natural water bodies—scenic Berry Pond and Tilden Swamp, a former bog turned into a beaver pond.

LOCATION
Pittsfield, Lanesborough, and Hancock, MA

RATING
Moderate

DISTANCE
5.4-mile loop

ELEVATION GAIN
1,000 feet

ESTIMATED TIME
3-3.5 hours

MAPS
USGS Pittsfield West, MA, and USGS Stephentown, NY; Massachusetts Department of Conservation and Recreation map: mass.gov/files/documents/2016/08/ut/pittsfield-summer.pdf

DIRECTIONS

From the intersection of US 7 and MA 9 at Park Square in the center of Pittsfield, turn west onto West Street and travel 0.5 mile. Make a left turn to continue on West Street. Drive for an additional 2.2 miles to Churchill Street on the right. Follow Churchill Street 1.7 miles then turn left on Cascade Street and drive 0.7 mile to the Pittsfield State Forest contact station (trail maps available). From there, continue another 0.7 mile to the Lulu Brook Day Use Area and a spacious gravel parking lot on the left. The trailhead is across paved Berry Pond Circuit Road at an iron gate. *GPS coordinates*: 42° 29.576′ N, 73° 17.927′ W.

TRAIL DESCRIPTION

Walk to the far (north) end of the parking lot and cross paved Berry Pond Circuit Road diagonally. Look for a brown iron forest gate near where Lulu Brook flows under the road. A sign marks the start of the 1.9-mile Lulu Brook Trail (not recommended in icy conditions). Begin your hike on this trail, marked with occasional blue blazes.

After only a couple of minutes, arrive at Lulu Cascade. This is not a large waterfall but enchanting nonetheless; the brook plunges into a crystal-clear pool surrounded by mossy boulders. Continue to follow Lulu Brook Trail along a schist ledge above the brook. Over the next mile or so, you'll be treated to additional smaller cascades. A big, egg-shaped milky quartz boulder, resistant to erosion and flecked with moss, will likely catch your eye. Walk

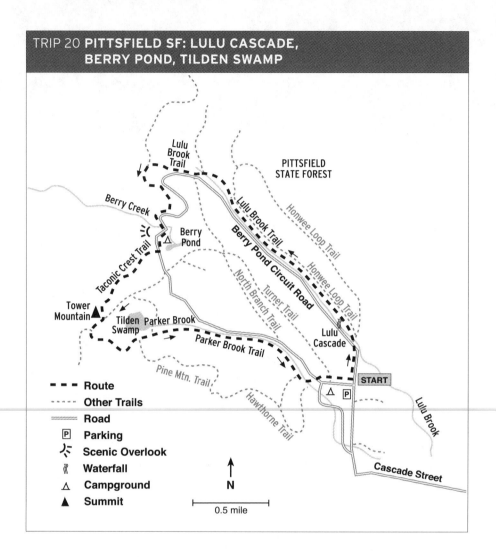

Lulu
Brook
Trail

PITTSFIELD
STATE FOREST

Berry Creek

Lulu Brook Trail

Honwee Loop Trail

Berry
Pond

Berry Pond Circuit Road

Honwee Loop Trail

Taconic Crest Trail

Turner Trail

North Branch Trail

Tower
Mountain

Tilden Parker Brook
Swamp

Parker Brook Trail

Lulu
Cascade

Pine Mtn. Trail

Hawthorne Trail

START

P

Lulu Brook

Cascade Street

- - - **Route**

- - - - **Other Trails**

===== **Road**

P **Parking**

☼ **Scenic Overlook**

≈ **Waterfall**

△ **Campground**

▲ **Summit**

N

0.5 mile

upstream on an undulating trail through a ravine cut by the brook under a canopy of hardwoods—oak, ash, maple, birch, and beech—joined by hemlock. Striped maple and hobblebush fill out the understory. Tall meadow rue—spindly stalks with thumbnail-sized leaves topped by starry white flowers—enlivens the banks in summer.

The trail alternately climbs along the leafy slope and dips to brook level. Watch for ground-hugging trailing arbutus (mayflower), the Massachusetts state flower, and partridgeberry along the upper level. At one point along the stream, a tilted schist ledge with flat slabs juts out. On humid summer days, fog may hang above the cold flow. The abundant moisture makes this a verdant place. Continue uphill, closely paralleling Honwee Loop Trail (which offers slightly easier walking) on the right. After crossing several wooden spans across minor

Scenic Berry Pond, at 2,150 feet above sea level, is the state's highest natural water body.

drainages, arrive at a stone wall composed largely of milky quartz. Tall white pines rise up and create a needle-cushioned path that levels out farther from the brook. Pass through a plantation of red pines with ramrod-straight, pinkish trunks, and arrive at a T intersection with an old woods road at the end of Lulu Brook Trail. Turn left on the woods road, walk a short distance to a rocky ATV track, and then turn left again and cross the brook on an ATV bridge. Turn right onto the paved circuit road and walk 150 feet to a blue-blazed path on the right that connects to Taconic Crest Trail. Turn right onto the path and soon bear left on a narrower path under birches, maples, and beeches. Below these trees are shiny-leafed clusters of the northern wildflower called goldthread.

At an unmarked intersection, bear left and amble easily along the slope for a few hundred feet, reaching Taconic Crest Trail (marked with white diamonds on blue squares) at a T intersection. Turn left on Taconic Crest Trail and climb past plush patches of shining club moss. The trail levels out under oaks and beeches, and a luxuriant growth of hay-scented fern blankets the ridgeline forest's floor. (This forest is stunted due to the thin soil and a harsh microclimate.) Pass a trail register box on the left. When you arrive at Berry Pond Circuit Road again, turn right and stroll 150 feet to a white-on-blue blaze for Taconic Crest Trail on the right, at a sign for Azalea Fields. Turn right and follow the path along the edge of a field where raspberry canes proliferate. Mountain azalea shrubs bloom pink in late May and offer a delicious aroma.

Enter young woodland with Canada mayflower and ferns and shortly arrive at a level clearing—just feet from the summit of Berry Mountain—and a T intersection. Shad trees, red maple, mountain ash, and several species of shrubs—arrowwood, bilberry, meadowsweet, lowbush blueberry, and azalea—thrive atop the bedrock. Descend through a tunnel of vegetation to the paved circuit road, where a vista at a gravel pullout at 2.4 miles offers a wonderful westerly view into New York all the way to the Catskills.

After taking in the scenery, walk downhill along the paved circuit road's grassy shoulder to the state's highest natural water body—Berry Pond (2,150 feet). Showy blossoms of fragrant white waterlilies dot its surface in summer. Close to shore, look for pumpkinseed sunfish fanning their tails to create circular depressions in which the female deposits her eggs for the male to guard. Continue along the shoreline and follow the gravel driveway past campsites.

Rejoin the paved circuit road and bear right on Taconic Crest Trail, which branches off the circuit road here and continues up the far side into beech, maple, and oak woodland. As the path levels out among the hardwoods, notice that some red oaks have twin trunks—the probable result of stump sprouting following logging. Begin an easy descent. Small light gaps are now filled with hay-scented fern and raspberries. Delicate maidenhair fern may attract your attention just before some eye-catching milky quartz ledge outcroppings softened by emerald-green mosses. Flutelike voices of hermit thrushes are often heard under this leafy canopy.

Climb moderately along the slope's flank, taking advantage of a few switchbacks, to reach a shrubby clearing on the summit of Tower Mountain (2,193 feet), approximately 1 mile from Berry Pond (2.5 miles overall). Regenerating woody vegetation has obscured this former vista. Abundant lowbush blueberry patches start producing ripe fruit by the end of June—a tasty consolation. No doubt black bears visit here as well. Taconic Crest Trail bears right at this Y intersection, but bear left instead to begin the 2-mile descent to the trailhead on the upper portion of Pine Mountain Trail, a narrow path that leads down through a shrubby growth of wild raisin and raspberry. Descend through fern growth from which young trees—especially black cherry, shad, and red maple—rise up.

Pass a couple of informal trails on the right and arrive at the intersection with a portion of Taconic Skyline Trail, a rutted gravel ATV road, under a mix of hardwoods and white pines. Turn right and follow the track a few hundred feet to the left to continue on blue-blazed Pine Mountain Trail, which leads toward Tilden Swamp. Follow it through a young, mostly deciduous forest with a fairly dense understory. A few American chestnuts have managed to reach 4 or 5 inches in diameter. These root sprouts are a sad reminder that this species dominated the forest community before the onset of the chestnut blight in the

1920s. Pass a trail that joins on the right and continue easily down the slope. The water's surface is visible through the trees—mostly beech, oak, birch, and white pine.

At the junction with Parker Brook Trail on the right, make a quick detour straight ahead to a view of Tilden Swamp. Since the mid-1990s, beaver activity has turned the former swamp (or more accurately, bog) into a pond. At the pond's southeastern end, you can inspect the tall, arched dam constructed by the world's second-largest rodent. Yellow bullhead lilies protrude from the water in summer; this peaceful spot is home to dragonflies, damselflies, pickerel frogs, and bullfrogs. Beaver ponds are part of a natural cycle, and one day Tilden Swamp may transition back to a bog.

Parker Brook is the outflow from the pond. Retrace your steps to the intersection and turn left on Parker Brook Trail. After just a few steps, unmarked Pine Mountain Trail branches left to a wooden footbridge across Parker Brook. Instead of taking it, continue straight to follow Parker Brook Trail downhill under beech, maple, birch, and oak. The narrow, water-cut gorge is quite deep, and the pliable branches of hobblebush are bountiful on its steep side slopes. Colorful woodland warblers are a treat for the eyes as they search for leaf-munching caterpillars and other insects in the foliage from late spring through summer. One such species found here is the lovely Canada warbler, which sports a necklace of black on its citron-yellow breast.

Continue a steady descent along a hillside graced with ferns and a cover of hardwood trees. Hemlocks increase in number before you reach an intersection with a trail on the right. Stay straight to continue on Parker Brook Trail at the junction with a multiuse path that runs up to Hawthorne Trail. Pass clumps of wintergreen and partridgeberry, whose red fruits are eaten by grouse. Head to a four-way intersection and turn left to cross Parker Brook on a wooden ATV span. Before turning, check out the angular schist outcroppings along the stream under an umbrella of hemlocks.

Continue to follow Parker Brook Trail past two paths that appear almost immediately beyond the brook—one on the left under oaks and then another on the right. Walk past campsites and more chestnut sprouts to the one-way, paved circuit road, where rows of Depression-era Norway spruces stand. Bear right on the circuit road, walk 50 feet, and turn left onto wide gravel Crossover Road, heading moderately uphill past a modern, seasonally open restroom building. Pass a number of side paths, including unsigned Turner Trail on the left. Mature oak trees tower on the right. After you pass a metal forest gate, reach the paved road and turn left, following it several hundred feet straight back to Lulu Brook Day Use Area and your vehicle.

DID YOU KNOW?

Classic bog species, including the carnivorous pitcher plant, round-leafed sundew, and leatherleaf, once grew profusely in the damp, acidic soil of Tilden

Swamp. Since the beaver flooding, however, only a few remnants of bog denizens currently survive along the largely inundated shoreline.

MORE INFORMATION

Open sunrise to sunset, year-round. A day-use parking fee ($5 MA residents, $10 out of state) is charged from early May to mid-October. Parking is free for ParksPass holders; vehicles with handicapped, POW, or disabled veteran plates/placard; and seniors ages 62 and older with the Massachusetts Senior Pass. Restrooms, open seasonally, are available at Lulu Brook Day Use Area. Skiing, biking, dogs, and hunting are allowed. Picnicking is permitted, but alcoholic beverages are prohibited on all state lands. Pittsfield State Forest, 1041 Cascade Street, Pittsfield, MA 01201 (413-442-8992; mass.gov/locations/pittsfield-state-forest).

NEARBY

The Berkshire Museum offers a unique array of art, history, and natural science exhibitions, activities, and attractions. An aquarium of native and exotic creatures is a favorite. Open Monday through Saturday, 10 A.M. to 5 P.M., and Sunday, noon to 5 P.M. Admission is $13 for adults ages 18 and older, $6 for children ages 4 to 17, and free for children age 3 or younger and museum members. The museum is at 39 South Street (US 7) in Pittsfield (413-443-7171; berkshiremuseum.org).

21

WARNER HILL

This enjoyable hike on the Appalachian Trail leads through northern hardwoods interspersed with evergreens. Warner Hill's partially cleared summit yields a pleasing view of Mount Greylock.

LOCATION
Dalton and Hinsdale, MA

RATING
Moderate

DISTANCE
6.3 miles round trip

ELEVATION GAIN
430 feet

ESTIMATED TIME
3–3.5 hours

MAPS
USGS Pittsfield East

DIRECTIONS

From the intersection of MA 9 and East Street in Pittsfield (1.25 miles east of the junction of MA 9 and US 7 at Park Square), follow East Street east for 3.0 miles to Division Road at the Dalton town line. East Street becomes South Street in Dalton. Drive north on South Street for 0.85 mile to Grange Hall Road on the right. Follow Grange Hall Road for 1.1 miles and park on the wide gravel shoulder on the left. Parking in winter along Grange Hall Road may not be possible because the road shoulder is not plowed. *GPS coordinates*: 42° 27.391′ N, 73° 09.711′ W.

TRAIL DESCRIPTION

This hike follows the white-blazed Appalachian Trail (AT), with a short side trip to Kay Wood Shelter. Cross to the south side of Grange Hall Road (watch for traffic speeding downhill around the curve) and ascend the rather steep slope on the AT, which is lined with white ash, red maple, black cherry, and American beech. Note the interesting step-like gneiss rock outcropping studded with quartz crystals. As the path levels out, prince's pine and cedar club moss—ancient nonflowering plants—add a fairyland quality to the forest floor. On the right stands a fine yellow birch, one of the classic indicators of northern hardwood forest.

After passing the remains of a fireplace chimney built of local stone and mortar on the left, the path descends into a shallow gully. Planted non-native Norway spruces

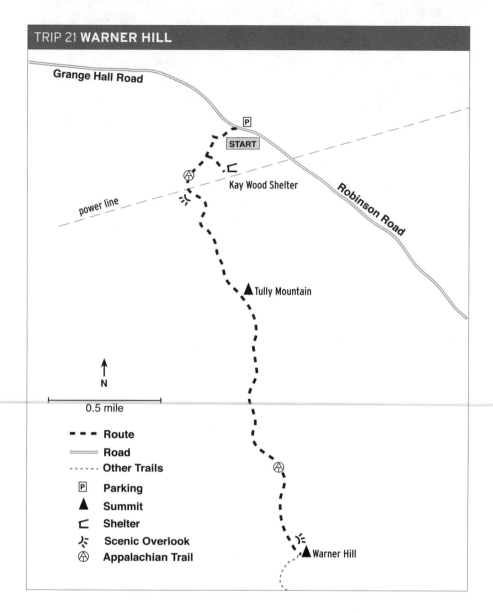

Grange Hall Road

P

START

Kay Wood Shelter

Robinson Road

power line

▲ Tully Mountain

N

0.5 mile

- - - Route
═══ Road
----- Other Trails
P Parking
▲ Summit
⊏ Shelter
⅄ Scenic Overlook
Ⓐ Appalachian Trail

Ⓐ

⅄
▲ Warner Hill

also indicate past human presence. After a moderate climb up the far side of the gully, reach a blue-blazed trail on the left at 0.3 mile that leads to Kay Wood Shelter, which has a privy and a picnic table. A metal box near the structure is designed to keep hikers' food safe from black bears. The shelter's picturesque setting on a moss-and-lichen-covered gneiss outcropping makes the 0.3-mile round trip worthwhile. You'll also pass a massive sugar maple on the left en route.

Return to the AT, turn left back onto it, and climb moderately along the slope. Screened views of the Taconic Range's rounded summits to the west are possible

Periodic clearing by volunteers keeps the summit of Warner Hill open, making it a fine spot for a rest break.

after leaf fall. Note the wind-thrown black cherry on the left whose root ball tenaciously grasps stones. Negotiate small boulder fields, their stones cleverly used in construction of this section of the trail. The hilltop appears grassy, but it's actually thickly vegetated with sedges, which are similar to grasses but bear triangular stems rather than round ones.

Cross a power-line gash about 0.1 mile beyond the Kay Wood Shelter side trail, filled with blackberry brambles and meadowsweet shrubs. Its elevation of 1,981 feet makes a nice view of Lenox Mountain possible. The path beyond the right of way is straddled by emerald clumps of club mosses and spinulose wood fern, both of which remain green year-round. Walk a gently undulating trail under a leafy canopy and through a shallow bowl. A dark-green hemlock grove to your left contrasts with the comparatively light-green shades of maples, cherries, and beeches. Past a tiny drainage rill, you'll come across an expansive growth of shining club moss, which emits a smoky cloud of microscopic spores if you brush against it in late autumn. (The highly flammable spores once provided the flash for early flash photography.)

Traverse damp areas on several series of plank bridges. Gray-barked shad (juneberry) shares the damp earth with yellow birch. Be alert for well-camouflaged ruffed grouse that you might encounter as you begin a gradual climb to the 2,085-foot summit of Tully Mountain, reached at 1.5 miles. (Unfortunately, this wooded peak does not offer long views.) Twin yellow birches stand trailside on the left. As you stride over an exposed chunk of gneiss bedrock, note the 6-inch-thick milky quartz intrusion that filled a fracture when the bedrock was buried deep underground hundreds of millions of years ago.

Along this high-elevation stretch are pockets of boreal evergreens—red spruce, specifically. In a damp swale, goldthread and wintergreen bloom in spring and summer, respectively. Both display white blossoms. Goldthread's are star shaped, and wintergreen's resemble tiny bells.

Follow along a ledge outcropping, the slope dropping off to the left, and descend into a hobblebush stand. The shrub's big, heart-shaped leaves are among the first to reveal their multiple hues in autumn. Conifers become more common now, interspersed with hardwoods. Cross two small streams about 60 feet apart, and then pass through a bowl hemmed in by dramatic gneiss ledges—a sort of miniature canyon that provides ideal den habitat for porcupines and other wildlife. Climb out at the far end, bearing left around a low outcropping, and pass an old woods road, where the trail levels out.

More screened views of forested ridges are to the right. Black birches are suddenly common as you descend into a col then amble up and cross a woods road. The trail bears right and descends gently to a ledge on the right that juts out like a ship's prow. Wild strawberries, whose small fruits are relished by many creatures, have gained a foothold in pockets of soil atop the rock. Following the AT all the while, continue left, then right, and pass a number of fallen stone walls before entering a scruffy woodland of gnarly old apple trees and viburnum shrubs. Cross an unmarked path and begin a gradual climb amid more apple trees and 6- to 8-inch-diameter shad trees.

The light-green fronds of hay-scented ferns wither and fade to an amber hue after frost ends their growing season; they fill the slope just below the summit of Warner Hill. A sign on a tree tells you that you've finally reached your objective: the 2,050-foot summit of Warner Hill at 3.3 miles. Sprouting gray birch and highbush blueberry spring from pockets of soil amid rust-stained gneiss bedrock, but this modest growth still permits fine views north 16 miles to the Greylock Range and west to the Housatonic Valley. The rotating white blades of wind turbines are visible on ridges to the north and northwest. Periodic clearing of brush by AT volunteers keeps the outlook open. The Trust for Public Land purchased 370 acres adjoining the summit in 2017, permanently protecting it from development. The National Park Service manages the land as part of the Appalachian National Scenic Trail corridor.

The AT turns right at this point and continues south (reaching Blotz Road in 0.9 mile), but retrace your steps northward 3.0 miles to your vehicle at Grange Hall Road to complete this hike.

DID YOU KNOW?

Kay Wood Shelter is named for Dalton resident Kay Wood ("Grandma Kay"), who hiked the entire AT from 1988 to 1990, completing it at age 71. She welcomed so many hikers into her home over the years that it became a recognized stop along the trail.

MORE INFORMATION

Motorized vehicles, biking, horses, and hunting are not permitted on or along the AT. Camping is allowed in designated areas only. The AT in Massachusetts is maintained by volunteers of the Appalachian Mountain Club Berkshire Chapter's Massachusetts AT Committee (amcberkshire.org/at; at@amcberkshire.org). For more information on the Trust for Public Land's involvement with Warner Hill, see the trust's website (tpl.org/our-work/warner-hill).

NEARBY

Mass Audubon's Canoe Meadows Wildlife Sanctuary in Pittsfield has 3.0 miles of walking trails along the Housatonic River and its associated wetlands. From the intersection of Dalton Division Road and East Street, follow Dalton Division Road south 1.6 miles. Turn right on Williams Street and continue for 2.0 miles to Holmes Road. Turn left and drive 0.3 mile to the sanctuary entrance on the left. Admission is free, but donations are appreciated. Open 7 A.M. to dusk, year-round (413-637-0320; massaudubon.org/get-outdoors/wildlife-sanctuaries/canoe-meadows).

TRAIL TRIBULATIONS

The Appalachian National Scenic Trail (the AT) is one of the most extensive continuous footpaths in North America. The first of several such continental trails, it was the brainchild of Massachusetts native Benton MacKaye. Although MacKaye conceived the idea in 1921, his dream was not fully realized until 1937. Stretching for 2,192 miles from Springer Mountain in northern Georgia to the craggy summit of 5,267-foot Katahdin in Maine's Baxter State Park, the AT is walked by hundreds of thousands of hikers annually. But only a few hundred hardy souls, known as thru-hikers, complete the roughly five-month journey in a single year. Numerous others complete state segments or spend a month or more on the trail every year until they have traversed its entire length.

A significant number of the hikes described in this guide follow portions of this fabled trail. Its 6-inch-high-by-2-inch-wide white blazes are iconic. The AT passes over some of the most scenic ridgelines in the Berkshires, from the Vermont border to the Connecticut line—about 90 miles. Many of the original segments have been relocated farther from roads and onto acquired conservation land. Changes and improvements continue.

Along the AT's 2,000-plus-mile route, rough shelters provide respite for long-distance hikers. In summer, you're likely to encounter at least a few of these thru-hikers on their way north or south. Many adopt an emblematic moniker or "trail name" that you'll find at the bottom of journal entries in trail registers along the AT. The majority set out from Georgia in March, before winter has fully retreated. Their goal is to reach Katahdin in September, before winter reasserts itself. Therefore, most pass through the Berkshires in June, some pausing to enjoy the relative luxury of Bascom Lodge atop Mount Greylock, Massachusetts's tallest peak, where hot showers and warm meals are a welcome change from their daily routines. If you can get a thru-hiker to stop long enough to chat, you'll almost certainly enjoy the experience.

Although the AT is under the jurisdiction of the National Park Service, which designated it a National Scenic Trail in 1968, in Massachusetts a cadre of dedicated, hard-working volunteers from the Appalachian Mountain Club's Berkshire Chapter maintains the AT for all of us. They deserve our considerable gratitude.

22

OLD MILL TRAIL

This out-and-back trail is steeped in the area's industrial history. It is also an enjoyable hike to take with children.

DIRECTIONS

From the north: From the intersection of MA 8, MA 8A, and MA 9 in Dalton, drive south on MA 8, entering the town of Hinsdale after 2.5 miles. Continue for another 0.4 mile to Old Dalton Road on the left (no sign). Follow Old Dalton Road for approximately 100 feet and turn left into the Old Mill Trail parking area, which has space for eight to ten vehicles.

From the south: From the intersection of MA 8 and MA 143 in Hinsdale, follow MA 8 north for 0.7 mile to Old Dalton Road on the right (no sign). Follow Old Dalton Road to the parking area. *GPS coordinates*: 42° 26.877′ N, 73° 07.831′ W.

TRAIL DESCRIPTION

Walk down to a map kiosk that relates the interesting industrial history of the area. The first 0.7 mile of the crushed stone path is wheelchair accessible, though it is not fully compliant with universal accessibility standards. The East Branch of the Housatonic River—a narrow stream here—borders the majority of Old Mill Trail, which is well blazed. Stroll beneath sugar maples and white ashes with distinctive crosshatched bark and past the 2-foot-tall, leafless green stems of scouring rush. Ostrich ferns, which produce edible fiddleheads when young, also thrive in the moist soil. A couple of flowering dogwood trees—more common to the south—stand on the left just before a fiberglass and wood bridge. Cross the bridge to follow the river downstream along its opposite bank.

Water-thirsty cottonwoods line the banks, while wild grapevines provide tasty meals for wildlife in late summer

LOCATION
Hinsdale and Dalton, MA

RATING
Easy

DISTANCE
3 miles round trip

ELEVATION GAIN
155 feet

ESTIMATED TIME
1.5-2 hours

MAPS
USGS Pittsfield East; Berkshire Natural Resources Council map: bnrc.org/wp-content/uploads/2016/10/OldMillTrail_TrailMap.pdf

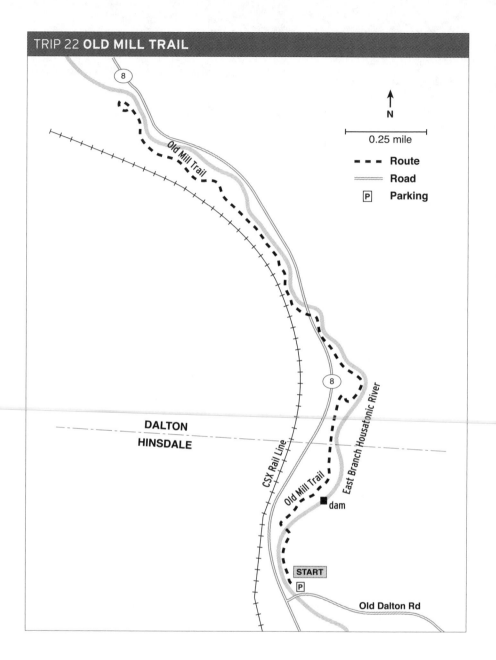

and early fall. In quick succession, cross two short bridges, one flanked by a dense stand of joe-pye weed. Nearby, goldenrods and asters provide nectar and pollen for insects. After reentering the maple woodland, notice a rusting automobile just beyond a quartzite boulder on the left. Three stones mark a short side path that leads 100 feet to the right, to the ruins of a breached dam upstream of the old Plunkett Brothers Mill, which produced textiles in the mid-nineteenth century. As you continue on the main trail, homes come into view through the

A portion of this trip's route follows an expertly built stone treadway along the East Branch of the Housatonic River.

maple and ash forest. For much of way, the route follows river terraces. Sometimes you walk near the water's edge and sometimes higher above the stream.

Enter a dense streamside hemlock stand, where a cooler microclimate is quite noticeable and gives rise to northern hardwood species, like yellow birch. The wide path follows the route of the original penstock, a channel that carried water from the dam down to the Renfrew Cotton Mill, where it powered the machinery. For a stretch, the trail is tunneled into the earth, but then turns right and heads down an easy hairpin turn to the river. The forest floor is almost devoid of vegetation beneath the dense evergreen shade. Red maples soon join the hemlocks, and a few patches of hobblebush pop up here and there. Continue on, passing several massive glacial boulders between the river and the highway. Patches of shining club moss poke up from the leaf litter. The accessible section ends at a trail register affixed to a hemlock, where visitors leave comments about their experiences.

The path narrows and soon leads over the top of a concrete penstock that once housed a large steel water pipe, the remains of which you'll soon see. Walk over a small bridge and carefully cross MA 8 at 0.7 mile. Pick up Old Mill Trail at the far end of the guardrail, where it parallels the road for a bit and then reenters forest. Follow along the base of the slope where boulders protrude. This is arguably the most picturesque portion of the hike. The path has been expertly fashioned from native stones into well-placed steps. (Watch your footing in icy conditions.) In contrast to this tranquil scene, an active CSX railroad line runs atop the slope on your left.

The trail climbs easily and moves temporarily away from the Housatonic River, crosses through a bramble-filled power-line cut, and reenters mixed forest of birch, beech, maple, and hemlock before returning to the river. Cross one final bridge over a feeder stream and continue to walk above the river. In spots, Christmas fern provides welcome color year-round. An imposing black cherry tree on the right is virtually hollow at the base. Yellow birches, with fine-peeling, brassy bark, become more numerous, and some are quite large. Note the clumps of plantain-leafed sedge, with evergreen leaves about 1 inch wide.

Follow the trail down to the river again and cross over quartzite boulders in the narrow floodplain. Invasive Japanese knotweed has established a foothold here. A patch of native shrub called leatherwood is also present. Its bark is so strong that American Indians once used it as rope and for bowstrings. Ahead in the river are concrete structures that once supported the penstock's 4-foot-diameter steel pipe. The path passes between more concrete supports that lead to what remains of the exposed penstock pipe on the left. The trail ends here, among large hemlocks. The land bordering is posted private, no trespassing. When you're ready to leave, retrace your steps upstream 1.5 miles back to your vehicle.

DID YOU KNOW?

The East Branch of the Housatonic River originates at Muddy Pond in the towns of Washington and Hinsdale, flows through the Hinsdale Flats Wildlife Management Area, and continues through downtown Dalton. It is one of three headwater tributaries that join in Pittsfield to form the main stem of the Housatonic.

MORE INFORMATION

Open during daylight hours. Skiing, biking, and leashed dogs are allowed. Motorized vehicles, fires, camping, littering, and cutting or removing vegetation are prohibited. Hunting, fishing, and trapping are permitted in season. Housatonic Valley Association (HVA) built the trail in 2010. Crane and Company donated the land to Berkshire Natural Resources Council (BNRC) in 2016. BNRC and HVA manage the property; MassWildlife (Massachusetts Division of Fisheries and Wildlife) holds the conservation restriction. BNRC, 20 Bank Row, Pittsfield, MA 01201 (413-499-0596; bnrc.org). HVA Massachusetts Office, 14 Main Street, P.O. Box 496, Stockbridge, MA 01262 (413-298-7024; hvatoday.org). MassWildlife, Western District Office, 88 Old Windsor Road, Dalton, MA 01226 (413-684-1646; mass.gov/locations/masswildlife-western-district-office).

NEARBY

Hinsdale Trading Company, at 371 Old Dalton Road (across from the Old Mill Trail parking area), offers pizza, sandwiches, and subs (413-655-0161).

23

SHAKER MOUNTAIN

This hike leads from the beautifully maintained Hancock Shaker Village to ruins and religious sites atop the neighboring hills in Pittsfield State Forest.

DIRECTIONS

From the intersection of US 7 and US 20 in the center of Pittsfield, follow US 20 west (West Housatonic Street) for 6.0 miles to the Hancock Shaker Village entrance road on the left. Park in the large paved lot and walk eastward to the visitor center to register. *GPS coordinates*: 42° 25.808′ N, 73° 20.429′ W.

TRAIL DESCRIPTION

When you register at the Hancock Shaker Village visitor center (restrooms available), you will be asked to give your name and contact information and to check in upon your return. Passes for hiking are given free of charge, but consider leaving a donation to support the organization's good work. Pick up or download an interpretive map and guide (see "Maps" for website), which give a great deal of information about this Shaker community and the trail. You might want to tour the village's many historical buildings now or upon your return, but be sure to leave sufficient time to complete your hike.

After registering, walk through the visitor center and out toward a round stone barn, a well-known village landmark. Turn left just before the barn, pass through a gap in the fence by some ocher-colored buildings, and cross US 20. (*Caution*: When crossing US 20, be sure to use the painted crosswalk.) On the other side of the highway, walk down a gravel farm road to the first interpretive sign on the left on the Shaker Trail, marked with a white circle in a green triangle.

LOCATION
Hancock, MA

RATING
Moderate

DISTANCE
5.8-mile loop

ELEVATION GAIN
790 feet

ESTIMATED TIME
3-4 hours

MAPS
USGS Pittsfield West; Massachusetts Department of Conservation and Recreation map and guide: mass.gov/files/documents/2016/08/nd/shaker.pdf

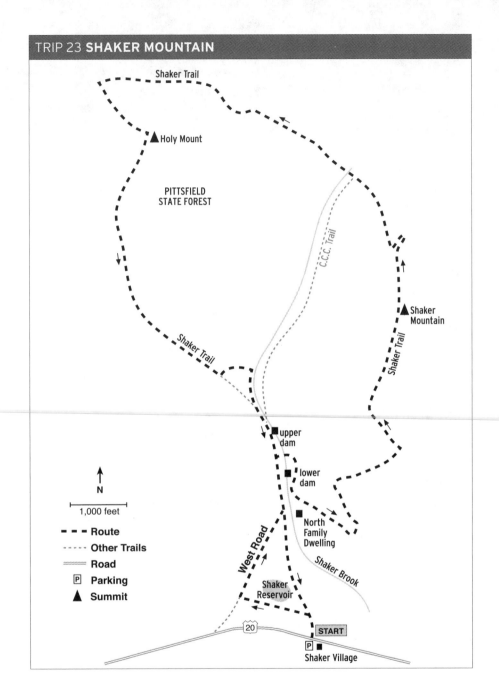

Shaker Trail

▲ Holy Mount

PITTSFIELD
STATE FOREST

C.C.C. Trail

Shaker Trail

▲ Shaker
Mountain

Shaker Trail

Shaker Trail

N

1,000 feet

- **Route**
- **Other Trails**
- **Road**
- P **Parking**
- ▲ **Summit**

West Road

Shaker Brook

■ upper
dam

■ lower
dam

■ North
Family
Dwelling

Shaker
Reservoir

20

START

P ■
Shaker Village

Bear left and walk up along the field edge. At gravel West Road, turn right and follow Shaker Trail along the road past 1-acre Shaker Reservoir, constructed in 1790 and enlarged in 1800. Continue straight on the mowed path and enter deciduous woodland, dominated by white ash and sugar maple. At the Y

Extensive stone walls enclose several fern-filled acres. One section is an impressive example of the stone wall builder's craft.

intersection, bear left on Shaker Trail and amble under a canopy of oak, maple, hickory, black cherry, and black birch along Shaker Brook. A low stone wall, the first of many, is on the left.

Pass the foundations of a bridge that once led over the stream to the North Family Dwelling site. A patch of native bloodroot blooms white in early spring on this side of the brook.

A bit farther up, arrive at the Lower Dam, which supplied water power to the village. A slope rises to the left, and yellow birch becomes evident as the road begins a gradual ascent. Cross a wooden footbridge over Shaker Brook to get to the eastern side. Here, the Shaker Trail loop begins at 0.7 mile. Follow green-and-white-blazed Shaker Trail in this counterclockwise direction rather than continuing straight, as blazes are less visible in that direction. Walk a short distance downstream on dirt East Road past Shaker Mill site foundations to the North Family Dwelling site, which dates to 1821. The site is named for the geographic location of this communal dwelling, which housed 20 to 40 or more people. An extensive carpet of shiny green periwinkle (*Vinca*) marks the location of a former garden. Follow the contours and switchbacks to ascend the moderately steep slope, where you'll encounter white pines—some large—and hemlocks mixed with oaks and beeches. In late spring, look for the yellowish pinecone-like form of squawroot—a parasite on oak roots. At a branch in the road, turn left. When you arrive at a four-way intersection with a steep woods road that leads to an airplane beacon near the summit, cross this rocky road and bear left; arrive at a second, higher intersection with the same road. Cross it again and continue steadily up Shaker Trail toward the Hancock Shaker community's Holy Ground atop Shaker Mountain, marked by an interpretive sign at 1.9 miles. In spring and fall, special religious services were held here. This brushy area has four sections of white picket fence demarcating the four corners of the site. American chestnut sprouts are numerous within, as are bracken ferns.

Continue uphill on an easy grade, passing young white pines and hemlocks. The predominant trees, though, are oak, black cherry, American beech, and white birch. Descend past dense hobblebush patches into hemlock woods on the contouring woods road. After a sharper descent, the path levels out through thick hay-scented ferns and reaches a four-way intersection with the multiuse C.C.C. Trail, which often shows heavy ATV travel (off-road vehicles are allowed in Pittsfield State Forest). Turn left and then immediately right (not straight ahead) to continue on blazed Shaker Trail toward the Shakers' Holy Mount. Bearing left leads down the ravine between the two promontories—the most direct route back to the village. Smooth gray schist bedrock protrudes from the path as you make your way across the head of the valley. Stately oaks rise where the stone walls on your right once bordered open pastures.

Reach an intermittent Shaker Brook tributary and cross it on stones; a stand of young hemlocks rises to your right. Hardwoods—white ash, sugar maple, and black cherry—thrive on the slope. After frost has killed other ferns, a luxuriant growth of spinulose wood fern has the forest floor to itself. (*Note:* ATV activity turns this path into a flowing brook during wet seasons as you head uphill.)

At the next intersection, turn left to continue on Shaker Trail. Many of the rocks in the adjacent stone wall contain white quartz, visible through the mossy covering. Beech trees become more common now among the oaks, and below them is a miniature "forest" of club mosses. These attractive nonflowering plants reproduce by spores as well as by runners (stemlike growths) and are indicators of once-pastured ground. On the left, beyond the rock wall, hay-scented fern grows profusely.

After you start climbing again, amid lowbush blueberries, turn right and pass through a gap in the stone wall (wide enough to permit a team of oxen to pass), entering a flat area of red maple, oak, cherry, and beech at 3.6 miles. This is the Holy Mount of the Shaker community of Lebanon, New York. Extensive stone walls demarcate a site of several fern-filled acres. Follow the stone wall to a side path on the left that leads 100 feet to the best example of the wall builder's craft on this hike. Once, this summit, like others in the area, was denuded of timber and long views were possible, but the trees have grown back enough to obscure those views.

Return to Shaker Trail and bear left. The path, which leads downhill, is needle-cushioned beneath a stand of young white pines. Encounter more stone walls with wide gaps as you descend moderately under oak and beech to the Sacred Gap, a natural amphitheater where the Shaker brethren gathered for prayer and reflection. A small rock dam impounded water from a spring. Turn left on the woodland path to head up through hardwood forest and then down, arriving at a fire road (open to motorized vehicles) that soon parallels Shaker Brook. Turn left and follow the rocky double track. An impressive black oak on the right bears the long scar of a lightning strike. A little farther, at the base of a white ash on the left, sharp-lobed *Hepatica* offers delicate lilac blossoms in early spring.

At the intersection with Griffin Trail, turn left and follow combined Shaker Trail and Griffin Trail uphill for the next 0.3 mile. Turn left and proceed uphill. Be mindful of loose rocks underfoot. A stone wall borders the path on the right. The route ascends fairly steeply for a bit and then descends under pines and mixed hardwoods to a major intersection. Shaker Brook is just beyond. Turn right and follow Shaker Trail downstream to the site of the Upper Dam, where an overgrown wooden staircase leads down to the brook. Dry masonry walls are visible on the opposite bank. The flow once powered a waterwheel built in 1810 (it was destroyed by flooding in 1976). A little more walking brings you back to the footbridge over Shaker Brook to close the loop. Continue straight to retrace your steps down West Road to the grassy Y intersection. Bear left to return to the village.

DID YOU KNOW?

During the early nineteenth century, the celibate religious sect known as the Shakers built a thriving community of 350 people at this site in Hancock, which they called City of Peace. Residents of a nearby Shaker community in New Lebanon, New York, are said to have called to their fellow Shakers across the 1-mile-wide valley between the two religious sites you encountered.

MORE INFORMATION

Open year-round for hiking. Hikers are asked to check in at the visitor center when open. Village hours are 10 A.M. to 4 P.M. mid-April to late June; 10 A.M. to 5 P.M. July to October; 10 A.M. to 4 P.M. in early November, on Thanksgiving weekend, and on December weekends (check the website for specific dates). Pets, motorized vehicles, firearms, hunting, and fishing are not permitted. Off-road vehicles and seasonal hunting are allowed in Pittsfield State Forest. Restrooms and a café are on village grounds. Hancock Shaker Village, 34 Lebanon Mountain Road, Hancock, MA 01237; P.O. Box 927, Pittsfield, MA 01202 (413-443-0188; hancockshakervillage.org). Pittsfield State Forest, 1041 Cascade St., Pittsfield, MA 01201 (413-442-8992; mass.gov/locations/pittsfield-state-forest).

NEARBY

To learn more about the Shakers, travel 4.2 miles west to the Shaker Museum and Library, a National Historic Landmark, in New Lebanon, New York. The 90-acre property and ten historical buildings are open to the public for walking and self-guided tours daily year-round; the visitor center is open 10 A.M. to 4 P.M. Friday to Monday, mid-June to mid-October. Call 518-794-9100 or visit shakerml.org for a schedule. The site is off US 20 at 202 Shaker Road in New Lebanon.

24

PLEASANT VALLEY WILDLIFE SANCTUARY: FIRE TOWER LOOP

On this trip, ascend Lenox Mountain's east-facing slope over narrow rocky ledges to its summit and then descend along gurgling brooks and tranquil hemlock ravines.

DIRECTIONS

From the south: From I-90 (Massachusetts Turnpike) in Lee, take Exit 2. Turn right at the end of the ramp and follow US 20 (which, just after Cranwell Resort, becomes US 7/US 20) west for 6.6 miles to West Dugway Road on the left (blue sanctuary sign). Follow the road (which junctions with West Mountain Road) for 1.6 miles to the sanctuary's gravel parking area and office.

From the north: From the center of Pittsfield at Park Square, drive south on US 7 for 4.9 miles to West Dugway Road on the right, and then follow the directions above. *GPS coordinates*: 42° 22.959′ N, 73° 17.939′ W.

TRAIL DESCRIPTION

After registering at the office (trail maps available here), cross the gravel drive and begin at the south end of Pike's Pond Trail, immediately opposite the office. Sanctuary trails are blazed blue outbound and yellow returning; trail intersections are clearly signed. Bear right and then turn left immediately to traverse a boardwalk through a boggy area of ferns and alders, where liver-colored spathes of skunk cabbage push up through the cold earth as early as February, and the shiny yellow petals of marsh marigolds fairly glow in May. After skirting a planted red pine stand, the path descends gradually toward namesake Pike's Pond, constructed in 1932 to increase the sanctuary's habitat diversity. Named in memory of William Pike, whose family funded construction, it is an excellent vantage point from which to observe beavers, especially at dusk.

LOCATION
Lenox, MA

RATING
Strenuous

DISTANCE
3-mile loop

ELEVATION GAIN
825 feet

ESTIMATED TIME
2 hours

MAPS
USGS Pittsfield West;
Mass Audubon map:
massaudubon.org/content/
download/6934/127564/file/
pleasant-valley-trail-map.pdf

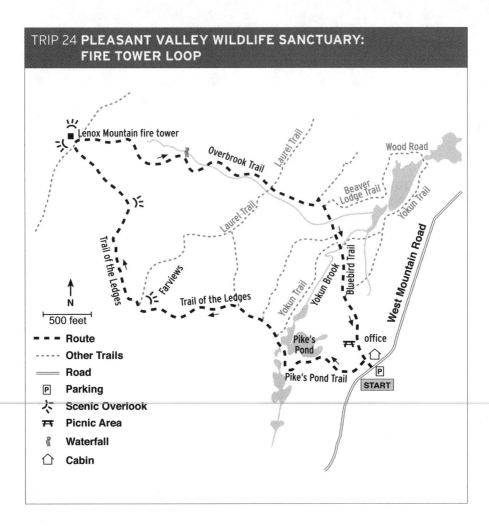

Lenox Mountain fire tower

Overbrook Trail

Laurel Trail

Wood Road

Beaver Lodge Trail

Yokun Trail

Laurel Trail

West Mountain Road

Trail of the Ledges

Farviews

Trail of the Ledges

Yokun Trail

Yokun Brook

Bluebird Trail

N

500 feet

Pike's Pond

office

Pike's Pond Trail

START

- - - Route
----- Other Trails
===== Road
P Parking
Scenic Overlook
Picnic Area
Waterfall
Cabin

Reach Yokun Brook on the left, which is a beaded necklace of small beaver ponds. Emergent bur reed with spiky inflorescences populates the shallows. A bridge leads across one pond to the foot of Lenox Mountain. After treading over a tilted outcropping of schist, turn left at 0.3 mile onto Trail of the Ledges, the start of your 1.3-mile ascent. Remnant stone walls attest to sheep grazing here as recently as 1909. When you arrive at the Waycross Trail intersection, continue straight up, remaining on Trail of the Ledges. Between here and an outlook called Farviews, at 1,850 feet elevation, you'll ascend 500 vertical feet in less than one-third of a mile. Beyond the Ravine Trail junction on the right, some slopes approach 45 degrees. As some over-rock scrambling is required, hikers are advised not to use this section to descend.

A transitional forest of oak, white pine, birch, beech, and maple clothes the lower slopes of the ridge. Crow-sized pileated woodpeckers seek out mature trees infested with carpenter ants, while yellow-bellied sapsuckers (the only

In spring and fall especially, enjoy the sight and sound of a 12-foot-high waterfall during your descent on Overbrook Trail.

local woodpeckers that regularly migrate long distances) dine on the sweet sap of birches and maples, as well as the insects that are also attracted to the flow. Mountain laurel increases as you gain elevation, and at Farviews, laurel and eastern hemlock predominate. From here you can gaze eastward all the way to October Mountain State Forest.

Although you are only about halfway to the top, you've achieved 60 percent of the total rise. The remaining section to the summit is not as steep, and the narrow trail leads to several more views to the east and north. As you continue up the slope, notice that the stature of the timber decreases as you go. Shallow soils and a harsher climate stunt growth. (As a rule of thumb, temperatures decrease 1 degree for every 400 feet one ascends.) Finally, reach the grassy summit at 1.6 miles, where the former state fire tower has been refurbished with state police communications equipment. The tower, on state-owned land and surrounded by a chain-link fence, is not accessible.

The red maples aren't tall but are high enough to block any easterly view. A nearby bench offers a nice spot to take in the vista. The best scenery from the

2,126-foot summit is westward toward the nearby Taconic Range, which runs the length of the New York–Massachusetts border. Almost directly below the viewpoint is Richmond Pond. The Taconics are among the continent's oldest mountain ranges, thrust up more than 400 million years ago when what is now Africa rammed into what is now North America. Geologically speaking, Lenox Mountain is considered to be an outlier of the Taconics. On a clear day, the Catskills, 40 miles to the southwest, are visible as a distant bluish ridge. Walk a few feet down the westward flank and gaze to your right (north) for a glimpse of Mount Greylock

When you are ready to descend, follow signs along the fence to the start of Overbrook Trail, marked with yellow blazes and a white sign on a tree indicating the return path to Pleasant Valley Sanctuary (1.3 miles to the trailhead). Amble through a mixed woodland and listen in summer for the ethereal song of the 7.5-inch-long hermit thrush. The grades are moderate at first with some steeper slopes along the way, but none approach the inclines of the ascent. Cross a shallow brook five times en route to the signed intersection with Laurel Trail. Just above the first brook on your descent is a picturesque 12-foot waterfall.

Hemlocks crowd the ravines, their needle-dense boughs weighed down by the accumulation of snow. The inner bark of hemlock was once used to tan leather, but these trees escaped harvest due to their location. It is hard to imagine now that most of the mountain was once denuded. Timber was cut for charcoal making, lumber, and firewood, and to clear land for pasture. Just above Laurel Trail, walk along the rim of a hemlock ravine where some of the conifers are massive. For this hike, however, pass by Laurel Trail.

At a four-way intersection with Laurel Trail, continue straight down on Overbrook Trail along a cascading stream among stately hemlocks. The trail bears left and widens into a dirt road, leading down to the junction with Bluebird Trail and Old Wood Road. In late spring and summer, the loud *teacher-teacher-teacher* refrain of the ovenbird is ubiquitous. This species builds a roofed nest with a side entrance, resembling an old-fashioned oven. Turn right on Bluebird Trail and pass the junction with Beaver Lodge Trail on the left. Cross short bridges over two brooks and head toward an imposing grove of white pines. Some are 3.5 feet in diameter and more than 100 feet tall; the tallest is a little more than 141 feet.

Arrive at Yokun Brook, the property's only year-round stream. Brook trout, two-lined salamanders, and dusky salamanders call it home. Louisiana waterthrushes are among the first warblers to return here from the tropics in mid-April; they construct their nests along its banks. The birds bob their hindquarters incessantly as they walk along. Continue over the brook and under more pines to a sloping field. Ahead on the left, clumps of common milkweed attract a myriad of butterflies in summer. From the intersection with Alexander Trail, continue about 200 yards along the field edge back to the office, passing two pole-mounted solar arrays on the right that provide one-third of the sanctuary's electrical power.

DID YOU KNOW?

The Lenox Fire Tower, built in 1970, was a Berkshire landmark until it burned in March 1995. Although the popular observation tower afforded 360-degree views, the 70-foot steel structure had not been staffed and used as a fire lookout since the 1988 fire season. The tower's old frame is still used to support emergency communications equipment.

MORE INFORMATION

Trails open dawn to dusk, year-round. Office hours: June to October, 9 A.M. to 4 P.M. daily; November to May, 10 A.M. to 4 P.M. Tuesday to Sunday. Fees: $5 for adults; $3 for children ages 2 to 12 and senior citizens age 65 or older. Access is free for Mass Audubon members and Lenox residents. Restrooms and potable water are available at the office. Pets, vehicles (including bicycles), horses, hunting, trapping, fishing, and collecting are not permitted. Pleasant Valley Wildlife Sanctuary, 472 West Mountain Road, Lenox, MA 01240 (413-637-0320; massaudubon.org/pleasantvalley).

NEARBY

Tanglewood Music Festival has been the world-renowned summer home of the Boston Symphony Orchestra since 1937. Each summer, hundreds of thousands of visitors flock to the Berkshires for the Tanglewood season. The main entrance is at 297 West Street in Lenox, about 2 miles from the sanctuary; call 888-266-1200 for ticket information (bso.org).

BRINGING BACK THE BEAVER

You won't find the beaver on a short list of most beloved animals. In fact, for many, the mere mention of its name engenders disdain. But why? The answer seems clear enough: North America's largest rodent is sometimes in direct competition with us for waterfront property. These herbivorous furbearers are adept at constructing engineering marvels that, in their own way, rival ours; their persistence and ingenuity are legendary.

From the time of European settlement, beavers were killed for their splendid pelts. Long, glossy guard hairs protrude above a dense, luxuriant underfur that insulates the animal against damp and cold—just the right attire for a creature that doesn't hibernate and spends a good portion of its waking hours submerged in cold water. Beavers constituted the bread and butter of the fur trade that provided impetus for the exploration of much of North America. By the late eighteenth century, though, beavers had been eliminated from Massachusetts.

In the late 1920s and early 1930s, some people sought to repatriate the former native. After an absence of almost 150 years, they felt it was time to recalibrate the balance of nature. Thus, in 1932, S. Morris Pell, warden of Pleasant Valley Bird and Wildflower Sanctuary, acquired—after considerable effort—one adult female and two adult males from the Blue Mountain Lake region of New York. Pell and his helpers constructed a sturdy fenced enclosure around 1.5 acres of willows and alders bordering Yokun Brook. The trio was introduced to their new quarters at 5 P.M. on October 8; by dawn the next morning, they had constructed their first dam and pond.

Beavers build ponds to safeguard themselves from land-bound predators. Although certainly not defenseless on terra firma, in its watery realm, the pudgy beaver transforms into a study in grace. An enlarged liver enables it to remain submerged for up to fifteen minutes. And just like humans, beavers use the water's buoyancy to float cargo, be it construction material for dams and their homes (called lodges) or food, in the form of leafy twigs.

Beaver wetlands have many virtues. They absorb storm runoff like the proverbial sponge and release it slowly, minimizing flooding. Wetlands serve as nature's purification plant for runoff entering groundwater aquifers. And beaver wetlands provide homes for a litany of other creatures, from mosquito-eating dragonflies to fish and wood ducks. If frogs could vote, beavers would win the popularity contest hands down.

25

PLEASANT VALLEY WILDLIFE SANCTUARY: BEAVER PONDS LOOP

Lying in a scenic valley on the east flank of Lenox Mountain, this sanctuary's 1,300 acres and 7-mile trail system offer wonderful hiking and wildlife observation opportunities. An active and easily observed (at dusk) beaver colony is a highlight of this outing.

DIRECTIONS

From the south: From I-90 (Massachusetts Turnpike) in Lee, take Exit 2. Bear right at the end of the ramp and drive west on US 20 (which, just after Cranwell Resort, becomes US 7/US 20) for 6.6 miles to West Dugway Road on the left. Follow West Dugway Road 1.6 miles to the sanctuary's gravel parking area.

From the north: From the center of Pittsfield at Park Square, drive south on US 7 for 4.9 miles to West Dugway Road on the right, and then follow the directions above. *GPS coordinates*: 42° 22.959′ N, 73° 17.939′ W.

TRAIL DESCRIPTION

All visitors are asked to register at the circa-1790 farmhouse that serves as the sanctuary office. Registration cards and trail maps are available inside (and sometimes outside, after hours). Check the board for recent wildlife sightings, and examine the nearby orientation panel, which includes a large artistic rendition of the trail system. Sanctuary trails are blazed blue outbound and yellow returning; intersections are clearly signed.

From the wide gravel drive, walk north toward a bright-red barn on the left, where attached public restroom facilities and potable water are available year-round. A picnic area is nearby. The wheelchair-accessible All Persons Trail/Sensory Trail begins here and ends at nearby Pike's Pond. Continue straight on Bluebird Trail past the

LOCATION
Lenox, MA

RATING
Easy

DISTANCE
1.5 miles round trip

ELEVATION GAIN
115 feet

ESTIMATED TIME
1 hour

MAPS
USGS Pittsfield West; Mass Audubon map: massaudubon.org/content/download/6934/127564/file/pleasant-valley-trail-map.pdf

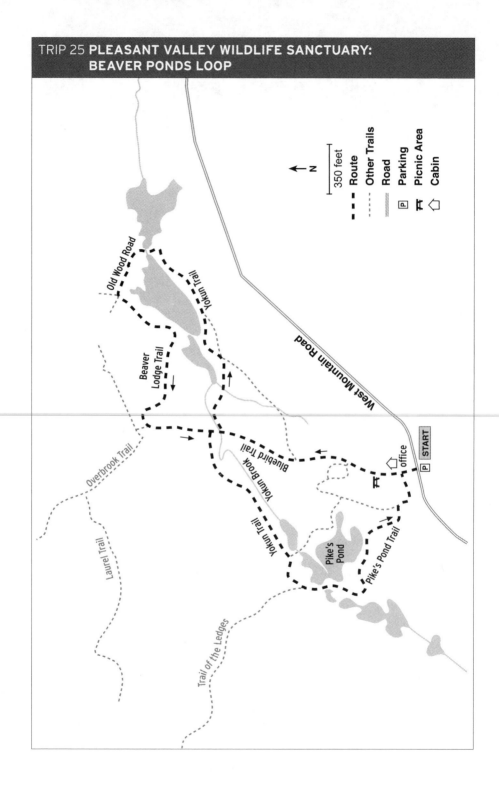

N

350 feet

Route
Other Trails
Road
P **Parking**
⚲ **Picnic Area**
◇ **Cabin**

Old Wood Road

Yokun Trail

Beaver
Lodge Trail

West Mountain Road

Overbrook Trail

Bluebird Trail

Yokun Brook

Yokun Trail

START
office

Laurel Trail

Pike's
Pond

Pike's Pond Trail

Trail of the Ledges

While beavers are the most visible large mammals at Pleasant Valley, lucky hikers occasionally stumble upon other mammals such as this white-tailed deer fawn.

education center and solar array. In the brushy field opposite, tree swallows and sometimes eastern bluebirds nest in wooden boxes. In July, the sweet-smelling pink flower heads of common milkweed lure a myriad of butterflies, including various hairstreaks, skippers, and monarchs. The looming Lenox Mountain ridge beckons.

Walk straight ahead past a formidable eastern cottonwood at the intersection with Alexander Trail, and through another field, prickly with raspberry canes, before entering a stand of tall white pines bordered by a remnant stone wall. Ahead is Yokun Brook, a tributary of the Housatonic River, and the sanctuary's only perennial stream. Rather than crossing the brook, turn right onto signed Yokun Trail. Both the trail and brook were named for a notable Mahican leader of the early eighteenth century. The path winds through low-lying woodland of white ash, black cherry, and birch. Opposite the far end of the short Alexander Trail, turn left onto a loop spur that leads to the first of a series of beaver ponds along Yokun Brook. Signs of the big rodents' handiwork are evident, including a sizable cherry tree felled years ago. In 1932, beavers were reintroduced at this location after an absence of almost 150 years. A bench, a fine spot for wildlife watching, sits near a well-vegetated beaver dam.

Continue on the short loop to rejoin Yokun Trail and turn left. Pass hollows on the right where gravel was once mined. To your left is a larger beaver-engineered pond and, near its far end, a conical mass of sticks and mud—a beaver lodge. Each lodge is home to one family. If you are here in early morning or at dusk, you may observe a curious beaver cruising about, with only its head and a bit of its back visible above the surface.

When you reach Old Wood Road, turn left and pause on a long wooden bridge that spans a small pond between two beaver dams. The semiaquatic beavers create ponds to protect themselves from predators. The upstream dam to your left is 3 to 4 feet high, while the smaller one on the right is lower. Glance down and you'll surely see beaver scat—oval pellets of compressed "sawdust." At the far end of the bridge, the blue-purple blossoms of bottle gentians bloom in September. Beyond the bridge grow a few mountain laurels and some impressive white pines. Spiny Japanese barberry shrubs—an invasive exotic—are abundant. Some have been uprooted, but many persist.

At the signed four-way intersection, turn left onto Beaver Lodge Trail. In the vicinity of the boardwalk, be alert in summer for the sudden launch of an American woodcock—a chunky "shorebird" sporting a nearly 3-inch-long, crochet hook-like bill with a flexible tip to adroitly pull earthworms from the moist soil.

Winterberry bushes have established themselves in a beaver-dug channel on the left, beyond the winding boardwalk. The coral-red berries add a welcome splash of color to the late fall scene. During warm seasons, a multitude of ferns (mostly New York fern) carpet the sunny openings. Pass the first beaver pond you reached, but from the opposite side. Here, the path curves right onto a low mound above another small pond, where the trail's namesake beaver lodge sits hidden by woody vegetation until after leaf fall. A bench near a couple of white pines, some 150 years of age, serves as a nice spot for a snack.

Continue on Beaver Lodge Trail around the swamp and into a stand of pines and hemlocks, where golden-crowned kinglets shelter during the cold months. At the shaded junction with Bluebird Trail, turn left and follow Bluebird Trail across another boardwalk. Now at the base of Lenox Mountain, cross a short span over an intermittent brook. Ahead of you towers a stand of cathedral pines—their straight, lofty trunks soaring 100 feet above the needle-cushioned forest floor. Their girth suggests considerable age. You'll discern a definite hushed atmosphere in their shade. Back at gushing Yokun Brook, turn right onto the southern section of Yokun Trail, and amble under a pine canopy to a point above the brook where the soothing sound of flowing water is omnipresent.

The trail continues through mixed woodland that now includes red oak and yellow birch. The vernal green leaves of pleated false hellebore pushing up through the brook's moist floodplain soil are a welcome sight in April after a long, snowy winter. Emerge into the sunlight at another beaver pond.

At the intersection, turn right onto Pike's Pond Trail. Green frogs emit shrieks as you approach, while in the woods, eastern chipmunks utter a fluty whistle and scamper for their burrows when danger threatens. They harvest the abundant acorns, beechnuts, and beaked hazelnuts for winter dining belowground.

The trail is bordered in places by mountain azalea shrubs that waft intoxicating perfume from their tubular pink flowers in late May. After the path crosses a protruding schist outcropping, it bears left to a picturesque bridge. Trailing arbutus, the Massachusetts state flower, blooms here from late April to early May, hence its other common name: mayflower. Its sandpaper-like leaves and delicate pink blossoms hug the ground in sunny openings.

Although not fragrant, mountain laurel clusters of nickel-sized white and pink blossoms are a sight to see in late spring or early summer. Beyond the bridge, the trail bears left to continue around the pond—best viewed as the path climbs a few feet to higher ground at two substantial sugar maples. Saw-billed hooded mergansers and wood ducks nest in big wooden boxes fastened to trees.

Move away from the pond and walk beneath a stand of planted Depression-era red pines, where high-strung red squirrels chatter. The trail curves left into a small shrub wetland traversed by a boardwalk that is bordered by alders, larches, and luxuriant ferns. Interrupted ferns stand shoulder high on drier ground, while royal and cinnamon ferns (the latter with cinnamon-hued, fertile fronds) crowd the decking. At the end of the boardwalk, turn right to walk a few feet back to the sanctuary office and parking area.

DID YOU KNOW?

Beavers are strict herbivores that do not hibernate through the depths of winter, but rather retrieve twigs that they have stockpiled in the pond mud near the lodge. Twigs (especially the nutritious bark) serve as their sole food until more succulent vegetation becomes available in spring.

MORE INFORMATION

Trails open dawn to dusk, year-round. Office hours: June to October, 9 A.M. to 4 P.M. daily; November to May, 10 A.M. to 4 P.M. Tuesday to Sunday. Fees: $5 for adults; $3 for children ages 2 to 12 and senior citizens age 65 or older. Access is free for Mass Audubon members and Lenox residents. Pets, vehicles (including bicycles), horses, hunting, trapping, fishing, and collecting are not permitted. Carry in, carry out rules apply. Pleasant Valley Wildlife Sanctuary, 472 West Mountain Road, Lenox, MA 01240 (413-637-0320; massaudubon.org/pleasantvalley).

NEARBY

The Arcadian Shop, at 91 Pittsfield Road (US 7/US 20) in Lenox, carries an assortment of outdoor and camping gear, shoes, clothing, guidebooks and maps, kayaks, mountain bikes, snowshoes, and other recreational equipment. Kayaks, bikes, snowshoes, cross-country skis, and paddleboards are available for rent. The shop's Trailside Café invites visitors to stay for a bite to eat (413-637-3010; arcadian.com).

26

JOHN DRUMMOND KENNEDY PARK

This fine hiking trip for the whole family features points of historical interest, including the site of the famed Aspinwall Hotel, a balanced marble rock, and long views.

DIRECTIONS

From the south: From I-90 (Massachusetts Turnpike), take Exit 2 in Lee. Bear right at the end of the ramp and follow US 20 (which later becomes US 7/US 20) west for 6.6 miles to West Dugway Road on the left (sign for Pleasant Valley Wildlife Sanctuary). Drive down West Dugway Road for a little more than 0.1 mile to the park's gravel parking area on the left, with space for approximately fifteen vehicles.

From the north: From Park Square in Pittsfield, drive south on US 7/US 20 for 4.9 miles to West Dugway Road on the right. Follow West Dugway Road for a little more than 0.1 mile to the park's gravel parking area on the left. *GPS coordinates*: 42° 22.975′ N, 73°16.717′ W.

TRAIL DESCRIPTION

John Drummond Kennedy Park features an extensive network of trails traversing wooded slopes once capped by the elaborate Aspinwall Hotel. Although almost all intersections are signed and posted with maps, the intricacy of the trail system requires attentiveness because junctions are numerous and the trails are not blazed.

A small picnic area is at the parking lot; a kiosk sits at the right-hand edge of the lot. From the kiosk, which contains use regulations and a brief history of the property, follow Cold Spring Trail into a forest of maple, ash, oak, birch, and cherry. Pass a side path on the left, and walk up a slight grade to the trail's namesake, a stone-lined, octagonal reservoir that captures and holds spring water. It once supplied the luxurious Aspinwall Hotel. Take a few minutes to investigate a short dead-end path to the spring's

LOCATION
Lenox, MA

RATING
Easy to Moderate

DISTANCE
4.8 miles round trip

ELEVATION GAIN
355 feet

ESTIMATED TIME
2.5–3 hours

MAPS
USGS Pittsfield West, USGS Stockbridge; Town of Lenox map: townoflenox.com/sites/lenoxma/files/uploads/kennedyparkmap2012_vemergency.pdf

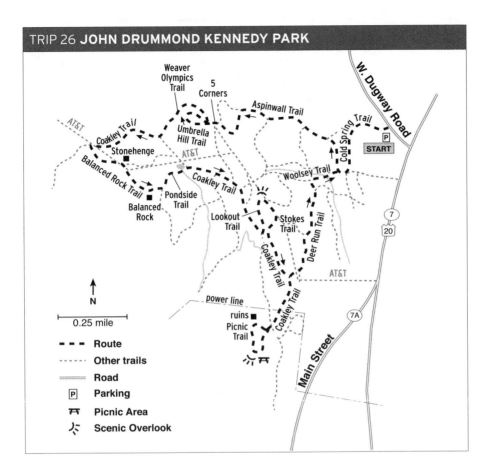

source on the right, where a dense growth of hardy kiwi festoons a grotto of marble boulders, reminiscent of Mayan ruins lost to the jungle!

Back on Cold Spring Trail, turn right and follow the old roadway, bearing right past kiwi-infested light gaps (see "Alien Invaders," page 145), which have been treated with herbicide to remove this non-native species. In late summer, ripe black cherries litter the path. Reach wide Woolsey Trail at a four-way intersection with a map kiosk and bench. Turn right onto it and almost immediately right again on Aspinwall Trail, named for the former 400-room hotel that succumbed to fire in 1931.

The dirt road becomes rougher as it bears left and continues up a gentle grade. Ignore the side paths. The still-numerous white and gray birches are being outcompeted by more shade-tolerant hardwoods. Rock outcroppings protrude from a slope on the left, and a sizable sugar maple stands opposite, at the fringe of a dark hillside grove of hemlocks and yellow birches. The easy climb soon steepens. Hemlock Trail joins from the left at a junction, but continue straight and then bear left on Aspinwall Trail at a marked junction where Nose Trail bears right. Beyond, there are boulders and gneiss ledges up to 15 feet high, with

Spring-fed Cold Spring reservoir once supplied water to the famed Aspinwall Hotel, which burned to the ground in 1931.

white quartz bands capped by the 7-inch fronds of common polypody fern. Lowbush blueberry shrubs are scattered about this drier forest floor.

Arrive at a five-way intersection known as 5 Corners. Continuing straight takes you, via a short loop of a few hundred feet, to the forested top of Umbrella Hill, the park's high point at 1,634 feet. After returning to 5 Corners, turn left onto wide, level Weaver Olympics Trail, named for Nordic skier and Olympian Patrick Weaver, from Lenox. A plaque in his honor is affixed to a boulder on the left. In late summer, white wood asters form a decorative fringe along these paths. Pass under a young canopy of red maple and black birch and, ignoring side paths, reach a Y intersection. Bear right and in 75 feet join T.F. Coakley Trail (or Main Trail). Thomas Francis Coakley was a renowned local horseman who developed most of the current trails and maintained them until his death in 1952.

Turn right and look for a wolf pine on the right that grew up in what was then an open field. Another tree worthy of attention is a massive, deeply furrowed oak farther along on the left. At a marked Y intersection, turn left on Balance Rock Trail and head up a wide, rough road past jumbled rock outcroppings, ignoring a descending side path on the right. Maple-leaf viburnum and sapling sugar maples pose an identification challenge; distinguish the two by the viburnum's fine-toothed leaves. A screened glimpse of Parson's Marsh is on the right, just before you pass an AT&T transcontinental telephone corridor. A thick patch of horse balm produces pointed, airy stalks with large leaves and pale yellow blossoms that appear vaguely orchidlike in late summer, but this plant is actually a member of the mint family.

At the next trail split, follow the left fork onto Stonehenge Trail, which leads left to a mound topped by twelve concrete pilings, each 4.5 feet high, and a presumably older pair of lower, concrete-and-stone footings. These two pillars may have supported two tanks that once fed water, by gravity, to the hotel. After exploring the site, return to Balance Rock Trail and continue in the direction you had been heading. Pass Kirchner Trail on the left, and bear right on the old roadway through oak woodland with a "grassy" ground cover of sedges. Note that the downslope margin of the roadway was fortified with stones. Pass little-used Ferncliffe Trail on the left, and arrive at a Y intersection where a short side path leads right to Balanced Rock. A grayish marble boulder rests atop a sculpted base of the same composition, creating a natural sculpture. Retrace your steps to Balance Rock Trail and a big white oak at the intersection. Turn right and continue moderately downhill on Balance Rock Trail, choosing either fork where it splits—both soon lead to Pondside Trail.

Bear left onto Pondside Trail, passing through remnants of a fallen stone wall, and walk down under beech, maple, and ash trees to reach a small, murky pond. At the next intersection, follow T.F. Coakley Trail right. Look for a small patch of wild ginger at the base of a mature big-tooth aspen on the right. Ginger's heart-shaped leaves obscure the ground-level maroon blossoms pollinated by beetles attracted to the fetid odor. Under Mountain Trail appears on the right, but continue straight on T.F. Coakley Trail past Aspinwall Trail on the left near an exposed bedrock ledge. Arrive at a major Y intersection with two benches. A sign attached to a tree trunk on the left reads "Woolsey." Continue on T.F. Coakley Trail, bypassing Cutoff Trail on the left by keeping straight on the old roadway that contours the hillside. Just past Red Neck Trail on the right, make a hard left turn onto Lookout Trail, a gravel road that morphs into a twin track through dry oak woodland. Your destination is a wooden gazebo built in 1992 at a 1,555-foot-high outlook for Mount Greylock and other promontories, but views are now almost entirely obscured by trees. The various summits and cardinal points are noted in the structure. Step out of the gazebo and turn left along the AT&T corridor. Ignore the subsequent left junction with Lookout Trail; instead, descend easily to signed Stokes Trail on the right. Follow Stokes Trail through attractive mixed woods and soon find yourself back on T.F. Coakley Trail. Bear left and remain on the wide roadway. After the trail levels out, pass the Upper Deer Run Trail junction on the left.

Walk through a power-line cut flanked by pleasing views of farms and forested ridges. At the major four-way intersection of Main Trail and Red Neck Trail, continue straight and head uphill on a paved section for approximately 50 feet before bearing right onto a narrow woodland path—Picnic Trail—past concrete structures, stone ruins, cellar holes, and foundations of Aspinwall Hotel outbuildings. A short side path labeled "Ruins" leads to foundations. Return to Picnic Trail and turn right to follow it up a steep, hemlock-shaded hillside with a precipitous drop on the right. The grassy former hotel lawn, now a picnic area and the site of the Kennedy Park Belvedere (a granite memorial to the doctor

Jordan Feldman) offers southerly views that include Monument Mountain (Trip 34) and Mount Everett (Trip 45). The hotel's hanging gardens once graced the slope below the low concrete wall, beyond which staghorn sumac is now prolific. Colorful woodland sunflowers bloom around the vista and forest edge (and along other trails) in midsummer.

Turn left and walk about 70 feet under white pines to a grassy rectangle where the posh hotel, built in 1902 and host to the rich and famous of that era, once stood. The panoramic view back across the picnic area is optimized from here. Continue across the field and onto an asphalt access road (T.F. Coakley Trail). A historical photograph of the hotel is posted near this junction. Turn left and amble down to a major intersection. Bear left, and when you reach the Y, take the right fork (T.F. Coakley Trail) back to the power-line cut. At Upper Deer Run Trail, turn right onto that trail. Bishop's weed (also called goutweed)—an invasive exotic with poison ivy–like leaves and flower clusters like Queen Anne's lace—forms a trailside monoculture. After the AT&T corridor, bear left at a signed intersection onto Deer Run Trail. A stone wall runs along below the rather inclined slope to your right. Pass Weaver Olympics Trail on the left. The stone wall continues close now on the right.

Deer Run Trail briefly passes between mossy outcroppings. Ignore Greenfield Trail on the right, and reach a T intersection with spacious Woolsey Trail. Turn right onto Woolsey Trail, cross a drainage, and descend easily past Wilderness and Aspinwall trails, both on the left. Back at the four-way intersection with the map kiosk, turn left onto Cold Spring Trail to return to your vehicle.

DID YOU KNOW?

Edward J. Woolsey bought the nucleus of what would become John Drummond Kennedy Park beginning in 1853 with a dozen land acquisitions totaling 500 acres. Originally known as Aspinwall Park, the property was renamed in 1973 to honor Kennedy, a longtime Lenox planning board member who played a key role in the town's acquisition of the property in 1956.

MORE INFORMATION

Open dawn to dusk, year-round. Dogs, horses, mountain bikes, and skiing are all allowed. Dogs must be under owner's control at all times. Motorized vehicles, alcohol, fires, tree cutting without permission, hunting, and trapping are prohibited. John Drummond Kennedy Park Restoration Committee, Town of Lenox, Lenox Town Hall, 6 Walker Street, Lenox, MA 01240 (413-637-5500; townoflenox.com).

NEARBY

Naumkeag, a 44-acre property of The Trustees at 5 Prospect Hill Road in Stockbridge, features a historical home and gardens with scenic views. Open seasonally June to late September. An elaborate winter light display is held during the holiday season. Visit naumkeag.thetrustees.org for hours, fees, and other information.

ALIEN INVADERS

They're green; they've arrived from far, far away; and they are threatening to take over. Little green beings from Mars? No, invasive exotic plants! Ask most land managers what their biggest concern is regarding species diversity, and it's a good bet they'll answer, "Invasive species." Continent-wide, invasive exotics are second only to habitat loss on the list of threats to biological diversity.

Well-known invaders include purple loosestrife, Eurasian water milfoil, the exotic form of the common reed, Japanese barberry, Oriental bittersweet, and garlic mustard. What makes a perfectly respectable plant (or animal for that matter) in one part of the globe such a menace in another? Plants translocated from their native haunts to foreign soil have no insect or mammal herbivores, fungi, or diseases to keep them in check. In their homelands, species face a long-evolving system of checks and balances to prevent rampant growth. When a species is transported (either by accident or on purpose) outside its range, the possibility exists that in its new home, sans controls, it will outcompete the local natives.

In Kennedy Park, the adjacent Pleasant Valley Wildlife Sanctuary, and a few other locations, a newly recognized threat has the potential to do serious damage to our forests. That threat is hardy kiwi (*Actenidia arguta*). If you've never heard of it, you're not alone. So recent is this realization that the species has yet to be added to the official state registry of invasive exotic plants.

Hardy kiwi hails from Southeast Asia, a region from which a number of other troublesome plants, including Oriental bittersweet, arrived. Both Oriental bittersweet and hardy kiwi have found our soils and climate to be welcoming because they mimic those of their homeland. Like bittersweet, hardy kiwi (related to the popular kiwi fruit available in grocery stores) is a climbing vine, but one that is even more aggressive. And that says a lot! Kiwi spreads mostly by runners, but it also produces tasty, grape-sized, seed-filled green fruits that are distributed by birds and mammals looking for a treat. Although it doesn't constrict the trunks of trees the way Oriental bittersweet does, it grows so prolifically as to completely engulf woody natives and rob them of sunlight. Kiwi-filled light gaps are a frightening vision of complete alien dominance, and native species have little chance against these invaders. Although currently restricted in its range, hardy kiwi is potentially a major threat to deciduous forests in the Berkshires. Massachusetts agricultural officials are considering banning growing or selling the fruit in the state; the decision was pending at the time this book went to press.

27

LENOX MOUNTAIN: BURBANK TRAIL

This enjoyable loop takes you through diverse woodland to a pleasing lookout on the southern slope of Lenox Mountain. A historical home site and an estate's reservoir add interest.

LOCATION
Richmond and Lenox, MA

RATING
Easy to Moderate

DIRECTIONS

From I-90 (Massachusetts Turnpike), take Exit 2 in Lee. Bear right at the end of the ramp and follow US 20 for 4.1 miles. (US 20 joins US 7 just after Cranwell Resort; the route then becomes combined US 7 and US 20.) Turn left at the traffic light onto MA 183 South (Walker Street). Drive for 1.1 miles to the monument in Lenox center and continue straight on MA 183 South for another 1.5 miles (past the entrance to Tanglewood Music Center). Bear right on Richmond Mountain Road and follow it uphill for 1.4 miles to a circular gravel parking area on the left at Olivia's Overlook. The lot is bounded on the left by a stone wall. *GPS coordinates*: 42° 21.109′ N, 73° 20.259′ W.

DISTANCE
3.2-mile loop

ELEVATION GAIN
540 feet

ESTIMATED TIME
1.5-2 hours

MAPS
USGS Stockbridge; Berkshire Natural Resources Council map: bnrc.org/wp-content/uploads/2016/10/YokunRidgeN_TrailMap.pdf

TRAIL DESCRIPTION

This excursion's best view is from the parking area at Olivia's Overlook and takes in Stockbridge Bowl (also known as Lake Mahkeenac) and the verdant ridges beyond. The lookout is named for Olivia Stokes Hatch, whose family donated the land to the Berkshire County Land Trust and Conservation Fund. A plaque atop an elegant stone wall explains that the Tennessee Gas Pipeline Company constructed the parking area in 1992.

Carefully cross Lenox Road and enter the woods at the trailhead on the north side of the road. A kiosk, complete with large trail map (and often a supply of printed maps), is about 50 feet into the forest. Walk up into diverse woodland of eastern hemlock, oak, ash, and red maple. Note the gray schist outcroppings veined with milky quartz. This erosion-resistant rock type forms the spine of the

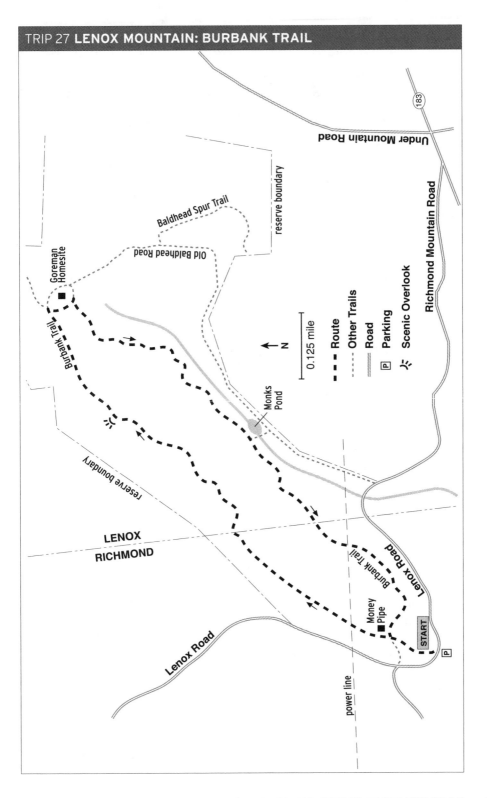

LENOX

RICHMOND

Under Mountain Road

Richmond Mountain Road

183

reserve boundary

Baldhead Spur Trail

Old Baldhead Road

Goreman Homesite

Burbank Trail

N

0.125 mile

- - - Route
- - - - Other Trails
——— Road
P Parking
Scenic Overlook

Monks Pond

reserve boundary

Money Pipe

Lenox Road

Burbank Trail

Lenox Road

START

P

power line

Opalescent Monks Pond once supplied water to Anson Phelps Stokes's Shadowbrook estate, which was later owned by Andrew Carnegie.

Lenox–Stockbridge Mountain ridge. Enter a darker forest in which hemlock predominates, joined by yellow, black, and gray birches as well as shade-tolerant American beeches and sun-loving oaks. In spring, a wet depression to the right is filled with a profusion of purple violets.

Follow the blue-blazed path and arrive at a signed four-way intersection. (*Note*: All Berkshire Natural Resources Council trails on Yokun Ridge are marked with blue blazes.) Continue straight ahead on Burbank Trail. Begin a moderate climb past schist outcroppings, and emerge into sunlight as you reach a power-line cut. Wintergreen on the left bears coral-red fruits in late summer and during fall. This sunny, dry, linear landscape also provides suitable growing conditions for pale corydalis, which bears tubular pink-and-yellow flowers in May. Eastern towhees are among the bird species that nest in such artificial shrublands. Listen for their *chewink* calls and *drink-your-tea* songs.

Back in the moister forest, the trail undulates under oaks, hemlocks, and mountain laurels. Woodland wildflowers here include *Clintonia* (blue-bead lily), Indian cucumber-root, and sessile-leafed bellwort (wild oat), which all produce yellow flowers. In time, the path climbs, gently at first and then more steeply, paved in spots with bedrock. Witch hazel, a spreading shrub, blooms here in autumn. Striped maples are the small trees with greenish bark. Even their flowers, produced in May, are green.

After a few more undulations through oaks and hop hornbeam, Burbank Trail arrives at a short side path that leads left to an outlook at 1.0 mile. The view to the northwest through a gap in the forest is limited but very nice. A nearby plaque indicates that the trail was named for Kelton (Kim) Burbank, a local attorney and conservationist. Lowbush blueberries thrive in the acidic soil beneath the pines and oaks. Return to Burbank Trail and turn left. Striped maple, red maple, and witch hazel abound beneath the oaks. Gaudy scarlet tanager males sing their burry refrains from high in the oaks in late spring and early summer. In contrast, their yellow-green mates blend in with the foliage. When you reach a signed path, turn right to continue the loop on Burbank Trail, heading toward Old Baldhead Road.

The route descends through a forest of white ash, big-tooth aspen, black birch and gray birch, red maple, and red oak. At 1.4 miles, reach a cellar hole on the left—all that remains of the Gorman homesite, occupied by that family from 1852 to 1892, although dates on a concrete marker indicate occupation from 1838 to 1898. The Gormans farmed this 44-acre hardscrabble lot until they sold it to Wall Street financier Anson Phelps Stokes to become part of his Shadowbrook estate. Philanthropist Andrew Carnegie later owned the property.

Blue-blazed Burbank Trail joins Old Baldhead Road and bears right. Shortly, reach an intersection and turn right to remain on Burbank Trail. Morrow's honeysuckle, an introduced exotic ornamental, outcompetes native shrubs here.

After crossing a series of bog bridges, bear left to continue a gradual descent to a stone wall composed of small pieces of schist. Reach a hemlock stand and drop into a shallow gorge through which a small brook spills. Some towering hemlock specimens border the stream. Gray birches, which preceded the conifers, have succumbed to the hemlocks' shade, but yellow birches thrive in the cool shadows. The wide path passes a sofa-sized boulder on the right.

Turn right at a log bench by the brook and amble under hemlocks and hardwoods. Traverse a bridge and bear left. The path changes to a wider old cart road and leads downslope to an opalescent pond in a serene setting on the left. This was the Shadowbrook estate's reservoir. During the twentieth century, it took on the name Monks Pond; a Jesuit order owned the property at the time. (The Kripalu Center for Yoga and Health, below Olivia's Overlook, now occupies the former monastery.) Reach a signed intersection at the far right end of the reservoir and bear right to remain on Burbank Trail, following it past the earthen dam's concrete spillway. The trail stays high above the flow, and ledge outcroppings make the scene picturesque. Listen for the call of the 21-inch-tall barred owl: *who cooks for you, who cooks for you all*. The path rises moderately along this steep hillside; the slope was reinforced with rock during construction, making for excellent footing. Cross the power-line corridor again, where tall mountain laurels bloom profusely in late June.

The trail undulates easily under hemlocks and then through deciduous woodland of birch, beech, maple, and oak before reentering evergreens. Before long, you are back at the first intersection. Turn left and retrace your steps across Lenox Road to your vehicle.

DID YOU KNOW?

During the eighteenth century, virtually the entire Lenox–Stockbridge Mountain ridge was denuded of timber. Much of the wood was reduced to charcoal to feed local iron furnaces—iron production was a thriving early Berkshire industry—until almost all the nearby timber had been harvested. As a result, coal became a cheaper source of fuel for the furnaces.

MORE INFORMATION

Open dawn to dusk, year-round. Hiking, skiing, mountain biking, horseback riding, leashed dogs, and hunting in season are permitted. Motorized vehicles, fires, camping, littering, and cutting or removing trees or plants are prohibited. Berkshire Natural Resources Council, 20 Bank Row, Pittsfield, MA 01201 (413-499-0596; bnrc.org).

NEARBY

Chill out at Stockbridge's Kripalu Center for Yoga and Health, visible below Olivia's Overlook. The center offers presentations, training, and workshops in yoga and healthy living. From the intersection of MA 183 and Richmond Mountain Road, follow MA 183 west 1.6 miles to the entrance on the right (866-200-5203; kripalu.org).

28

WEST STOCKBRIDGE MOUNTAIN: CHARCOAL TRAIL

West Stockbridge Mountain is the main attraction of the southern portion of Yokun Ridge Reserve. This enjoyable loop trail leads through mature woodlands and features a couple of pleasing vistas.

DIRECTIONS

From the center of Lenox, at the intersection of Walker Street, MA 183, and US 7A (Main Street), follow MA 183 (West Street) for a little more than 1.5 miles then turn right onto Richmond Mountain Road and drive 0.4 mile to a gravel parking area on the left at Olivia's Overlook. This is the same parking area as for Burbank Trail (Trip 27). *GPS coordinates*: 42° 21.109′ N, 73° 20.259′ W.

TRAIL DESCRIPTION

From the west end of the parking area, begin by following blue-blazed Charcoal Trail across a gas pipeline corridor flush with grasses, goldenrod, catchfly, and other forbs in summer. (*Note*: All Berkshire Natural Resources Council [BNRC] trails on Yokun Ridge have blue blazes.) Cross a short wooden span to a map kiosk at the edge of a shady forest, where the Charcoal Trail loop begins. Turn left and follow blue blazes along a wide old roadway under hemlocks and oaks. The path descends gently along a ravine for the first portion of the route.

White oak, whose leaves have rounded lobes, joins the deciduous woodland mix, while witch hazel and American chestnut sprouts form a trailside understory. Stride across stretches of schist bedrock as you continue an easy descent through abundant mountain laurel that blooms in mid-June to early July. Pass the signed intersection for Brothers Trail on the left—it leads to Baldhead and Monks Pond—and continue straight. At the BNRC property boundary, Charcoal Trail turns right (roughly halfway

LOCATION
Stockbridge,
West Stockbridge, and
Richmond, MA

RATING
Moderate

DISTANCE
1.6-mile loop

ELEVATION GAIN
530 feet

ESTIMATED TIME
1-1.5 hours

MAPS
USGS Stockbridge;
Berkshire Natural Resources
Council map:
bnrc.org/wp-content/
uploads/2016/10/
YokunRidgeS_TrailMap.pdf

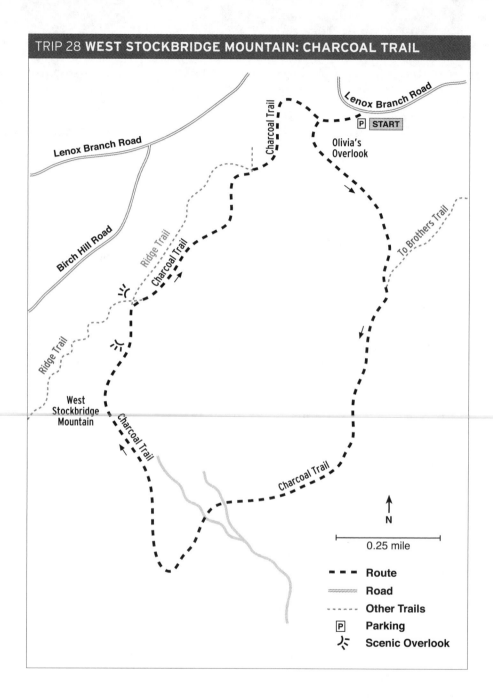

Charcoal Trail

Lenox Branch Road

P START

Olivia's
Overlook

Lenox Branch Road

Birch Hill Road

Ridge Trail

Charcoal Trail

To Brothers Trail

Ridge Trail

West
Stockbridge
Mountain

Charcoal Trail

Charcoal Trail

N

0.25 mile

- - - Route
===== Road
- - - - Other Trails
P Parking
Ⅹ Scenic Overlook

through the 1.6-mile loop). Listen for the deeply resonant drumming or mania-
cal call of the big pileated woodpecker and the mellow tremolo of the wood
thrush. Shade-tolerant black birches become common, while evergreen Christmas ferns enliven the woodland year-round.

A split log bench resting on vertically tilted schist offers a view south to Monument Mountain and Butternut Basin ski area beyond.

Begin an easy climb through mixed deciduous and coniferous woods—a variety of oak, black birch, and hemlock. The deep shade and acidic soil prohibit the growth of virtually any other plant life. Drainage streams have dissected the slopes and carved small ravines of varying depths. Cross several on well-placed rockwork. White ashes, sugar maples, and mature oaks here are impressively tall and straight. Stride up a stone staircase amid fallen hemlocks and reach an angular boulder where the path levels out briefly and then climbs easily. Cross a trickling drainage and pass remnant stone walls to your right. A few massive white pines escaped the lumberman's ax here. Wend along the base of an outcropping studded with mosses and ferns, including hay-scented fern, spinulose wood fern, and rock-loving common polypody.

Higher up the slope, the trees—American beech and red maple—are of much smaller stature due to the thin soil. Stone steps lead to a fern glade near the height-of-land, and lowbush blueberries and Canada mayflower grace the forest floor. The hoarse, singsong voice of the male scarlet tanager fills the late spring and early summer air, but the bird itself is seldom seen.

At about 1.1 miles from the trailhead, reach a rocky bald where a bench offers a view south to Monument Mountain and the Butternut ski area beyond (but the best view is yet to come). Note that the schist bedrock is tilted vertically. Continue straight on Charcoal Trail to a signed intersection just north of the summit. Turn left to reach nearby Vista Point, a rocky perch with a bench, where you can take in a gorgeous vista west across a wooded valley. The outlook is part of Ridge Trail, which runs roughly parallel to Charcoal Trail along the reservation boundary, entering private land just south of the summit. A few small sassafras saplings, with mitten-shaped leaves, grow here. When you're ready, return to Charcoal Trail, or continue north on Ridge Trail, marked with periodic red blazes. Descend through oak, hemlock, and laurel. Blueberries and Canada mayflowers thrive in the acid soil, while common polypody ferns cap some boulders. At times, the downward angle increases. *Clintonia*, a native lily, and bush honeysuckle bloom yellow, while the small shrub maple-leaf viburnum adds its umbels of whitish-pink blossoms in late spring.

From the lower junction of Ridge Trail and Charcoal Trail (marked with signs for Charcoal Trail only), continue on Charcoal Trail. Drop down easily and pass more angular outcroppings on the left under an oak canopy. A few additional twists and turns lead you back to the map kiosk and the trailhead at Olivia's Overlook.

DID YOU KNOW?

Olivia's Overlook is named for Olivia Stokes Hatch, who, with her husband, John D. Hatch Jr., and her brothers, Anson Phelps Stokes Jr. and Isaac N.P. Stokes, donated the land. Tenneco Inc. of Houston funded the construction of the overlook.

MORE INFORMATION

Open dawn to dusk, year-round. Hiking, skiing, mountain biking, horseback riding, leashed dogs, and hunting are permitted. The reserve is owned and managed by Berkshire Natural Resources Council, a regional land trust founded in 1967 that protects more than 22,000 acres of conservation land in the Berkshires. Berkshire Natural Resources Council, 20 Bank Row, Pittsfield, MA 01201 (413-499-0596; bnrc.org).

NEARBY

The Mount, at 2 Plunkett Street in Lenox, is the former home and 113-acre estate of Pulitzer Prize–winning novelist and short story writer Edith Wharton (1862–1937), best known for her ghostly tales. The home and its public gardens are open to the public 10 A.M. to 5 P.M. daily May through October and on weekends November to February. Check the website for other seasonal hours. An admission fee is charged. The Terrace Café is available seasonally for dining. The property closes early some days for events and programs (413-551-5111; edithwharton.org).

29
SCHERMERHORN GORGE

From the still waters of wildlife-rich Woods Pond to the cascading flow of Schermerhorn Brook, flanked by massive trees, this hike provides dramatic contrasts.

DIRECTIONS

From I-90 (Massachusetts Turnpike), take Exit 2 in Lee. Bear right at the end of the ramp and follow US 20 west through Lee (US 20 joins US 7 just after Cranwell Resort) for 4.6 miles to Housatonic Street in Lenox. Turn right onto Housatonic Street and drive 1.3 miles to where the pavement makes a sharp turn to the right. Leave the pavement and continue straight ahead on gravel, parking on the right between the railroad tracks and the pedestrian bridge, where there is space for approximately four vehicles. (*Note:* Do not block the driveway to the private residence on the left, and do not obstruct access to the canoe landing on the pond edge to the right.) Parking is also available outside the railroad tracks, on the right, but be aware that this is an active rail line. *GPS coordinates*: 42° 20.985′ N, 73° 14.638′ W.

TRAIL DESCRIPTION

Cross the arched steel-and-wood pedestrian bridge at the south end of Woods Pond and admire the sight of October Mountain. The reflection off the pond is especially eye-catching during fall foliage season in early to mid-October. The Housatonic River plunges over Woods Pond Dam—which backs up the river's flow to create the 100-acre pond—about 200 yards to the right (south). Exotic Morrow's honeysuckle lines the gravel roadway beyond the bridge.

Bear left upon reaching gravel Woodland Road and pass under power lines. If you visit from May to early July,

LOCATION
Lenox, Lee, and Washington, MA

RATING
Moderate to Strenuous

DISTANCE
3.7 miles round trip

ELEVATION GAIN
620 feet

ESTIMATED TIME
2–2.5 hours

MAPS
USGS East Lee; Massachusetts Department of Conservation and Recreation map: mass.gov/files/documents/2016/12/qw/october_4.pdf

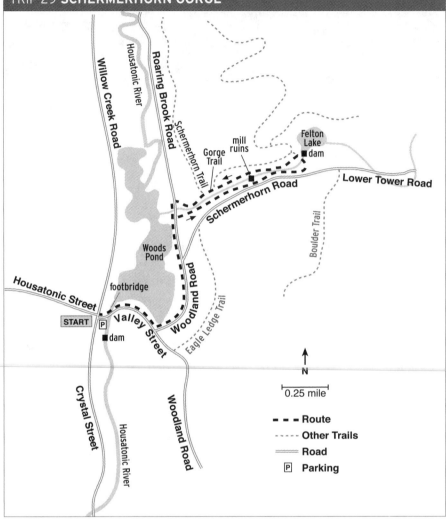

you'll be impressed by the exuberance of birdlife. Yellow warblers and a myriad of other avian life forms abound in and around the pond, including belted kingfisher, Canada goose, wood duck, mallard, and warbling vireo.

The road hugs the pond shore, affording views of the water and surrounding hills. The bucolic scene belies the fact that Woods Pond holds the highest concentrations of carcinogenic polychlorinated biphenyls (PCBs) in the Housatonic River system, caused by twentieth-century industrial pollution upstream in Pittsfield. Bear left at another gravel road to continue around the pond. Primarily young woodland of white ash, sugar maple, and gray, black, and yellow birch stand above the water body. A few massive white pines tower in stark contrast to

A handsome keystone arch spans Schermerhorn Brook soon after it leaves October Mountain State Forest's Felton Lake.

the young deciduous growth. The body of one multitrunked giant lies where it crashed to earth. Walk past a huge red oak on the right and then encounter more impressive trees.

Pass two woods roads on the right separated by a modest high-gradient stream flowing down the hillside into the pond. Reach the state forest boundary to your right shortly before the intersection with paved Schermerhorn Road, also to the right. Continue straight on Woodland Road, paralleling the boundary of the George Darey Wildlife Management Area along the Housatonic on the left. Giant oak trees grow in the valley's nutrient-rich soil.

The sound of Schermerhorn Brook heralds your arrival at the trailhead, 1.1 miles from where you parked. Turn right at a small wooden sign on blue-blazed Gorge Trail to begin a moderate climb under sugar maples, ashes, and oaks. The brook to your left gushes over and around boulders of gneiss and quartzite. American yew—a low evergreen shrub—thrives in the shade near the cascade.

The trail turns right, continues to climb, and then bears left to ascend above the flow; watch your footing here. A two-step waterfall is soon visible below. The rugged slopes of the gorge hold some impressive oaks and hemlocks. One hemlock trunk is 3 feet across. The trail moves farther from the stream as the incline eases. Eventually, the trail levels out and rejoins the brook, perhaps 30 feet above it.

Mountain maple, a small understory tree similar in size to striped maple but with brown bark and smaller, toothier leaves, grows in the gorge along the flowage.

Tread up stone steps and past a jumble of big gneiss boulders as the streambed continues to be very rocky. After a bit, reach the partial stone foundation of what was probably a millhouse long ago. Along the way, note the characteristic alternating dark and light bands of the gneiss. In spring and early summer, the loud, ringing notes of the bobbing, striped Louisiana waterthrush can be heard even above the roar of the water; these warblers winter in the tropics and nest along fast-flowing upland streams. On the right, a hemlock grows from a rock crevice, inexorably breaking the rock apart. The brook soon splits in two, forming a narrow floodplain.

Emerge briefly into a brighter patch of young maples; Schermerhorn Road is very near. After reentering shady hemlock forest, pass a 100-year-old fallen tree cut years ago to accommodate the trail. White pines and a mammoth oak stand on the left a few feet farther along. The steepness of these slopes made timber harvesting here less economical, resulting in some truly impressive specimen trees remaining today. The reverberating drumming of the crow-sized pileated woodpecker is an increasingly common percussion in such mature Berkshire woodlands. Even if you don't hear or see one of these memorable birds, you will likely come across the deep, rectangular cavities they excavate to reach carpenter ant colonies.

The gorge deepens again, and soon Gorge Trail approaches close to the brook. After the brook negotiates a 90-degree bend to the left, the well-blazed trail follows it up to a gravel road. A keystone arch bridge built of native stone lies ahead, beneath which flows Schermerhorn Brook, the outlet stream from Felton Lake. Turn left to cross the bridge at 2.0 miles. An earthen dam to your right impounds the water body. Three-inch-long bullfrog tadpoles sometimes swim in the concrete spillway. You will return along the opposite side of the gorge.

Blue-blazed Gorge Trail continues at a sign just beyond the far end of the bridge, under planted Norway spruces. The path follows the stream and passes a small, derelict shack some 100 feet to your right. The gorge seems deeper from this side, and the descent is moderately steep. Light gaps are filled with hobblebush, maple-leaf viburnum, and bush honeysuckle. Patches of young American beech appear as the trail again closely approaches the brook. The ruins of the millhouse are more easily observed from this side. Walk under a mixed canopy of hemlocks, oaks, and northern hardwoods; cross an intermittent tributary stream on large, flat stones; and continue downward along Schermerhorn Brook.

The woodland is more predominately deciduous in this area—especially rich in oaks. Hobblebush shrubs bloom here in early May. Both Solomon's seal—with greenish flowers hanging down from each leaf node—and false Solomon's seal—with white blossoms at the tip of the stalk—thrive on the forest floor. The brook tumbles over moss-cushioned boulders, and its roaring intensifies with the gradient. A few stone steps take you down to brook level again.

The yellow trumpets of bush honeysuckle are numerous. Blue cohosh, which has oddly purple-green leaves, blooms in spring in a sunny canopy gap. Your descent steepens as the gorge narrows markedly and the brook drops precipitously. As you proceed downward, the cascades become more dramatic. One four-step section is particularly picturesque. Finally, bear right, away from the brook. Amble down more excellent stone steps and negotiate a series of short switchbacks down the slope. Reach the brook again, pass a huge oak on the right, and arrive back at Woodland Road. Turn left and retrace your steps to Woods Pond (bearing right at the intersections), the pedestrian bridge, and your vehicle.

DID YOU KNOW?

The George Darey Wildlife Management Area and the adjoining western slopes of October Mountain State Forest constitute a significant portion of the 12,280-acre Upper Housatonic Area of Critical Environmental Concern designated by the commonwealth in 2009. It is home to 32 state-listed endangered or threatened species and dozens of vernal pools.

MORE INFORMATION

Open sunrise to 30 minutes after sunset, year-round. Access is free. Pets are permitted but must be on a 10-foot-maximum leash and attended at all times. Proof of rabies vaccination required. Motorized vehicles are not permitted on Gorge Trail. October Mountain State Forest, 317 Woodland Road, Lee, MA (413-243-1778; mass.gov/locations/october-mountain-state-forest).

NEARBY

Railroad buffs will enjoy the Berkshire Scenic Railway Museum, at 10 Willow Creek Road in Lenox, within view of where you parked. Cross the railroad tracks, turn right onto Willow Creek Road, and walk 100 yards to the museum on the right. The restored 1903 Lenox Station once welcomed Gilded Age "cottagers" to their Berkshire summer homes. Open Saturdays, 10 A.M. to 2 P.M., Memorial Day weekend to Labor Day. Hoosac Valley train rides on the historical Adams Branch are offered weekends and holidays Memorial Day weekend to late October departing from Adams Visitor Center, 3 Hoosac Street, Adams (413-637-2210; berkshiretrains.org).

30

STEVENS GLEN

Towering trees and cascading Lenox Mountain Brook make Stevens Glen one of the area's most appealing walking destinations in any season.

DIRECTIONS

From the center of Lenox, at the intersection of MA 183, US 7A (Main Street), and Walker Street, travel southwest on MA 183 for 1.5 miles to Richmond Mountain Road on the right (where MA 183 curves left). Follow Richmond Mountain Road for 1.6 miles, past Olivia's Overlook on the left, to Lenox Branch Road on the left. Turn left and drive for 0.6 mile to a signed pull-off on the right with parking for five or six cars. Additional parking is available about 100 yards farther on the right, opposite Deer Hill Road. *GPS coordinates*: 42° 21.026′ N, 73° 20.895′ W.

TRAIL DESCRIPTION

Portions of the loop trail were temporarily closed due to severe erosion at the time this guide went to press. BNRC plans to reconstruct the trail and crossings. Visitors may do an out-and-back walk to the falls (please be alert for signs marking closed or rerouted sections).

Stride down wooden steps under the shade of a yellow birch to a kiosk where trail maps are often available. The unnamed trail, marked with blue blazes, leads right, through a balsam fir plantation. The trees are tall and straight, their bark marked with resin "blisters." Herb-Robert, a geranium relative with pink blossoms, blankets the forest floor in early summer. The dirt path leads easily down, past invasive garlic mustard. Turn right at a Y intersection to begin the loop; you'll return along the other pathway.

Little sunlight penetrates the fir boughs, and as a result, not much grows beneath them, but pockets of spinulose

LOCATION
West Stockbridge and Richmond, MA

RATING
Easy to Moderate

DISTANCE
1.2 miles round trip

ELEVATION GAIN
320 feet

ESTIMATED TIME
1-1.5 hours

MAPS
USGS Stockbridge; Berkshire Natural Resources Council map: bnrc.org/wp-content/uploads/2016/10/StevensGlen_TrailMap.pdf

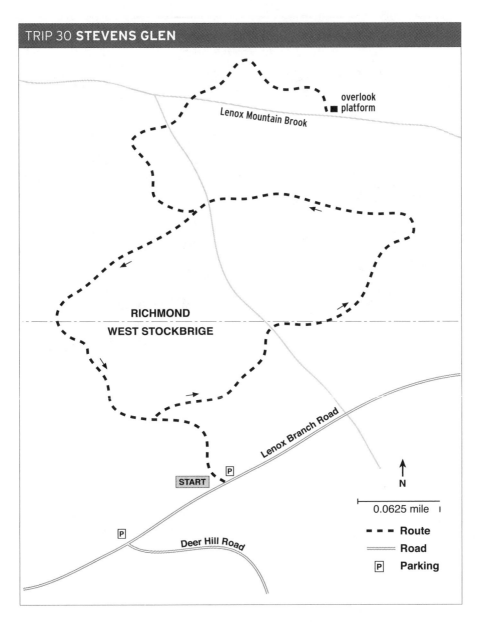

wood fern add splashes of color year-round. Cross a damp spot on bog bridges and begin an easy descent under a deciduous canopy of white ash, basswood, big-tooth aspen, and eastern hemlock. Turn right to cross a bridge over an unnamed high-gradient tributary stream. Moss coats the span's handrails. Dark green, paired leaves of partridgeberry form a creeping ground cover beneath hemlocks; black, yellow, and white birches; impressive ashes; and sugar maples. In early summer, partridgeberry produces twin fuzzy, white star-shaped flowers, which are replaced by bright red berries.

Porcupines dine on leafy greens in summer and den in rocky crevices.

Sizable white pines loom here—trees that pioneered this ground when it was open and sunlit. Bear left at a log bench (the first of many), and just before entering a power-line cut, be alert for poison ivy on the right. A mowed path leads through the shrub-filled linear clearing, decorated with showy red-flowering raspberry in early summer. Back in the forest, note the hemlock scarred by a lightning strike. By the time you reach another log bench, you can hear the sound of flowing water. Descend and bear left over another bridge over the tributary. Some big boulders in the streambed are moss covered. Wild ginger tops one on the left.

When you arrive at a signed intersection with the one-way trail to Stevens Glen, turn right off the loop and pass a sizable sugar maple and a multitrunked oak on the left. The trees are impressively tall and straight in this mature woodland. At 0.7 mile, traverse a short bridge over the tributary, which joins Lenox Mountain Brook a short distance below. The cool ravine offers a refreshing break from summer heat. A cascade is visible to the right as you cross a longer span. A massive hemlock stump and trunk lie just beyond it to the left.

More picturesque cascades appear as you proceed. Watch for several species of spring wildflowers here, including shinleaf, Canada mayflower, foamflower, and maidenhair fern. You'll encounter the first real ascent as you stride up over two series of schist steps, but the path levels out before too long. After a few more rock steps, climb down a sturdy metal stairway to a well-situated platform overlook at 0.9 mile. A brass plaque on the outcropping relates the history of the property's acquisition. From the platform, enjoy the fabulous sight of Lenox Mountain Brook careening steeply down a fissure barely a couple of feet wide in places. The almost-deafening roar is a major part of the ambience.

When you are ready, retrace your steps—uphill this time—back to the signed junction. Turn right and follow the slope contour past a mossy, striated boulder that resembles a ship's hull. Christmas ferns become numerous just before you reenter the power-line cut. At the Y intersection, turn right to return to your vehicle.

DID YOU KNOW?

In the nineteenth century, farmer Romanza Stevens, whose family had owned the glen since 1760, built a series of bridges to enable guests to have access to its wonders and charged 25 cents for the privilege. Stevens Glen was a major tourist attraction then for wealthy Berkshire residents and summer visitors. The site eventually lost popularity and faded into obscurity until Claire and Millard Pryor and Zora and Frederick Pryor donated the land and a conservation restriction in 1995.

MORE INFORMATION

Open dawn to dusk, year-round. Stay on existing trails. Mountain biking, skiing, leashed dogs, and horseback riding are allowed. Hunting is allowed in season. Motorized vehicles, fires, camping, littering, and cutting or removing trees or plants are prohibited. Berkshire Natural Resources Council, 20 Bank Row, Pittsfield, MA (413-499-0596; bnrc.org).

NEARBY

For an eclectic mix of coffee shop, café, bakery, art gallery, store, and event space in an old train station, try No. Six Depot, 6 Depot Street, in West Stockbridge for breakfast or lunch; open daily 8 A.M. to 4 P.M. (413-232-0205; sixdepot.com).

31

OCTOBER MOUNTAIN STATE FOREST: FINERTY POND

From a busy highway, this route follows the Appalachian Trail over a couple of wooded promontories to a serene pond ringed by mountain laurel in Massachusetts's most expansive state forest.

DIRECTIONS

From the west: From I-90 (Massachusetts Turnpike), take Exit 2 in Lee. Turn left at the traffic light at the end of the ramp, and follow US 20 (Jacob's Ladder Scenic Byway) east for 4.2 miles to a paved pullout on the right and the Appalachian Trail parking area at the Lee–Becket town line. The gravel lot accommodates seven cars.

From the east: From MA 8 North/US 20 in Becket, follow US 20 west for 7.8 miles to the paved pullout and Appalachian Trail parking area on the left. *GPS coordinates:* 42° 17.577' N, 73° 09.684' W.

TRAIL DESCRIPTION

This is the same parking area and trailhead as the Upper Goose Pond hike (Trip 32). From the kiosk, which has display maps of the Appalachian Trail (AT) route, walk east to the pedestrian crossing sign on the left. Do not walk along US 20; this is very hazardous as there is no shoulder in spots. Use caution crossing the highway. A narrow, blue-blazed access trail leads into a forest of American beech, eastern hemlock, and white pine. The tiny and fuzzy paired white blossoms of partridgeberry bloom in ground-hugging mats here in early summer.

The route parallels US 20 for about 100 yards. Bits of rusted barbed wire embedded in tree trunks on the left are evidence of former livestock pasturing. Upon reaching the AT at a Y intersection, turn left and follow the white-blazed trail northbound, uphill, under red and sugar

LOCATION
Becket and Washington, MA

RATING
Moderate

DISTANCE
6 miles round trip

ELEVATION GAIN
870 feet

ESTIMATED TIME
3.5 hours

MAPS
USGS East Lee; Massachusetts Department of Conservation and Recreation map: mass.gov/files/documents/2016/12/qw/october_4.pdf

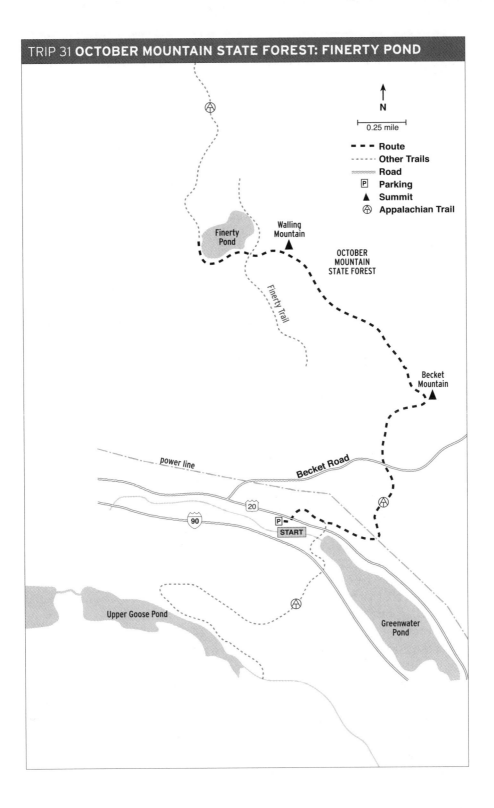

N

0.25 mile

- - - **Route**
.... **Other Trails**
≈≈≈≈ **Road**
Ⓟ **Parking**
▲ **Summit**
Ⓐ **Appalachian Trail**

Finerty
Pond

Walling
Mountain ▲

OCTOBER
MOUNTAIN
STATE FOREST

Finerty Trail

Becket
Mountain ▲

power line

Becket Road

⑳

㊿ 90

Ⓟ
START

Ⓐ

Upper Goose Pond

Ⓐ

Greenwater
Pond

maples; bear left at an especially large sugar maple. Cross a damp area filled with light-green sensitive fern, a species characteristic of wetlands. A sign attached to a tree gives distances to various landmarks along the route. A probable vernal pool lies in a depression a bit farther on the right. Climb stone, then log, steps up a slope covered with maple, hemlock, birch, and oak. A mammoth twin white pine commands attention on the left. Canada mayflowers bloom in spring beneath the pines. Abundant beech saplings, often sprouting in clones from the same rootstock, populate the understory.

Cross the first of several boulder fields. The gneiss rocks are banded alternately light and dark. A moderate climb brings you to a level woods road where the route turns right. The sound of flowing water should be evident as you cross two wide snowmobile trails in rapid succession near their junction. Continue to follow the white blazes as the AT skirts a dark hemlock ravine cut by a brook. The trail soon bears left, away from the woods road, and enters a power-line right of way. Various ferns and yellow loosestrife flourish in the sunny depression. Rejoin the brook under a canopy of hemlocks and cross it on moss-covered stones. The soothing sound of running water replaces the mechanized din of the highway and turnpike.

The trail climbs gradually through mixed rock-strewn woodland. Mingling with the dominant beeches are multitrunked oaks, which indicates that the species may have been selectively logged here a century ago, because multiple stems sprout from cut oak stumps. Recent logging off the trail has created open habitat for wildlife. Cross a shallow brook on stones and follow the level path up to paved Becket (Tyne) Road at 1.1 miles. Cross the road and climb easily under hardwoods that edge a boulder field on the slope to your right.

For a bit the AT parallels an old skid road over which logs were once hauled out. A gray gneiss boulder on the left, next to a dead beech, has weathered into tiers. Unfortunately, the vast majority of the American beech trees in this forest are diseased and dying. Beech scale insects make tiny incisions to get at the tree's sap. *Nectria* fungus invades the tree through the holes and wreaks havoc on its circulatory system. An outward symptom is rough, broken black bark all over instead of smooth, gray bark.

Bear right and pass over a knoll with some big, non-native Norway spruces. The narrow trail leads through young beech woods and ferns, traversing striated bedrock in spots. High winds have snapped many of the beech trunks.

A short climb takes you to the top of Becket Mountain (elevation 2,178 feet), where the path levels out in a hay-scented fern glade at 1.6 miles. Concrete footings are all that remain of a tower that stood here when the summit was fully open. A trail register hangs from a tree. Turn left, remaining on the AT, and pass a cluster of gneiss boulders to begin an easy descent through a beech, birch, and maple woodland. A rectangular, flat-topped boulder on the right is capped by wild oats (lilies, not grasses) that flower pale yellow in spring.

Continue over gently rolling terrain past another jumble of rocks. In early summer, red-berried elder shrubs sport crimson fruits. Zigzag up another slope

A short side trail leads to a pond access point where in late June and early July mountain laurel puts on a fine show.

and amble through a hay-scented fern glade under broad-leafed trees. The trail begins another easy descent and levels out among hobblebushes in rocky woods. The large, heart-shaped leaves of the hobblebushes shade black-throated blue warbler nests. Soon the character of the forest changes markedly. Scattered maple trees on this flat ridgeline permit enough light to reach the forest floor for a dense layer of raspberry, ferns, elderberry, and climbing false buckwheat to thrive.

The trail climbs again and levels out on top of Walling Mountain. It might be difficult to tell that you're at 2,200 feet above sea level, given the minor elevation change since the last bump along the ridge. Pass car-sized hunks of gneiss and the woodland wildflowers *Clintonia* and Indian cucumber-root. The latter has modest but beautiful flowers, with recurved yellow petals hanging from a second tier of whorled leaves.

From here, the descent gets a bit rougher. Patches of shining club moss, a non-flowering fern relative, form a green carpet on the forest floor. Wood frogs and red efts wander in search of invertebrate prey as the path switchbacks down.

When you reach Finerty Trail, a woods road used by all-terrain vehicles, cross it. Finerty Pond is visible through the trees ahead. The AT widens and leads down to a 10-foot-high laurel bush on the right; then it turns left to follow near the shore. If you pass this way in late June or early July, you'll be treated to a fantastic laurel flower show. About 100 feet past the laurel, a short side path leads to the best shoreline access point. Beavers have felled a couple of hardwoods here, and one of their lodges is visible on the far shore.

In summer, bullfrogs bellow and green frogs announce your arrival with a little *eek* as they flee. An impressive old yellow birch stands on the left just before you follow a cushioned path past an angular boulder and beneath hemlocks to a contemplative spot near the water's edge, bordered by abundant laurel shrubs. Listen for the dry, rattling call of the belted kingfisher (about 12 inches long, with a shaggy crest) from somewhere across the pond.

Here, the AT swings away from the shore. Take some time to linger and enjoy the serenity, and then retrace your steps some 3 miles back to the parking area. Near the end of the hike, be sure to bear right on the blue-blazed path rather than turning left to follow the AT down to US 20. It's much safer to walk back on the path than along the highway.

DID YOU KNOW?

October Mountain State Forest, at 16,500 acres, is the largest state forest in Massachusetts. Writer Herman Melville, whose home (called Arrowhead) in Pittsfield afforded a fine view of the mountain, is reputed to have coined its name. The commonwealth purchased the initial 11,000 acres of the forest from the Whitney estate in 1915. William C. Whitney served as President Grover Cleveland's secretary of the navy.

MORE INFORMATION

Carry out all litter. No motorized vehicles, mountain bikes, horses, tree cutting, or fires permitted. Camping allowed in designated areas only. The AMC Berkshire Chapter's Appalachian Trail Management Committee is responsible for maintenance, management, and protection of the nearly 90 miles of the AT in Massachusetts; volunteers do this work, with assistance from the Massachusetts Department of Conservation and Recreation. Massachusetts AT Committee, AMC Berkshire Chapter, P.O. Box 2281, Pittsfield, MA 01201 (amcberkshire.org/at; at@amcberkshire.org). October Mountain State Forest, 317 Woodland Road, Lee, MA 01238 (413-243-1778; mass.gov/locations/october-mountain-state-forest).

NEARBY

Jacob's Pillow, on a 220-acre former farm in Becket (358 Carter Road), is internationally renowned as a focal point for contemporary dance. A National Historic Landmark and National Medal of Arts recipient, Jacob's Pillow is home to America's longest-running dance festival, founded in 1933 by Ted Shawn. The summer season runs from mid-June to late August (413-243-0745, box office; jacobspillow.org).

ASH UNDER SIEGE

Ash trees are a crucial component of eastern forests, providing food and cover for wildlife, material for a variety of forest products, and shade and decor for landowners and municipalities. American Indians have traditionally used the wood to make baskets, canoes, musical instruments, and medicines. Nearly 70 percent of Massachusetts's 45 million ash trees grow in the Berkshires. Sadly, all of the region's ash species (mostly white, black, and green ash) are threatened by the emerald ash borer (EAB, *Agrilus planipennis* Fairmaire), one of North America's newest and deadliest forest pests.

EAB, named for its metallic green color, is a half-inch long beetle native to Asia. It has relatively little impact in its home range, where trees have evolved resistance over thousands of years and there are several natural predators. Such is not the case in North America, and since being introduced to Michigan in the late twentieth century, EAB has rapidly spread across the continent, killing hundreds of millions of ash trees in just twenty years. EAB disperses less than 2 miles per year naturally, but humans have unwittingly conveyed it long distances by transporting infested firewood, lumber, and nursery stock.

The infestation process begins when females lay eggs on ash bark during the summer. Larvae feed on the inner bark tissues, disrupting circulation of nutrients and water and killing most trees within just two to five years. Adult beetles emerge in spring and fly from May to September, searching for new host trees. EAB causes near 100 percent mortality, but a small percentage of trees have shown natural resistance. Symptoms include exposed light-colored bark caused by woodpeckers feeding on infested trees (known as "blonding"), dead upper branches, D-shaped exit holes chewed by adults, discolored leaves, and unusual root and trunk sprouts. These signs are difficult to detect in early stages, and EAB is often present for several years before being discovered.

The first confirmation of EAB in Massachusetts was in August 2012, when Massachusetts Department of Conservation and Recreation researchers discovered an adult beetle in a trap (designed to lure EAB during the summer flight season) in the town of Dalton, in the western part of the state. EAB quickly spread throughout the central Berkshires and is rapidly becoming well-established in other regions of Massachusetts and New England.

Eastern forests, already ravaged by pests and diseases such as hemlock woolly adelgid, gypsy moths, chestnut blight, and Dutch elm disease, stand to lose an entire genus of trees, with significant consequences for the ecosystem. According to a study published in *American Entomologist,* ash is a preferred food source for 100 invertebrate species, including several moths now potentially threatened with extinction. Wood frogs, cavity-nesting birds, and small mammals all use ash for food and cover.

From an economic standpoint, EAB has already cost wood producers hundreds of millions of dollars nationwide and will likely have similar impacts in

New England. Massachusetts officials forecast the loss of ash will cause overall losses of $500 million, and the Maine Forest Service estimates ash harvests are worth $140 million annually. Ash wood, coveted for its strength and elasticity, is well-suited for many products including furniture, flooring, and baseball bats. Replacing infested shade and ornamental trees is a considerable expense for municipalities and landowners.

Scientists haven't given up on ash yet, though. The United States Department of Agriculture and state agencies are working collectively on biocontrol measures using introduced wasps that prey on EAB in its native range. Preliminary findings indicate slower infestation rates, allowing young trees to survive and produce seeds. USDA researchers are also cloning trees that have shown natural resistance. Insecticides can be used on individual trees, through treatments are expensive. You can do your part by not transporting firewood or other potentially infested materials. Report signs of EAB to local officials and the Massachusetts Introduced Pests Outreach Project (massnrc.org/pests/eabreport.htm).

32

UPPER GOOSE POND

This out-and-back hike on the Appalachian Trail reaches one of the Berkshires' most scenic ponds, in a serene location reminiscent of northern New England.

DIRECTIONS

From the west: From I-90 (Massachusetts Turnpike), take Exit 2 in Lee. Turn left at the traffic light at the end of the ramp, and follow US 20 east for 4.2 miles to the Appalachian Trail parking area on the right at the Lee–Becket town line. The gravel lot accommodates about seven cars.

From the east: From MA 8 North/US 20 in Becket, follow US 20 west for 7.9 miles to the Appalachian Trail parking area on the left. *GPS coordinates*: 42° 17.577′ N, 73° 09.684′ W.

TRAIL DESCRIPTION

This is the same parking area and trailhead as the October Mountain State Forest hike (Trip 31). From the kiosk with a display map, walk east a short distance to the pedestrian crossing sign at US 20. Do not walk along US 20; this is very hazardous because there is no shoulder in spots. Use caution crossing the highway. A narrow, blue-blazed access trail on the north side of the highway leads through a forest of American beech, eastern hemlock, and white pine. It parallels US 20 for about 100 yards and then joins the Appalachian Trail (AT). Turn right and follow the white-blazed AT southbound down to the highway.

Cross US 20 again, pass through a gap in the guardrail, and proceed down wooden steps. Old orchard trees litter the ground with apples in fall. A brown AT directional sign indicates that the side path to Upper Goose Pond Cabin is 1.6 miles away. Cross a wooden bridge over Greenwater Brook at a former mill site, and arrive at the earthen dam

LOCATION
Becket, Lee, and Tyringham, MA

RATING
Moderate

DISTANCE
3.7 miles round trip
(4.7 miles including Upper Goose Pond Cabin)

ELEVATION GAIN
385 feet

ESTIMATED TIME
2.5 hours

MAPS
USGS East Lee

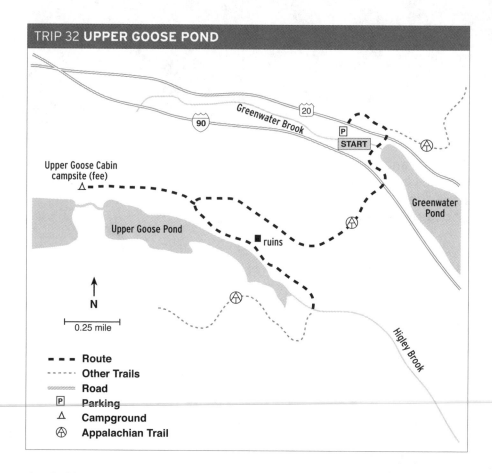

Upper Goose Cabin
campsite (fee)

Greenwater Brook

Greenwater
Pond

Upper Goose Pond

ruins

Higley Brook

N

0.25 mile

- - - Route
----- Other Trails
===== Road
P Parking
△ Campground
Ⓐ Appalachian Trail

that holds back the waters of Greenwater Pond. Turn right and follow the AT toward the Massachusetts Turnpike; bear left under the bridge and circle up and around to cross above the westbound lanes of I-90. Cross a second concrete span above the eastbound lanes. The October Mountain plateau looms behind you.

Reenter woodland at 0.5 mile. At a trail split, continue to follow the white-blazed AT by taking the left fork (the right fork is a snowmobile corridor). Ascend fairly steeply under a canopy of sugar and red maple, white ash, yellow birch, and red oak. A metamorphic rock ledge (gneiss) pops up on the left. Bear left around the ledge and up over stone steps, passing more outcroppings amid the steady roar from the interstate. Ferns and green-trunked striped maple saplings, hobblebush shrubs, and beech sprouts shade evergreen club mosses. Higher up, red oak becomes more common. After the trail levels out briefly, watch for an impressive white ash more than 2.5 feet in diameter on the left, which bears an AT blaze. Ashes provide the sturdy lumber required for ax handles and baseball bats. Unfortunately, many are succumbing to the emerald ash borer, which arrived in the area in 2012 (see "Ash Under Siege" on page 169).

As you begin climbing once again, young, shade-tolerant beech trees cover the north-facing slope along with birches, maples, and oaks. At the boundary of the

So close to the Massachusetts Turnpike, yet appearing to belong in northern New England, Upper Goose Pond is a gem.

Upper Goose Pond Natural Area, the height-of-land, find an AT trail register. You may want to peruse the register for interesting insight into the exploits of AT thru-hikers and other trail users. From here, descend gradually through small patches of hobblebush, identifiable by its big, paired, heart-shaped leaves. It features clusters of small white flowers in spring, red fruits in summer, multi-hued foliage in autumn, and large, straw-colored buds in winter. The din of the highway fades away, and you'll feel you're in a different world.

As you head to the right, an impressive gray ledge—uptilted at 30 degrees—juts out to your right. The woodland now includes mountain laurel and its tiny relative, wintergreen. This south-facing slope encourages a dominance of oaks, through which a screened view of a ridgeline is possible. Follow the slope contour, then descend more steeply and follow an impressive 250-foot exposed gneiss ledge. Brown and black rock tripes (lichens) cling to its vertical face, turning green only after absorbing moisture. Descend again and soon reach a signed junction indicating that Upper Goose Pond Cabin is 0.5 mile down the blue-blazed side path. If you have time, it's worth a visit. The cabin, which offers overnight accommodation for thru-hikers, is on a laurel-studded slope above the lake. Privies are available at the cabin and at the designated camping area.

Back on the white-blazed AT, continue straight on what is now an old woods road through beech, oak, black birch, and mountain laurel. Turn right, off the road, where the AT's white blazes lead down toward the pond. Reach Upper Goose Pond and turn left to follow the trail as it hugs the shoreline on its way toward Higley Brook at the pond's eastern end. Stunning views of the 45-acre pond (elevation 1,465 feet) abound through gaps in the vegetation. Arrive at the site of a former sportsmen's lodge—the Mohhekennuck Club—constructed in the first decade of the twentieth century. A fallen chimney and a few foundation stones are all that remains. A short path leads to a tiny gravel beach popular as a canoe landing. Continue on the southbound AT along the shoreline through mountain laurel, which blossoms pinkish-white in late June.

A thick growth of shining club moss carpets the forest floor at one spot on the right. White Indian pipes—parasitic on oak roots—bloom here in summer. The hardwood forest is also home in summer to many species of colorful wood warblers, vireos, and thrushes. The path moves away from the water before arriving at Higley Brook, which is spanned by a modest wooden bridge. Golden Canada lilies bloom along this permanent water source for the pond in early July. Goose Pond Road is 1.9 miles farther, but this is the end point for your hike. Retrace your steps approximately 0.5 mile to the lodge ruins and then 100 yards beyond to where the AT bears right, up the slope. Pay attention, as this intersection can be easily missed. Get on the AT and follow it back to the beginning of the hike.

DID YOU KNOW?

The Mohhekennuck Club, a gathering of sportsmen, was incorporated in 1909 and operated for 72 years. In 1981, the club conveyed its lands along Upper Goose Pond to the National Park Service to become part of the Appalachian Trail corridor and serve as a wilderness preserve in perpetuity.

MORE INFORMATION

Upper Goose Pond Cabin, while open to all AT visitors, is managed primarily for long-distance hikers (outdoors.org/lodging-camping/camps-cabins/upper-goose). Volunteer caretakers are present mid-May through mid-October. Camping is allowed at two designated campsites near the cabin. Biking is not allowed. The AMC Berkshire Chapter's Appalachian Trail Management Committee is responsible for maintenance, management, and protection of the nearly 90 miles of the AT in Massachusetts. Volunteers do this work, with assistance from the Massachusetts Department of Conservation and Recreation. AMC Berkshire Chapter's Massachusetts AT Committee, P.O. Box 2281, Pittsfield, MA 01202 (amcberkshire.org/at; at@amcberkshire.org).

NEARBY

Camping is available from mid-May to mid-October at nearby October Mountain State Forest in Lee. This primitive camping area has 47 nonelectric tent and RV/trailer sites on three levels, including three yurts. Reservations are required through Reserve America (reserveamerica.com/explore/october-mountain-state-forest/MA/32615/overview); fees apply. October Mountain State Forest, 317 Woodland Road, Lee, MA 01238 (413-243-1778; mass.gov/locations/october-mountain-state-forest).

SECTION 3
SOUTHERN
BERKSHIRES

The southern Berkshires remain the most agricultural part of the Berkshires. Hayfields and dairy barns dot the landscape of the broad Housatonic River valley, and the valley's marble bedrock fosters lime-loving plants. The southern Berkshires combine quaint towns and villages, pastures dotted with cattle, forests in which mountain laurel puts on a dazzling show, and summits and ridgelines that offer endless views. Some consider this area to be the most scenic in the region.

The eighteen excursions in this section include steep climbs, pastoral settings, impressive waterfalls, and even some old-growth giants. For instance, magical Ice Glen (Trip 33) offers a cool respite from summer heat; Guilder Pond and Mount Everett, the region's highest summit (Trip 45), offer a laurel bloom second to none; Alander Mountain (Trip 46) boasts one of the most expansive vistas in the Berkshires; and the quartzite peak of Monument Mountain (Trip 34) is a beloved destination for many. Southern Berkshires waterfalls are justly popular as well. Bash Bish Falls (Trip 43) is the commonwealth's most spectacular, but Upper Race Brook Falls (Trip 44) and Sages Ravine (Trip 49) are evocative in their own right. For an easier ramble, try lovely Lime Kiln Farm (Trip 47) or the botanically renowned Bartholomew's Cobble Reservation (Trip 48). Whatever your preference of scenery or level of difficulty, the southern Berkshires have it all.

33

ICE GLEN AND LAURA'S TOWER

This primordial, rocky cleft, studded with mammoth hemlocks and pines, holds pockets of ice into summer. An intersecting trail leads to a summit, topped by Laura's Tower, with pleasing views.

DIRECTIONS

From I-90 (Massachusetts Turnpike), take Exit 2 in Lee. Turn left at the exit ramp traffic light, and then take the first right onto MA 102. Follow MA 102 for 4.6 miles to the intersection with US 7 at the Red Lion Inn in Stockbridge. Turn left and follow US 7 south approximately 0.4 mile to Ice Glen Road on the left (immediately after crossing the Housatonic River and the railroad overpass). Drive up Ice Glen Road for 0.5 mile to a small pull-off parking area on the left, adjacent to a gravel driveway and a small sign for Ice Glen. Do not block this private driveway! Parking is limited to four vehicles. Alternate parking is available at the end of Park Street (take the second left at the Mobil gas station following the left turn at the Red Lion Inn). *GPS coordinates*: 42° 16.255′ N, 73° 18.674′ W.

TRAIL DESCRIPTION

Walk about 250 yards up the private gravel driveway, lined by white pines; the driveway soon turns to asphalt as the grade increases. Where the asphalt turns right, bear left on Ice Glen Trail, a woodland path leading toward the mouth of Ice Glen, home to one of Massachusetts's most accessible old-growth forests. If you visit in summer, you'll notice a refreshing drop in temperature as you reach the trail. A jumble of large boulders and the twin pillars of a white pine on the left and an eastern hemlock on the right serve as a kind of portal to the glen. The oldest hemlocks here are more than 300 years old. Truck- and cabin-sized

LOCATION
Stockbridge, MA

RATING
Moderate

DISTANCE
1.9 miles round trip

ELEVATION GAIN
580 feet (610 feet if climbing tower)

ESTIMATED TIME
1.5 hours

MAPS
USGS Stockbridge; Laurel Hill Association map: laurelhillassociation.org/sites/default/files/laurel-hill-trail-map.pdf

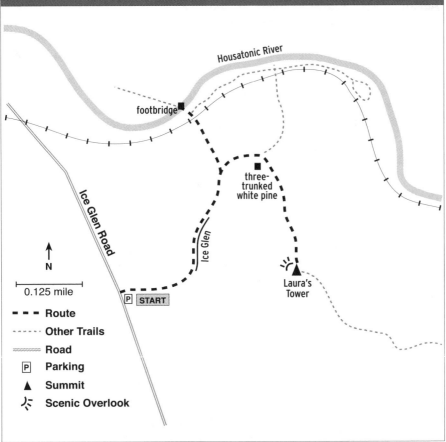

boulders are green with moss and topped by ferns. Mosquitoes are often plentiful in this area, so be prepared.

Native stone steps, artfully placed by nationally renowned trail builder Peter Jensen, lead into the defile; the slopes that create the glen rise abruptly on both sides. Ice Glen inspires a sense of awe. Occasional blue blazes on trunks and rocks are helpful guides, but the best way to stay on the route is to follow the numerous stone steps, which are so expertly arranged that their placement seems totally natural. The cool microclimate in this north-to-south-trending cleft, shaded by towering evergreens and insulated by massive quartzite boulders, is quite amazing. On a sultry summer afternoon, the air temperature in the glen's cold pockets may be 20 to 25 degrees (Fahrenheit) cooler than the surrounding areas. If you gaze down into the crevices between the boulders, don't be surprised to see remnant ice there, even in summer. In fact, it is so cool that atmospheric moisture condenses in the ravine to form an eerie ground fog.

Although the glen is less than 0.25 mile long, don't rush through this haven of tranquility, with its narrow crevices and twists and turns. Watch your footing—the rocks often are wet and a bit slippery in spots. Still, this is not a dangerous place to walk if you have the proper footwear and use caution.

According to geologists, the final act of the glen's creation began some 15,000 years ago during the last ice age. The meltwater from a receding glacier just north of here, as well as the effects of freezing and thawing over a multitude of years, loosened chunks of quartzite from the opposing hillsides. The pieces subsequently tumbled down into the cleft between the hillsides.

Listen to the vocalizations of hermit and wood thrushes (characterized by flutelike phrases), the trill of dark-eyed juncos, the effervescent tune of the tiny winter wren, and a multitude of other songs from warblers and vireos. Birdsong adds to the atmosphere here in late spring and early summer, as do the massive, straight tree trunks that reach for the sky. Four of the state's tallest white pines are in Ice Glen—one is 151 feet high! The oldest are between 170 and 200 years of age.

Some trunks of fallen trees, covered in moss, serve as "nurseries" for tree seedlings that have taken root in their decaying wood. Low spots collect pools of tannin-stained water. Shoulder past one massive boulder on the left that is decorated with rock tripes (lichens), which are leafy and green when wet, but platy and brown when dry.

The trail levels out and emerges into a bowl. Some 30 feet to the left is an inscription on the moss-covered rock face that commemorates David Dudley Field's donation of the property to Stockbridge in 1891. Birches, maples, and ashes (some massive) merge with the evergreens here. Begin a gradual descent and soon arrive at an intersection with unmarked Laura's Tower Trail at a gigantic, triple-stemmed white pine at 0.5 mile. Turn right onto Laura's Tower Trail. Going straight takes you down to the Housatonic River.

Years ago, a violent windstorm snapped off a number of mature pines, as evidenced by dead snags. Young deciduous trees compete for light under the remaining pines. At the signed Y intersection, turn right toward Laura's Tower and begin a gradual 0.4-mile ascent of Laurel Hill. Large maples and ashes (and a few oaks) thrive here. The grade increases as the trail winds past cabin-sized boulders. Big-tooth aspens, with their straight, furrowed trunks, are members of this woodland, which also includes red oaks, birches, red maples, beeches, and far more undergrowth (mostly mountain laurels and sapling striped maples) than is found beneath the shade of pines and hemlocks. Climb the slope on a few moderate switchbacks.

At 0.9 mile, reach a sturdy 30-foot tower, its base 1,465 feet above sea level. The tower, designed by local engineer Joseph Franz, was installed in 1931 and still serves hikers well today. It was named for David Dudley Field's daughter-in-law, Laura. Climb the steel staircase to a viewing platform just about even with a low canopy of oak, red maple, cherry, birch, and ash. A 360-degree panorama was

Pockets of ice often persist into June within the crevices formed by the massive boulders of Ice Glen.

once possible, but tree growth on adjoining property has obscured much of the view to the south. A horizontally mounted brass locator disk is inscribed with the names of promontories, their elevations, and the airline distances to them. The most prominent feature to the northwest is West Stockbridge Mountain (Trip 28), 4.5 miles away. Mount Greylock lies 25.5 miles to the north.

A yellow-blazed trail opposite the path you ascended leads to Beartown State Forest, several miles distant, but retrace your steps to the signed Y intersection. Turn right for a brief excursion to the Housatonic River and cross a footbridge. Descend easily through a stand of monolithic white pines and listen for the high-pitched, cheerful whistle of brown creepers, which nest behind slabs of loose bark. Road noise becomes more evident as you reach a power-line right of way filled with raspberry bushes.

Cross the Housatonic Railroad line (this is an active line—use caution!) to a stone arch and steel suspension bridge built in 1936 by the aforementioned Joseph Franz, 0.8 mile from Laura's Tower. Walk across the wooden decking to enjoy a fine view of the Housatonic River. A brass plaque announces that this bridge replaced the original one given to Stockbridge in 1895 by Mary Hopkins Goodrich, founder of the Laurel Hill Association. A trail sign is on the far side of the river at an accessible trailhead at the Park Street cul-de-sac. Eight to ten vehicles can park there.

A 1.2-mile (round trip, out and back) wheelchair-accessible path—the Mary V. Flynn Trail—was created along the river in 2003 on a former trolley line. If you are inclined to add mileage to your route, follow it between the railroad tracks and the Housatonic. Benches are placed along the route, and a stand of maidenhair fern delights the eye near the looped end.

When you're ready, retrace your steps to return to your vehicle. After crossing the railroad and entering the forest, you can return via the blazed switchback trail on the left or the older, unmarked path straight up the hill (stay straight when you get to the giant, triple-stemmed white pine).

DID YOU KNOW?

The Laurel Hill Association, the oldest existing village beautification society in America, was founded in 1853 by Mary Hopkins Goodrich, the great-grand-daughter of Stockbridge missionary founder John Sergeant. The association, which has acquired almost 500 acres in town over the years, seeks to improve the quality of life and the environment in Stockbridge.

Engineer Joseph Franz had many talents. In addition to designing the Shed at Tanglewood Music Center and the Ted Shawn Theatre at Jacob's Pillow, he figured out how to transmit electricity through buried power lines in downtown Stockbridge, built one of the earliest hydroelectric generating plants in the world (in West Stockbridge), and supervised construction of many other buildings and electrical systems throughout the United States.

MORE INFORMATION

Trails open sunrise to sunset, year-round. Access is free. The trailheads have no restroom facilities. Vehicles, horses, camping, and fires are prohibited. Ice Glen Trail, Laura's Tower Trail, and Mary Flynn Trail are maintained by the Laurel Hill Association, P.O. Box 24, Stockbridge, MA 01262 (413-298-2888; laurelhillassociation.org). Ice Glen is owned by the town of Stockbridge (Stockbridge Town Hall, 413-298-4714).

NEARBY

The Red Lion Inn, an iconic Berkshire landmark, is one of only a few continually operating inns from the eighteenth century. Established in 1773, the inn was rebuilt in 1897. It has 125 rooms and offers formal and informal dining and live entertainment. The inn is at 30 Main Street in Stockbridge (413-298-5545; redlioninn.com).

34

MONUMENT MOUNTAIN RESERVATION

It would be difficult to name another hike as steeped in history as one on Monument Mountain. Some 20,000 hikers annually enjoy a pilgrimage to the fabulously picturesque summit of jagged quartzite boulders capped by pitch pines.

DIRECTIONS

From the east: From I-90 (Massachusetts Turnpike), take Exit 2 in Lee. Turn left at the traffic light at the end of the ramp, and then take the first right on MA 102. Continue 4.6 miles to the intersection with US 7 at the Red Lion Inn in Stockbridge. Turn left and drive south on US 7 for 3.0 miles to the reservation entrance and a large gravel parking area on the right.

From the south: At the junction of US 7 and MA 23 in Great Barrington, take US 7 north for 5.9 miles to the reservation on the left. *GPS coordinates*: 42° 14.598′ N, 73° 20.121′ W.

TRAIL DESCRIPTION

Begin at the map kiosk shaded by Depression-era red pines, where trail maps are sometimes available. Visitors are encouraged to support the nonprofit Trustees of Reservations with a donation. From the kiosk, turn right and head north on blue-blazed Hickey Trail. White pines, black cherry trees, red maples, red oaks, and white ashes tower above sapling American beeches, witch hazel, and striped maples with smooth, greenish trunks. Given that Monument Mountain Reservation was established in 1899, the forest here has had more than 100 years to regenerate. As a result, many white pines and oaks are of impressive proportions. However, many of the shade-intolerant pioneering gray birches are dying out. The well-trodden trail initially

LOCATION
Great Barrington, MA

RATING
Moderate

DISTANCE
2.7-mile loop

ELEVATION GAIN
765 feet

ESTIMATED TIME
2 hours

MAPS
USGS Great Barrington, USGS Stockbridge; The Trustees of Reservations map: thetrustees.org/assets/documents/places-to-visit/trailmaps/Monument-Mountain-Trail-Map.pdf

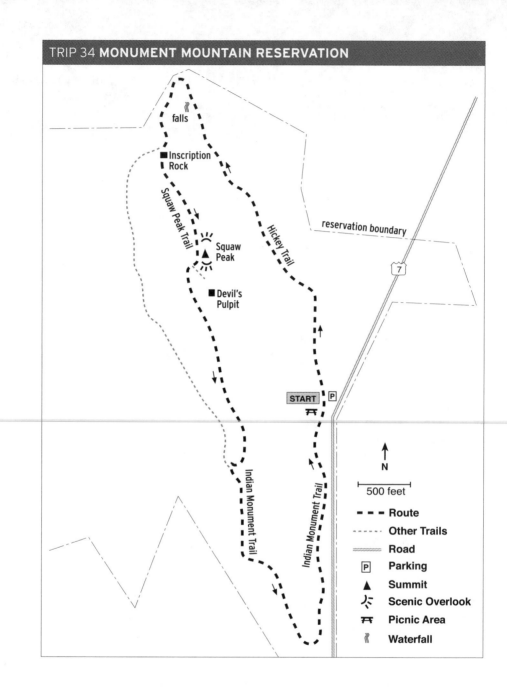

parallels the contour of the slope and passes a twin white oak near a quartzite boulder. White oaks produce sweet acorns relished by wild turkey and deer.

The trail soon bears left to begin a moderately steep climb. Pass a white-blazed path on the right and continue uphill. Note a massive red oak, fully 3 feet in diameter, on your right. Red oak acorns are bitter with tannic acid, unlike white oak acorns. Enter the year-round shade cast by eastern hemlocks at the junction with a wider woods road; bear right here. The grade becomes gentler for the time being. Gray, angular quartzite boulders become more numerous, and a cabin-sized boulder hems in the trail. Crusty lichens and little polypody ferns have colonized the rock's rough, erosion-resistant surface.

A talus slope, created by repeated freezing and thawing over eons, is visible after leaf fall to the left. This jumble of massive quartzite boulders reposes at the foot of the mountain. Talus (meaning "toe" in Greek) slopes like this are rare in the region. The hard, gray rock is actually 600-million-year-old beach sand compacted under tremendous heat and pressure deep underground. A verdant mat of ferns caps some slabs.

Follow Hickey Trail right, then left, under columnar hemlocks and pines, to continue the moderate climb. A mature white pine produces thousands of winged seeds relished by birds and small mammals. At a point where the trail turns left and ascends more steeply, the flowing water of a small, crystal clear brook has carved an attractive hemlock ravine. The trail levels out at the top of the ravine and traverses a log bridge over the brook. A short spur path on the left leads to a close-up view of a modest seasonal waterfall. In winter, mammoth icicles in frozen flow drape the outcropping. On your right, the tall, straight tree reaching skyward is a tulip tree, a southern species near its northern range limit here.

Return to Hickey Trail and climb more steeply now. Hemlocks, red maples, and oaks mix as you push up the ravine. The trail narrows and ascends to the reservation's northern boundary, marked by red blazes on the right. Turn left at the big outcropping; the trail levels out among mountain laurel shrubs. After negotiating another log bridge, head up through boulders decorated with flaky rock tripes; these lichens green up after rains.

Reach the signed intersection with Indian Monument Trail on the right at 0.8 mile, but continue straight on what is now called Squaw Peak Trail. To the right rests Inscription Rock, which commemorates Virginia Butler's donation of the property in October 1899, in memory of her elder sister, Rosalie. From here, Squaw Peak Trail winds up and over quartzite staircases and among boulders to the summit at 1,642 feet. Gnarly pitch pines, white pines, and mountain laurels dominate these craggy heights.

Watch your footing, especially in winter, as you wend your way among the quartzite blocks. A number of excellent viewpoints invite visitors to relax and enjoy the scenery. To the north is the bluish double hump of Mount Greylock, almost 30 miles distant. Much closer, at the foot of Monument Mountain, sprawl the vegetated waters of Agawam Marsh. The Housatonic Valley, lined with erodible marble, spreads out below to the south, and Mount Everett looms in the southwest. These landmarks are not all visible from the same perch, so move about (carefully) to get the full effect. When you reach a well-signed intersection with a blue-blazed spur path on the left leading to a viewpoint for Devil's Pulpit, ascend another rock staircase to gaze down upon this columnar formation, a

Hikers gaze down on Devil's Pulpit, a columnar formation that is a favorite perch of turkey vultures.

favorite haunt of turkey vultures. (*Note*: The summit can be a fine place to witness the spring hawk migration up the valley in late April.)

When you're ready to resume the hike, continue on Squaw Peak Trail as it descends moderately, climbing over rocks on the west flank of the mountain. In early summer, listen for the sweet trill of yellow-and-olive pine warblers that nest among the pine boughs. The male's song is similar to that of the dark-eyed junco, another breeder here. The path levels out as you reach a signed intersection at 1.5 miles. Turn left here on Indian Monument Trail and pass under towering white pines, hemlocks, large oaks, red maples, beeches, and black birches. This old woods road has a gentle grade, and many hikers use this longer route in reverse to reach Inscription Rock and the summit.

The trail turns left to parallel Route 7 and undulates over rocks and beneath hemlocks as it follows along the eastern talus slopes at the foot of the mountain. A triple-trunked chestnut oak stands on the left, recognizable by its rough, platy bark and wavy-edged leaves. Evergreen wood fern and the smaller polypody thrive among the boulders. Some slabs have impressive dimensions and rusty faces where oxidation has revealed the iron content of the rock.

When you arrive back at the picnic area under the red pines where you began, look for pileated woodpecker excavations (foraging holes) on the tree trunks.

DID YOU KNOW?

On August 5, 1850, writers Nathaniel Hawthorne and Herman Melville made a now storied picnic excursion on Monument Mountain. A thunderstorm forced them to take shelter in a boulder cave. It is said that Melville's conversations with his friend Hawthorne that day inspired his seafaring novel *Moby-Dick*.

MORE INFORMATION

Open sunrise to sunset year-round. No fee for Trustees members (parking code required); $5 parking fee at a self-serve kiosk for nonmembers. Picnic tables are available, but no restrooms are on-site. Skiing is allowed. Dogs must be leashed at all times. Motorized vehicles, mountain bikes, rock climbing, and fires are prohibited. Hunting is allowed in season. The Trustees of Reservations, (413-298-3239; thetrustees.org/places-to-visit/berkshires/monument-mountain.html).

NEARBY

Taft Farms, specializing in pesticide-free, sustainable agriculture since 1961, has a produce retail store, greenhouse, and deli. Located at 119 Park Street North in Great Barrington, Taft Farms is open daily, 8 A.M. to 6 P.M. (413-528-1515; taftfarmsgb.com).

WRITTEN IN STONE

The great natural beauty of the Berkshires has for centuries drawn creative minds to these hills and valleys. Look no further than the Tanglewood Music Festival as proof. Whether in music, art, or literature, "the purple hills," as geographer and author Roderick Peattie called them, have inspired many writers and artists. Best known among them is a triumvirate of nineteenth-century authors: Nathaniel Hawthorne, Herman Melville, and Henry David Thoreau.

No doubt the single most chronicled meeting of literary minds ever to occur in the Berkshires took place on August 5, 1850, when Nathaniel Hawthorne and Herman Melville hiked Monument Mountain. There, it is said, they became fast friends. As the story goes, Hawthorne, who had a home in Lenox, gave Melville inspiration for *Moby-Dick*, his most famous work, while they huddled together in a cave during an electrical storm. Perhaps the bedrock ledge, over which a falls drops during the wet months, was their shelter. Each year on August 5, a group of aficionados re-creates the hike of these literary giants.

Melville wrote his masterpiece while residing at Arrowhead (which now houses the Berkshire Historical Society), his home on Holmes Road in Pittsfield. Literary lore has it that the sight of Mount Greylock, or Saddleback Mountain as it was known then, dusted with snow, inspired the idea of the giant white sperm whale.

Influential nature writers have tromped Berkshire paths, Henry David Thoreau foremost among them. Thoreau hiked to Mount Greylock's summit on the still-extant Bellows Pipe Trail (Trip 9) and wrote about it in *A Week on the Concord and Merrimack Rivers*. William Cullen Bryant, who spent ten years in Great Barrington, wrote about Monument Mountain in his poem by the same name in 1824. He penned many other works with natural history themes at his home in nearby Cummington. Closer to the present day, author Hal Borland, a longtime resident of Connecticut's Litchfield Hills, wrote evocatively about the bucolic landscape he so loved. A trail at Bartholomew's Cobble Reservation (Trip 48) is named in memory of Borland, who passed away in 1978.

A quote from Thoreau seems like a fitting motto for the hiker: "An early morning walk is a blessing for the whole day." Perhaps hiking the Berkshires will inspire you as well.

35

ALFORD SPRINGS

This less traveled segment of the Taconic Mountains features wooded ridges with outstanding wildlife habitat. An upland forest management area and several lookouts provide scenic views of the Alford Brook valley and Mount Greylock from multiple angles.

DIRECTIONS

From Exit 2 on the Massachusetts Turnpike, follow MA 102 west 4.6 miles to the intersection with US 7 in Stockbridge. Turn left on US 7 south and travel 3.9 miles to Great Barrington. After passing Monument Mountain, turn right and follow West Stockbridge Road for 0.5 mile. Turn right on MA 183 north, and then take the next left on Division Street and continue for 3.0 miles. Turn right on Seekonk Road and continue 3.1 miles to the intersection with Mountain Road. Turn right on Mountain Road, bear left past a driveway on the right, and continue 0.7 mile to the parking area at the junction with Old Village Road. *GPS coordinates*: 42° 14.877′ N, 73° 26.721′ W.

TRAIL DESCRIPTION

Alford Springs encompasses 900 acres of ridges and cascading streams in the picturesque Taconic highlands along the New York state line. Most of the land was slated to become a housing development in the late twentieth century, but the project never happened after the market slowed. Berkshire Natural Resources Council and Mass-Wildlife (Massachusetts Division of Fisheries and Wildlife) acquired the various parcels between 2002 and 2018.

This outing combines Father Loop, a 4.3-mile circuit leading to the highest point and best view, with a short detour to a vista on Mother Loop, a 2.4-mile circuit in the southeastern portion of the reserve. The well-graded woods roads and trails are ideal for snowshoeing and for

LOCATION
Alford, MA

RATING
Moderate

DISTANCE
5.1 miles round trip

ELEVATION GAIN
940 feet

ESTIMATED TIME
2.5-3 hours

MAPS
USGS State Line MA/NY; Berkshire Natural Resources Council map: bnrc.org/wp-content/ uploads/2016/10/ AlfordSprings_TrailMap.pdf

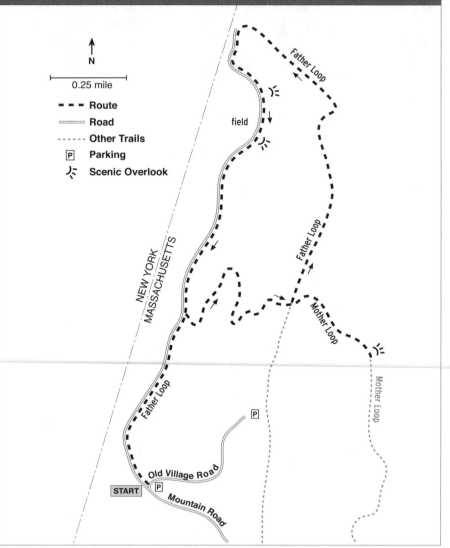

intermediate to experienced cross-country skiers comfortable with moderate grades. Maps are posted at the trailhead and at junctions. Several lookouts were partially screened by trees as of 2019, but Berkshire Natural Resources Council (BNRC) plans to maintain the views.

From the information sign at the Mountain Road trailhead, follow a woods road past the first of many stream and brook crossings (all via culverts). These waterways, draining into Alford Brook on the east side of the ridge and Green River to the south, are the source of the property's name, though there are no true springs. In late spring and summer, you'll likely be greeted by the *pee-a-wee* call of eastern wood pewees, flycatchers that breed near forest openings, such as the trailhead. A large, four-trunked sugar maple rises above the path on the right. Basswood trees, with large, heart-shaped leaves, thrive in moist upland valley forests like the one this hike explores.

At 0.2 mile, reach a former log landing near the New York state line. Clusters of tiny bluet wildflowers, also known as little bluets, azure bluets, or Quaker ladies, bloom amid the rocks in spring. From the right-hand side of the clearing (avoid the dirt road to the left), continue on Father Loop, following another woods road past another brook crossing. Begin an easy to moderate ascent of the west side of the ridge. Midspring to late spring wildflowers include golden rag-wort, an aster that favors wet areas, and wild geranium, a familiar sight in open woods and along trail edges. Common dandelions, though often perceived as lawn weeds, are a food source for bees and other pollinating insects.

The circuit portion of Father Loop begins at a three-way intersection at 0.6 mile. Following it counterclockwise avoids elevation gain on the return, so be sure to turn right and follow blue-blazed Connector Trail over the crest of the wooded ridge. Spoonlike leaves of Canada mayflower color the forest floor in spring. As you begin descending, a gap in the trees affords a glimpse of Alford Brook valley to the east, which is especially visible when the leaves are down. The trail, designed for cross-country skiing, winds down the east slope at an easy to moderate grade, passing glades of ferns and an old sugar maple on the right. A network of stone walls is evidence that these woods were once cleared for pastures by early settlers; the land was abandoned by the early twentieth century.

At the base of the descent, reach a four-way junction (with a posted map and wooden bench) where Father Loop intersects with the north end of Mother Loop at 1.5 miles. The reserve's Old Village Road entrance (see "More Informa-tion" below) is 0.3 mile from the gate on the right. Here, you have the option of adding the full Mother Loop (2.4 miles and about 1.25 hours walking time) to the hike or making a quick out-and-back detour to a vista, as described here.

Follow blue-blazed Mother Loop straight past a "Horses Prohibited" sign and mossy logs, then bear right and ascend easily through hardwood forest inter-spersed with mountain laurels and white pines. American chestnut saplings—holdover sprouts from the blight fungus that essentially eliminated the species in the early twentieth century—are a reminder that these woods are continually stressed by introduced pests and diseases. Eastern chipmunks actively gather food during the warm months before hibernating in winter. Like other small mammals, they are affected by cyclic variations in acorn and nut crops. At 0.4 mile from the junction, reach an outlook with a posted map and a partial view to Tom Ball Mountain's ridge on the eastern side of Alford Valley.

Retrace your steps to the four-way junction and turn right to rejoin Father Loop, heading north and downhill along the base of the ridge. The wide, grassy path serves as edge habitat for a variety of flora and fauna, including blue violet colonies in spring. Common garter snakes bask along the sunlit opening during the warm months. Many colorful dragonflies, including common whitetails and eastern meadowhawks (the last species on the wing in late October and

A ridge-top timber harvest at Alford Springs provides wildlife habitat and views to Mount Greylock and West Stockbridge Mountain.

November), are present from midspring through fall, especially near wet areas. You may surprise deer feeding at the forest edge, especially early or late in the day.

Cross a hemlock-shaded stream and continue downhill along its ravine. The trail opening affords a glimpse of a wooded ridge to the north. More streams and creeks drain the adjacent slopes as the road reaches its lowest point. The reserve's vernal pools provide crucial breeding habitats for Jefferson's salamanders, a species of large gray salamanders found mostly in western Berkshire County and the Connecticut River valley in Massachusetts. They are listed as a species of special concern by MassWildlife because populations are threatened by habitat loss. The quack-like calls of wood frogs, often well camouflaged amid fallen leaves, are a welcome early sign of spring.

Bear left and begin the ascent to the ridgetop, following the road past stone walls, an old sugar maple, and an overgrown trail on the right. Rocky areas with shrubby cover are ideal habitats for bobcats, which are fairly common in the Berkshires but highly secretive. Watch for their tracks, with four rounded toes and no claw marks, in snow and around muddy areas. Smooth-barked beech trees often display scratch marks left by black bears.

Climb along a stream valley and bear left (south) along the property boundary at the New York state line. The grade steepens on the upper slopes, but the road, originally built as part of the proposed development, provides good footing. At 3.8 miles, enter a 25-acre management area, cut in 2016 to promote a healthy forest and create early successional habitat for wildlife. Seven acres are being permanently maintained as open meadow, and the rest is gradually reverting to forest. American woodcocks, indigo buntings, common yellowthroats, ruffed grouse, pearl crescent and monarch butterflies, and white-tailed deer are among the many species benefiting from the regenerating vegetation. Common (also known as Allegheny) blackberry, which grows in disturbed areas, forest edges, and fields, is a food source for many birds and mammals, including black bears.

As you ascend through the sunlit clearing, the hike's best views unfold. Mount Greylock's distinctive profile is about 30 miles away on the northeast horizon. More prominent is Yokun Ridge, the site of several other BNRC properties, which rises above Maple Hill in West Stockbridge. A rounded, wooded peak along the adjacent Taconic ridge is on your left. From the edge of the timber harvest, continue along the paper birch–lined path to the height-of-land, where a lookout on the left offers a partial easterly glimpse across the valley.

From here, it's a fairly quick descent back to the trailhead through upland hardwood forest. Calls of black-and-white warblers, ovenbirds, red-eyed vireos, and other migratory songbirds echo from the treetops in spring and early summer. Sugar maples and birches display colorful foliage in early to mid-October; red oaks, white oaks, and chestnut oaks peak later in the month. Eastern coyotes, which arrived in Massachusetts during the 1970s, often leave droppings along trails to mark their territories. At 0.4 mile from the ridge crest, complete the circuit at the junction with Connector Trail. Retrace your steps downhill at a steeper grade to the clearing, and bear left to return to Mountain Road.

DID YOU KNOW?

In addition to the Alford Springs reserve, BNRC has protected 206 acres on Tom Ball Mountain's northern summit since 2018. The property abuts 200 acres of protected land in West Stockbridge. A trail was being planned as of this writing.

MORE INFORMATION

Open year-round. Access is free. No restrooms are available. Skiing, biking, leashed dogs, and hunting are allowed. The three-season Mother Loop trailhead (not maintained in winter) is at the end of Old Village Road, 1.6 miles from the intersection with Mountain Road at the main entrance. Berkshire Natural Resources Council, 20 Bank Row, Pittsfield, MA 01201 (413-499-0596; bnrc.org/trails-and-maps/top-berkshire-trails/alford-springs).

NEARBY

The Green River was part of a travel corridor used by American Indians and early European settlers. During the American Revolution, Colonial soldiers led by Henry Knox used the route to move artillery from Fort Ticonderoga to Boston, which precipitated the British evacuation of that city. A historical marker on MA 71 at the state line is one of 56 sites on the Henry Knox Cannon Trail, a National Heritage trail established by the states of New York and Massachusetts in 1927.

36

TYRINGHAM COBBLE RESERVATION

This wonderful loop trail takes you through bucolic pastures to a pair of ancient erosion-resistant promontories, known as cobbles, with splendid views of Tyringham Valley.

DIRECTIONS

From I-90 (Massachusetts Turnpike), take Exit 2 in Lee. Turn left at the traffic light at the end of the ramp, and then take the first right onto MA 102. After 0.1 mile, turn left onto Tyringham Road (which becomes Main Road in Tyringham), and follow it through the valley for 4.2 miles to Tyringham. Turn right onto Jerusalem Road and drive 0.2 mile to the gravel parking lot on the right, with space for about fifteen vehicles. *GPS coordinates:* 42° 14.589′ N, 73° 12.332′ W.

TRAIL DESCRIPTION

After reviewing the information posted on the map kiosk, walk through a wooden gate to your right toward a small red cattle barn, and turn left to follow along the edge of an expansive hayfield, where eastern bluebirds raise their young in nest boxes provided for them. After passing through another gate at the foot of the cobble, turn right and walk along a row of venerable sugar maples. Cobble Loop Trail, which begins as a mowed path, is marked with circular blue-paint blazes on wooden posts.

The lower slopes of Cobble Hill, first cleared for pasturage by Colonial farmers in the late eighteenth century, are now clothed in grasses, goldenrods, asters, crab apple trees, and white pine seedlings. Upon reaching a signed fork, turn left to walk uphill on Cobble Loop Trail (continuing straight on Pavilion Trail leads to a metal footbridge over tumbling Hop Brook and a pavilion on Main Road, just north of the village center). One hundred yards

LOCATION
Tyringham, MA

RATING
Easy to Moderate

DISTANCE
2-mile loop

ELEVATION GAIN
380 feet

ESTIMATED TIME
1.5 hours

MAPS
USGS East Lee; The Trustees of Reservations map: thetrustees.org/assets/documents/places-to-visit/trailmaps/Tyringham-Cobble-Trail-Map.pdf

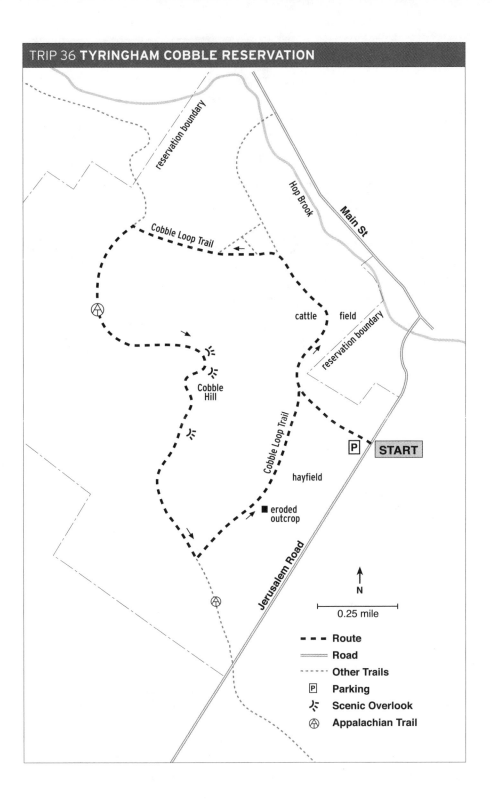

reservation boundary

Hop Brook

Main St

Cobble Loop Trail

cattle field

reservation boundary

Cobble Hill

Cobble Loop Trail

P START

hayfield

■ eroded outcrop

Jerusalem Road

N

0.25 mile

- - - Route
═══ Road
- - - - - Other Trails
P Parking
ʎ Scenic Overlook
Ⓐ Appalachian Trail

A pockmarked block of stone—disconnected from the underlying bedrock—has been weathered into a fantastic form.

beyond, Cobble Loop Trail turns left and ascends steeply, then swings right and enters a white pine stand at a barbed wire fence. Pass through a wooden gate, turn left, and walk uphill, following blue blazes on trees that include white ash, sugar maple, and black birch. Beware of poison ivy in this section.

The trail levels out after a short climb on a wide path among an all-too-thick growth of winged euonymus (an invasive exotic shrub, also known as burning bush) and Japanese barberry. Several species of woodpeckers frequent these woods, including hairy and red-bellied woodpeckers and yellow-bellied sap-suckers. Sapsuckers forsake the north in autumn. Omnivorous red squirrels col-lect and store pine seeds, gather mushrooms, and relish the occasional meal of bird's eggs or nestlings. The trail climbs easily under good-sized white ash trees. Walk through a stone-wall gap and then pass an eroded and closed trail on the left under a canopy of sugar maple, black cherry, birch, and hemlock.

At a junction with the white-blazed Appalachian Trail (AT) at 0.7 mile, bear left, following the combined AT and Cobble Loop Trail among white pines, cherry trees, white ashes, and fern growth. Green-barked striped maple and sap-ling American beech populate the forest understory layer as this easy climb con-tinues, leading through a disturbed woodland characterized by more invasive shrubs and vines: winged euonymus, buckthorn, Japanese barberry, and Orien-tal bittersweet. The trail steepens and enters a shady hemlock stand. Amble past a magnificent oak on the left as the path switchbacks up the slope. Turn left at a gneiss boulder and follow along a stone wall built of flat chunks of the same material. More sizable oaks appear; one on the right—more than 3 feet in girth—still has rusty barbed wire embedded in it.

Reach an intersection (the other end of the closed trail), turn right, and pass through a wooden gate into a small meadow at the crest of the first cobble. From this grassy summit, you can see fine views of the valley nearly 500 feet below. Continue over the top, negotiate another wooden gate, and enter a shallow wooded saddle between the two cobbles. A layered gneiss ledge on the left may catch your eye before you climb amid hemlocks. (The gneiss rock's stubborn resistance to erosion created these cobbles.) Turn left to continue along the second hill's contours. Note the large hop hornbeam with a dead limb that juts into the path on the left. At more than 20 inches in diameter, this is a giant of the species. You've now completed roughly half of the 2-mile loop.

The route crosses ledges that sport a growth of common polypody ferns—a species almost always anchored to rock. The scant soil atop Cobble Hill's true summit (elevation 1,340 feet) restricts the growth of trees, making for a wind-swept woodland of low-stature oak and hemlock and a prickly field form of juniper. Enjoy excellent views of the valley and the Union Church, built in 1844 and listed on the National Register of Historic Places, from atop the partially open ledge on the left.

The combined AT/Cobble Loop Trail begins to descend, reaching a brushy field at a low bedrock outcropping littered with mica crystals. Idyllic views of the valley may convince you to linger for a bit. Follow the trail through the field, where buckthorn thrives. Bear left, heading gently downhill past fuzzy stems of staghorn sumac, juniper, crab apple, raspberry, and goldenrod.

Bear left again, following the margin of the field until you reach a signed intersection where the AT and Cobble Loop Trail part ways. Turn left on blue-blazed Cobble Loop Trail and cross an old orchard that still holds apple and crab apple trees. Reenter the woodland and pass through a swinging wooden gate, then turn right and amble downhill to Rabbit Rock. Over eons, the forces of wind and water have pockmarked this soft sandstone outcropping to form the shape of a rabbit.

Follow the base of Cobble Hill and soon reach an unmarked junction. Turn left to continue on the loop trail, climb briefly, then drop back down, and bear left. The parking area comes into view as you reach a fence line and parallel the upper edge of the hayfield. More Japanese barberry indicates human disturbance as you pass through a wooden gate at a barbed wire fence. Continue down a short distance to close the loop. Turn right and retrace your steps back to your vehicle.

DID YOU KNOW?

Tyringham Cobble Reservation has a very intriguing geologic history. The rock atop the formation is 500 million years old, older than the layers beneath it!

Geologist Daniel Clark made that discovery in 1895, surmising that a chunk of a nearby mountain had broken off and flipped upside down.

MORE INFORMATION

Open year-round, daily, sunrise to sunset. Free admission; an on-site donation from nonmembers is welcome. The reservation is owned and managed by The Trustees of Reservations. Skiing and leashed dogs are allowed; mountain biking is prohibited. Seasonal hunting is permitted. The parking lot is not plowed during winter. The Trustees of Reservations, Berkshires Regional Office, 1 Sergeant Street, Stockbridge, MA 01262 (413-298-3239; thetrustees.org/places-to-visit/berkshires/tyringham-cobble.html).

NEARBY

The best-known structure in Tyringham is Santarella, or the Gingerbread House. It was the home of English sculptor Sir Henry Hudson Kitson (1865–1947), who lived and worked in the United States. He created many representations of American military heroes, including the famous Minuteman statue in Lexington, Massachusetts. The structure, at 75 Main Road, once housed an art gallery. It is not currently open to the public but is available for rent (413-243-0840; santarella.us).

37

BECKET LAND TRUST HISTORIC QUARRY AND FOREST

The Becket Historic Quarry is a place frozen in time. This hike takes you past rusting vehicles, sheds, and other abandoned artifacts of the granite quarry, used from the 1860s to the 1960s. A well-marked trail network winds through northern hardwood forest, among granite boulders, and over a small brook, leading to a panoramic vista.

DIRECTIONS

From the west: From I-90 (Massachusetts Turnpike), take Exit 2 in Lee. Turn left at the traffic light at the end of the ramp, and follow US 20 east for 12.1 miles to the intersection with Bonnie Rigg Hill Road in Becket. Turn right and follow Bonnie Rigg Hill Road uphill for 1.3 miles to the intersection with Quarry and Algerie roads. Turn left onto Quarry Road and drive 0.9 mile to the gravel parking area on the right.

From the east: From Exit 3 off I-90 (Massachusetts Turnpike) in Westfield, follow US 20 west for 12.2 miles through Westfield, Russell, Huntington, and Chester, and into Becket to the intersection with Bonnie Rigg Hill Road on the left. From this point, see directions above. *GPS coordinates*: 42° 15.082′ N, 73° 01.216′ W.

TRAIL DESCRIPTION

A kiosk with trail map and trail register sits at the far end of the circular gravel parking area—visitors are asked to sign in and out. Your education begins at interpretive panel 1 on the parking lot island, where a Sullivan drill rests. The device was used to drill the holes into which explosive charges were placed. The site is where granite blocks were loaded before final processing in the neighboring town of Chester.

LOCATION
Becket, MA

RATING
Easy to Moderate

DISTANCE
3 miles round trip

ELEVATION GAIN
400 feet

ESTIMATED TIME
1.5-2 hours

MAPS
USGS Otis, USGS East Lee; Becket Land Trust map: becketlandtrust.org/ historic-quarry/ forest-trail-map/

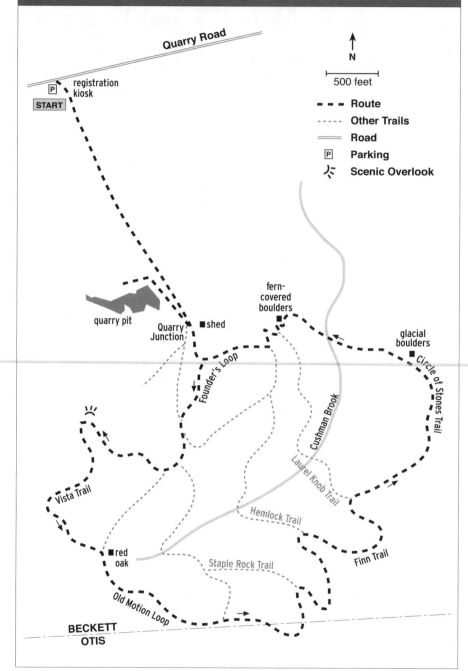

TRIP 37 BECKET LAND TRUST HISTORIC QUARRY AND FOREST

Quarry Road

↑
N

500 feet

- - - Route
----- Other Trails
═══ Road
P Parking
Scenic Overlook

P registration
kiosk
START

quarry pit

Quarry
Junction

shed

fern-
covered
boulders

glacial
boulders

Circle of Stones Trail

Founder's Loop

Cushman Brook

Laurel Knob Trail

Vista Trail

Hemlock Trail

red
oak

Staple Rock Trail

Finn Trail

Old Motion Loop

BECKETT
OTIS

To begin, walk past the cable and up the old roadway beneath a canopy of oaks, maples, American beeches, yellow birches, and eastern hemlocks. In spring, a stunning wildflower display includes trout lily and red trillium. Reach the grout pile, a tall heap of granite chunks, on the right. This is the waste material from decades of quarrying. Do not climb the pile, as it can be unstable and dangerous. In summer, when warm, moist air comes in contact with the cold air flowing from the bottom of the pile, it condenses to form fog. A bit farther, on the left, is a smaller grout pile. Soon, reach Quarry Junction.

Several old roadways and an interpretive trail radiate from here. The skeleton of an electrical generator shed and the rusting hulks of two trucks—one hauled the granite to Chester for processing, and the other had a large tank with compressed air that powered the drills—are visible (interpretive stations 5 and 7). The upper portion of the quarry interpretive trail, well worth the detour, leads to a restored derrick and winch and a scenic view from the top of the quarry. Use caution in rocky areas. You can explore the impressive water-filled quarry pit, a short distance to the right, now or when you return here later. To continue the hike, follow the leftmost road past the shed, and immediately reach an intersection at the stiff-leg derrick site. Opposite the derrick, on the right, is the rail grade to motion—a small quarrying site where granite blocks were cut. Stay left to proceed past rusting artifacts of a bygone era; the quarry operated 100 years, from the 1860s until the 1960s.

At 0.6 mile turn right onto Founder's Loop, blazed with blue diamonds, which heads gently uphill among granite boulders. Rocks seem more abundant than trees here! Reach a junction with the old roadway again at a wall of massive granite blocks; turn left. The rock is the same hue as the beech trunks. On the right is a rusty section of rail. When you reach a Y intersection where Founder's Loop Trail bears left, go straight on red-diamond-blazed Old Motion Loop Trail. Unfortunately, after leaf fall, the din of traffic on the Massachusetts Turnpike is audible here. At a fork in the trail, follow the right path, which leads gently uphill approximately 100 feet to green-diamond-blazed Vista Trail. Turn right onto Vista Trail.

The hillside is clothed in oak and beech. A fungal disease that blackens the bark of beeches disfigures many of them here. One larger specimen among the mostly young trees displays claw marks left by a black bear that climbed this tree for its tasty nuts. After walking 0.5 mile from the Founder's Loop Trail junction, arrive at an outlook and a granite bench—a nice spot to linger. Tree clearing has opened up a fine view of Round Top Hill to the east.

Bear left around the bench and pass the first of several recently logged areas. The cutting is being done in collaboration with the Massachusetts Division of Fisheries and Wildlife (MassWildlife) and the U.S. Department of Agriculture Natural Resources Conservation Service to create shrubland for species that favor brushy edge habitats, including the endangered New England cottontail.

The former Chester-Hudson Quarry, one of the region's most distinctive historical sites, is now part of a 300-acre preserve in the wooded hills of Becket.

A few young red maples show scars where a moose tore off strips of outer bark with its incisors to get at the nutritious inner bark. The fact that the bark was torn off to a height of 7 feet is a telltale sign. A gentle descent leads past a gray granite outcropping on the right. A few red spruce and hemlock appear, but American beech still rules this woodland. Beech sprouts prolifically from cut stumps and by means of runners. Rejoin red-diamond-blazed Old Motion Loop Trail. Across from you, perhaps 50 feet away, leans a massive red oak. The giant—more than 4.5 feet in diameter—is pocked with cavities where branches have rotted out, creating potential den sites for raccoons and other wildlife.

Turn right on Old Motion Loop Trail and soon pass a large, multitrunked white pine on the left that is more than 3.5 feet in diameter. Amble along easily through beech and hemlock woodland. Granite was quarried at what is now a depression on the right where big, angular blocks are piled. Sullivan drill marks are evident on some. The depression, rimmed by winterberry shrubs, fills with water and may well serve as a vernal pool for mating salamanders in spring.

Reach an intersection on the right with Staple Rock Trail, which is blazed with purple and yellow diamonds; follow it to descend gradually. At a hemlock-shaded junction with pink-diamond-blazed Finn Trail, turn right onto that trail. Walk down the wide old road past pockets of hay-scented fern, which yellows and dies after frost. Descend briefly and turn left onto a single-track, following Finn

Trail. Note the hobblebush shrubs. Shining club moss and ferns carpet the ground. Follow the rocky contour of the hill and reach an intersection with Hemlock Trail, blazed with both white and light-green diamonds, at a small boulder field. Turn right to continue on Finn Trail. A slope drops off on the left to a flat terrace. Large, rotting stumps are testimony to logging decades ago. Young beech trees and red maples are now dominant.

After an old roadway joins Finn Trail on the left, reach a three-way intersection with yellow-blazed Laurel Knob Trail on the left and orange-diamond-blazed Circle of Stones Trail on the right. Turn right onto Circle of Stones Trail, and soon cross short wooden bridge sections over a small brook. (*Note*: You may want to cross on stones because the wooden spans are in disrepair.) The shady woodland is home to singing hermit thrushes from spring through fall and to tiny spring peepers year-round. These little tree frogs blend in marvelously with the leaf litter. Bear right to briefly walk along the edge of a logged area filled with beech sprouts, and then reenter woodland.

Descend through more hemlocks and cross a tote road. A cabin-sized glacial boulder protrudes from the forest floor at the edge of a small clearing, and the tall common reed stalks hint at a wetland to the right. Cross flowing Cushman Brook on flagstones. Hemlock and red maple thrive in the boggy soil.

Pass a forest management area that has been logged to remove diseased beech trees and create space and sunlight to induce the growth of red and white oaks. The trail then leads up through granite boulders—most capped by a luxuriant growth of polypody fern, spinulose wood fern, and club moss, giving this spot the feel of a temperate rainforest. The rock crevices provide den habitat for porcupines. Now walk more steeply uphill and reach a wider, unsigned roadway. Circle of Stones Trail bears left and then away from the faint road, widens again, and reaches an intersection with Laurel Knob Trail. Continue to the right and head uphill on Circle of Stones Trail, which soon reaches a more obvious and signed intersection with Founder's Loop Trail. Turn right onto Founder's Loop Trail and follow the blue-diamond markers to the plaque erected to recognize the donors who made acquisition of this land possible. Turn right to retrace your steps to Quarry Junction.

Just past the generator shed, turn left and walk past the guy derrick site (interpretive station 6) toward the base of the quarry, lined 65-foot-high granite walls. Watch your footing and stay back from the edge. Granite steps lead up to a terrace where you'll see granite blocks into which quarry workers cut their initials and the years 1868 and 1894. When you're ready to leave, retrace your steps 0.6 mile back to the parking area.

DID YOU KNOW?

When the Labrie Stone Products Company announced plans in 1999 to obtain the land and restart large-scale quarrying operations, hundreds of local concerned citizens donated the funds that enabled the Becket Land Trust to purchase the 300-acre property.

MORE INFORMATION

The Becket Land Trust Historic Quarry and Forest is owned and maintained by the Becket Land Trust, which invites public participation and support. The site is open year-round, 10:00 A.M. to 7:00 P.M. A $10 parking fee, collected by a parking lot attendant, is charged to nonmembers of the Becket Land Trust between Memorial Day and Labor Day. Visitors enter at the property at their own risk. Pets must be kept under control. Hunting is permitted in season. Collecting or disturbing historical artifacts is prohibited. Motorized vehicles are not allowed. Becket Land Trust also has a quarry exhibit (open in summer by appointment) in the Mullen House Education Center, at the junction of MA 8 and Brooker Hill Road in North Becket. Becket Land Trust, 456 Quarry Road, P.O. Box 44, Becket, MA 01223 (becketlandtrust.org; landtrust@becketlandtrust.org).

NEARBY

The Becket Arts Center is a multidisciplinary community arts facility in historic Seminary Hall, Becket's first consolidated school, built in 1855. The center, at 7 Brooker Hill Road (at the intersection of MA 8 and Main Street) offers events, workshops, and exhibitions (413-623-6635; becketartscenter.org).

38

McLENNAN RESERVATION

Though only a short distance from a paved road, this nearly 600-acre property feels remote. An enchanting walk through tranquil woodland, beside a cascading brook, takes you to a picturesque beaver pond.

DIRECTIONS

From I-90 (Massachusetts Turnpike), take Exit 2 in Lee. Turn left at the traffic light at the end of the ramp, and then take the first right onto MA 102. After 0.1 mile, turn left onto Tyringham Road (which becomes Main Road in Tyringham), and continue south through Tyringham Valley for 4.2 miles to Tyringham. From the intersection with Jerusalem Road on the right, continue 0.9 mile to Fenn Road on the left. Park on the right along Main Road, off the pavement, where there is room for several vehicles. Hikers may also drive down Fenn Road and park at the reservation sign. Fenn Road is not plowed in winter. *GPS coordinates*: 42° 13.331′ N, 73° 10.998′ W.

TRAIL DESCRIPTION

Carefully cross Main Road onto gravel Fenn Road. Follow the bucolic lane across Camp Brook and enter a hardwood forest. The roadway is lined by majestic sugar maples, which may be outfitted with plastic tubing for sugaring season. Eastern hemlocks soon create a dense shade as the path curves right and heads steadily uphill. A slope rises rather steeply to the left. Barbed wire engulfed by expanding tree trunks and stone walls—built of tough quartzite and gneiss rocks—confirms an agricultural past and the former presence of livestock, most likely sheep. The route splits as you attain its high point; bear right to stay on Fenn Road. (*Note*: Be sure to remain on Fenn Road because it is bounded on both sides by posted private property.)

LOCATION
Tyringham and Otis, MA

RATING
Easy to Moderate

DISTANCE
2.5 miles round trip

ELEVATION GAIN
448 feet

ESTIMATED TIME
1.5-2 hours

MAPS
USGS Monterey

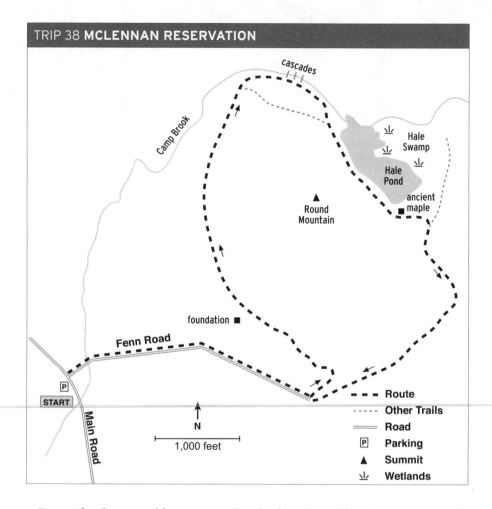

cascades

Camp Brook

Hale Swamp

Hale Pond

ancient maple

▲
Round Mountain

foundation ■

Fenn Road

P

START

Main Road

N

1,000 feet

- - - **Route**
- - - - - **Other Trails**
═══ **Road**
P **Parking**
▲ **Summit**
⊻ **Wetlands**

Except for the venerable sugar maples, the forest is uniformly quite young. In addition to maple, black cherry, white ash, American beech, and bitternut hickory form the canopy. An enormous white ash on the right is noteworthy. As the path begins to bear left and split, reach the signed trailhead on the left at 0.5 mile. Regulations are posted, but there is no map kiosk. Begin the 1.5-mile loop by following a yellow-blazed trail uphill under hardwoods, including oaks, and scattered hemlocks. The trail, bordered by ferns and prince's pine (a club moss), is shaded in summer by black birch, beech, maple, and oak. Be aware that some of the older blazes along the route are white. The trail, bordered by ferns and prince's pine club moss, is shaded in summer by black birch, beech, maple, and oak. Climb moderately at first, and then advance more steeply for a bit, following a low stone wall to its terminus, at which point the trail turns left. Ledge outcroppings of quartzite and a few chunks of milky quartz add variety to the landscape. Above them hang the thick, ropelike vines of wild grape. Sugar maples predominate.

Stride through a gap cut through a fallen oak and soon arrive at a mammoth living specimen on the right, fully 4 feet in diameter. The angular mound of Round

High-gradient Camp Brook cascades over bedrock slabs and into a series of small, dark pools.

Mountain—visible from this part of the level path—is a rock-strewn talus slope. Proceed past the end of a rock wall to the large fieldstone foundation of a former farm building on the left. Some blocks are massive and must have presented quite a challenge to the hardy farmers moving them into place. Lengths of rusty pipe protrude from the earth here and there. Beyond the foundation, young deciduous forest contrasts with the shaded hemlock woods along the mountain slope.

Continue a gradual climb on the yellow-blazed loop trail, still bounded by remnant barbed wire, and enter a darker forest of hemlock and shade-tolerant black birch, skirting the base of Round Mountain. Before long, the pleasant murmur of flowing water is audible from the left. Catch glimpses of high-gradient Camp Brook through the foliage as you climb and bear right. Creeping partridgeberry sports coral-red fruits here in late summer. At approximately 1.2 miles, follow the loop trail left at a Y fork and amble down to the brook, which cascades over bedrock and into small, dark pools. Continue up, along the bank, on a needle-cushioned path past a natural quartzite staircase over which the stream flows to pleasing effect. The brook and trail soon turn sharply left and make their way to Hale Pond, an on-again, off-again beaver pond.

Emerge from the shadows to the bright light of the shrub-filled pond at a beaver dam. A lodge—home to the big rodents—sits just upstream of the dam. The rounded form of Long Mountain rises above the wetland. In autumn, fiery red maples add vibrant color along the pond shore, making for a picturesque setting. The route resumes through forest briefly before exiting left through a stonewall gap and following a narrow path amid young growth along the pond margin. Watch for mammal tracks and droppings, known as scat, on the path. Signs of river otters include droppings with fish scales or crayfish parts, and long slide marks through snow or mud at wetland edges. Soon reenter woodland on a level section, leaving the pond behind. The forest morphs to northern hardwoods as you reach a huge sugar maple at the end of a stone wall on the left, its massive arms seemingly reaching out to embrace you.

Bear left around the behemoth, following the wall and fern-lined path to a signed T intersection. Turn right to follow the yellow-blazed loop trail downhill on a woods road (an extension of Fenn Road) beneath abundant hardwoods. The road becomes rocky where it drops more steeply and bears right. At the bottom of the hill to your right, glimpse the stone and concrete walls of an abandoned springhouse surrounded by a wire fence. Some pipe sections are visible in the road. Pass through a small, goldenrod-filled light gap to a trail split. Bear right to continue on the more prominent loop trail. After passing some hanging grapevines, bear right again. Several immense boulders repose above on the hillside to the right. At the end of the loop, turn right on Fenn Road and retrace your steps 0.5 mile back to your vehicle.

DID YOU KNOW?

According to author Charles W.G. Smith, Camp Brook is named for the maple sugar camp the Mahicans established along the brook each March. They tapped the trees, collecting the sap in birch-bark buckets. After transferring the sap to larger containers, they used hot stones to boil off the excess water.

MORE INFORMATION

Open sunrise to sunset, year-round. Free admission; donations from nonmembers are welcome. The property is owned and managed by The Trustees of Reservations. Leashed dogs and skiing are allowed; mountain biking is not allowed. Seasonal hunting is permitted. The Trustees of Reservations, Berkshires Regional Office, 1 Sergeant Street, Stockbridge, MA 01262 (413-298-3239; thetrustees.org/places-to-visit/berkshires/mclennan-reservation.html).

NEARBY

Ashintully (a Gaelic word meaning "brow of the hill") Gardens, also owned by The Trustees of Reservations, is at the intersection of Main Road and Sodem Road in Tyringham. The 120-acre property features award-winning plantings by composer John McLennan and walking trails through picturesque meadows. Dogs and bikes are not allowed. The site is open 1 to 5 P.M. Wednesdays and Saturdays from the first Wednesday in June to the second Saturday in October. Admission is free for individuals; a fee is charged for group garden tours (413-298-3239; thetrustees.org/places-to-visit/berkshires/ashintully-gardens.html).

POOL PARTY

In many ways, vernal pools are oddities. They're called pools, but they usually dry up by midsummer. They're referred to as "vernal" because the breeding frenzy they host happens in early spring, sometimes while snow still coats the ground. As ephemeral as they are, vernal pools are absolutely essential to a group of creatures able to reproduce nowhere else. These include mole salamanders, wood frogs, and fairy shrimp. None can exist without these fleeting woodland water bodies.

Mole salamanders spend the bulk of their lives beneath the leaf litter. They emerge during the first early spring rains, when temperatures are about 40 degrees Fahrenheit (late March or early April in the Berkshires), and head for depressions flush with snowmelt and vernal moisture. The pools must contain leaves, sticks, and other woodland detritus that forms the basic energy source for the minute creatures that provide food for the salamander larvae.

The mating ritual of spotted and Jefferson salamanders is really something to behold as the animals writhe and twirl in love's embrace. The males drop packets of sperm that females pick up with their cloacae (short body tubes). Then the females lay a fist-sized mass of gelatinous eggs that they attach to twigs beneath the vernal pool's surface. The eggs hatch into gilled salamander larvae, which must reach sufficient size to survive on dry land before the pool disappears under the blazing summer sun.

But why rely on such undependable water sources? Well, because vernal pools by definition don't contain fish. Fish eat salamander (and wood frog) eggs and larvae. Only the toxic red-spotted newt of local beaver ponds is able to coexist with the finned tribe. Many salamander species breed in brooks, bogs, or other locations out of the reach of fish. So it is only the large yellow-polka-dotted spotted salamander and the less common blue-flecked Jefferson salamander that put all their eggs in one basket, so to speak.

If you have the opportunity to get out during what biologists call "big nights," when the bulk of salamander movement to vernal pools occurs, wear your rain slicker, take a flashlight, and prepare to be amazed by the spectacle of dozens of mole salamanders and wood frogs, driven by age-old instincts, crossing highways and country lanes en route to breeding pools they may have visited each spring for ten or fifteen years. "Big nights" generally occur during the first soaking rain when the temperature is above 45 degrees in early spring. It's a sight you won't soon forget.

39

BENEDICT POND AND THE LEDGES

This loop includes circumambulation of one of the Berkshires' most scenic ponds, spiced up with a fine laurel bloom in late June, and a splendid viewpoint from the Ledges.

DIRECTIONS

From the intersection of US 7 and Monument Valley Road (near Monument Mountain High School) in Great Barrington, turn onto Monument Valley Road. Drive for 2.0 miles to Stoney Brook Road on the left. Turn onto Stoney Brook Road and follow it 2.7 miles to Benedict Pond Road on the left. It is 0.5 mile to the day-use area on the right. The first and larger parking area is at the boat ramp, the second at the beach. *GPS coordinates*: 42° 12.226′ N, 73° 17.403′ W.

TRAIL DESCRIPTION

From the Beartown State Forest parking area at the beach at Benedict Pond, head left past a kiosk with trail maps and along a wooden fence and concrete retaining wall at the pond shore to an observation deck spanning the dam's spillway. Interpretive leaflets may be available (the interpretive trail begins at the boat launch parking lot and ends here). Turn left onto blue-blazed Pond Loop Trail. Descend a few wooden steps, and then turn right to follow the trail under a canopy of mixed hardwoods—especially oaks. Witch hazel, scattered mountain laurel, and striped maple dot the rocky woodland beneath the canopy; ground-hugging wintergreen is abundant. At informal trail splits, remain on the blue-blazed trail, which generally follows the pond shore past tenting sites with picnic tables.

Cross a multiuse trail (open to snowmobiles in winter). Although predominately oak, the forest now includes red maple, black birch, and a few hop hornbeams. At the

LOCATION
Great Barrington and Monterey, MA

RATING
Easy to Moderate

DISTANCE
3 mile round trip

ELEVATION GAIN
240 feet

ESTIMATED TIME
1.5-2 hours

MAPS
USGS Great Barrington; Massachusetts Department of Conservation and Recreation map: mass.gov/files/documents/2016/12/qw/beartown.pdf

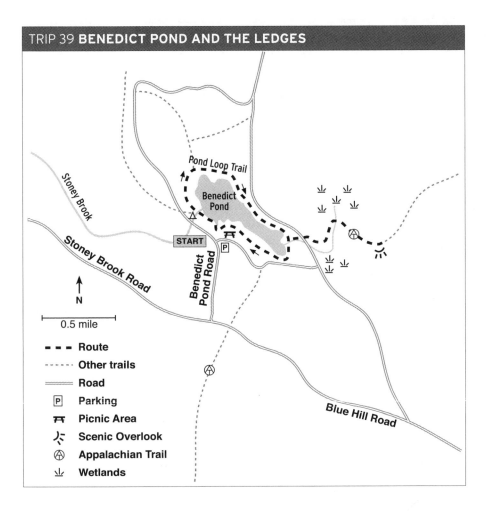

Legend:
- **- - - Route**
- **⋯⋯ Other trails**
- **═══ Road**
- **P Parking**
- **⊼ Picnic Area**
- **Scenic Overlook**
- **Ⓐ Appalachian Trail**
- **Wetlands**

junction with Mount Wilcox Trail, stay straight on Pond Loop Trail and enjoy glimpses of 35-acre Benedict Pond through the trees. Pass through a couple of low, wet areas marked by cinnamon and sensitive ferns—wetland indicators. Sensitive fern has persistent brown, bead-like spore capsules. Pointed stumps, cut by beaver, are also in evidence. Witch hazel and mountain laurel border the path. Ten-foot-high arrowwood shrubs, with arrow-straight branches and blue berries, line the route as you traverse bog bridges and a small wooden span through damp ground vegetated with tall reed canary grass.

As you round the northwest end of the pond, red maples become common. Pass some white pines and a patch of trailing arbutus (the state flower) on the left that blooms delicate pink in May, hence its other moniker: mayflower. A wooden bench at the water's edge invites a pause. In winter, ice anglers seeking pickerel, largemouth bass, yellow perch, and bluegill dot the otherwise featureless white expanse. Tilted gray gneiss bedrock outcroppings pop into view on the left.

Towering straight white pines grew up in woodland crowded by others of their kind. White ashes, black cherry trees, yellow and gray birches, and beeches join the mix, although massive oaks still rule. Camouflaged brown creepers hitch their way up the furrowed pine trunks, looking for insect eggs and larvae hidden in bark crevices.

Cross another small wooden span and continue under pines and oaks. Patches of delicate maidenhair fern soon appear. An 18-foot-high gneiss outcropping juts up 50 feet to the left. After another dampish area with a few small spruces, hobblebushes, and beaked hazelnut shrubs, arrive at a second wooden bench with a fine view. A modest clump of low-growing sheep laurel just left of the bench is easy to overlook, while highbush blueberry hugs the shore. Watch for a beaver lodge. The trail undulates past taller mountain laurels and enters a dense hemlock stand, where common polypody fern is anchored to a picturesque ledge. Water dripping from and through crevices in the rock creates a fantastic icicle display in winter, but watch your footing if visiting then, as this section can be very icy!

Continue to follow Pond Loop Trail on a woods road multiuse trail at 1.0 mile, bearing right as it descends gently. To your left are another tilted gneiss spine and a few white paper birches. Black birches populate the rising slope beyond. After passing a stand of spruces on the right, arrive at the Appalachian Trail (AT) intersection at 1.2 miles. Turn left to follow the white-blazed AT north toward the Ledges, about 0.75 mile, or 15 minutes distant. Walk uphill easily at first, under oak, maple, and birch. As the trail levels out, observe more ledges— some dotted with leafy brown rock tripes, lichens that turn green when wet.

Bear left and ascend rocky steps tight along a rock face for the hike's first real elevation gain. The path wends through oaks and laurels above the left slope of a rocky ravine. At the head of the ravine, turn right to cross a wooden bridge over an outflow stream that originates nearby at a sizable wetland known as Beaver Pond. A short detour straight ahead leads to the swamp edge and the opportunity to see beavers, river otters, muskrats, and other wildlife. Clamber over bedrock, bearing right, and walk along the opposite side of the 40-foot-deep defile near the verge, amid oaks and pines. After leaf fall, distant blue ridgelines become evident. Lowbush blueberry and tiny, shiny-leafed wintergreen thrive in the acidic soil beneath the trees—of shorter stature here on the bony ridge top.

Watch for more trailing arbutus just before reaching a bench-like outcropping at a gap in the woody vegetation. You have arrived at the Ledges, a rocky lookout with splendid views that is an ideal spot for a snack break. Mount Everett, at 2,624 feet high, is the high point along the third ridgeline to the southwest. In winter, the Butternut and Catamount ski areas are also visible.

When you're ready, retrace your steps to the wide roadway, turn left, and walk over a wooden bridge set on handsome mortared stone abutments to cross the brook. Then turn right to follow the combined AT and Pond Loop Trail

Enjoy splendid views of the rounded form of Mount Everett from the bench-like outcrop known as The Ledges.

(blue-and-white-blazed) around the southeast end of the pond. After passing a small spruce stand and a large yellow birch, negotiate the soggy ground safely via a series of bog bridges. Northern white cedar trees, or arbor vitae, between the path and the pond are unusual for this area. These flat-needled evergreens are generally bog denizens. After a minor brook crossing, the trail bears right to hug the pond shore. At an intersection where the AT veers left and up to the woods road, walk straight ahead to continue on Pond Loop Trail. The Benedict Pond shoreline is bordered here by a dense growth of evergreen mountain laurel that blooms luxuriantly in late June.

Although not as showy as laurel, hobblebush has conspicuous ocher buds in winter and white flower doilies in spring. The flower heads include both tiny fertile flowers and larger infertile ones that attract the attention of pollinators. Pass through a hemlock grove and by picnic tables—a sure sign that you are back at the boat ramp. A kiosk is at this end of the loop (trail maps and interpretive leaflets may be available). At the paved road (0.5 mile from the AT junction), turn right toward the beach parking area and your vehicle.

DID YOU KNOW?

Benedict Pond, built by the Civilian Conservation Corps in 1934, is named for Fred Benedict, a local dairy farmer who owned the surrounding land. In 1921, the commonwealth acquired the property from lumber dealer Warren H. Davis, who had cleared much of the timber, and the former estate of Fred Pearson.

MORE INFORMATION

Open sunrise to sunset year-round. A parking fee ($8 MA residents, $15 out of state) is charged Memorial Day weekend through Labor Day weekend. Restrooms and drinking water are available seasonally at the day-use area, and a composting toilet is available year-round at the campground. Biking is not allowed on the Appalachian Trail but is permitted on other trails. Pets must be on a 10-foot-maximum leash at all times, and owners must have proof of current rabies vaccination. Camping is available in the designated area year-round; reservations are required mid-May through mid-October. Off-season camping, mid-October through April, is on a first-come, first-served basis. All-terrain vehicles are permitted on designated trails May through November only. Snowmobiles are permitted with 4 inches minimum of hard-packed snow base. Alcoholic beverages are prohibited. Hunting allowed in season. Benedict Pond, Beartown State Forest, 69 Blue Hill Road, Monterey, MA 01245 (413-528-0904; mass.gov/locations/beartown-state-forest).

NEARBY

Gould Farm Roadside Store and Café, at 275 Main Road (MA 23) in Monterey, serves breakfast and lunch Wednesday to Saturday, 7:30 A.M. to 2 P.M. The farm's Harvest Barn Bakery, at 100 Gould Road, sells maple syrup, cheese, chocolates, ice cream, baked goods, and other products. The bakery is open Saturday and Sunday, 9 A.M. to 3 P.M.; self-service retail available Wednesday to Friday, 10 A.M. to 3 P.M. (413-528-2633, café; 413-239-5350, bakery; gouldfarm.org).

40

CLAM RIVER RESERVE

This remote, deeply wooded river valley possesses a true wilderness character. Stone foundations, wolf trees, and an old mill site offer insights into the landscape's past.

DIRECTIONS

From Massachusetts Turnpike (I-90) Exit 2 in Stockbridge, follow MA 102 west for 0.1 mile. Turn left on Tyringham Road (becomes Main Road in Tyringham, and Tyringham Road in Otis) for 9.6 miles to the junction with MA 23. Continue straight on Town Hill Road for 4.8 miles to the intersection with MA 57 (Sandisfield Road) in Sandisfield. Turn left (east) on MA 57 and continue 1.5 miles to trailhead parking at the Sandisfield Town Hall Annex (66 Sandisfield Road) on the left. *GPS coordinates*: 42° 06.541' N, 73° 06.791' W.

TRAIL DESCRIPTION

Clam River Reserve, in the largely undeveloped upper Farmington River watershed in Sandisfield, is one of the Berkshire region's newest hiking destinations. The 550-acre property comprises land donated by conservationist Bob Thieriot in the late 1990s and additional parcels acquired by Berkshire Natural Resources Council between 2000 and 2012. The trail network, completed in 2017, features two loops linked by the 1.2-mile Clam River Trail. The trails are marked with blue blazes; junctions have posted maps. This trip, starting at the main entrance at the Sandisfield Town Hall Annex on MA 57, combines all three segments. The walking is mostly easy, with some modest elevation gain in the northern section.

Begin at a trail sign on the east side of the parking lot, next to a fenced enclosure erected to keep local black bears away from the town hall's garbage cans. Wild strawberry blooms along the forest edge in middle to late spring. From

LOCATION
Sandisfield, MA

RATING
Easy to Moderate

DISTANCE
5.5 miles round trip

ELEVATION GAIN
860 feet

ESTIMATED TIME
3 hours

MAPS
USGS Tolland Center;
Berkshire Natural
Resources Council map:
bnrc.org/trails-and-maps/
top-berkshire-trails/
clam-river

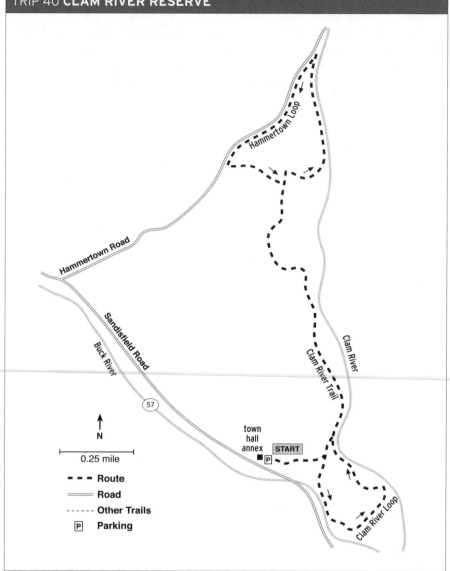

the information sign (where a trail map is posted), follow Clam River Loop Trail over a low knoll, where eastern starflower and Canada mayflower, familiar flora of cool upland forests, bloom in spring. A large, spreading gray birch rises just off the trail on the right.

Although the land is densely wooded now, there are many signs of past use, including stone walls, former cart roads, old pine plantations and apple trees, and multitrunked trees (indicators of logging). Sheep farming was especially popular in the early to middle nineteenth century, before the wool market declined. Rocky soil (evidenced by scattered glacial boulders) and lack of a nearby railroad made agriculture impractical here in the long term. Today nearly 90 percent of Sandisfield, the Berkshires' largest and least densely populated town, is forested.

Descend to a three-way junction at 0.2 mile, where the circuit portion of Clam River Loop Trail begins. Turn right, following an old woods road through a mixed forest of hemlock, white pine, and hardwood. Clusters of winterberry add evergreen color to the forest floor. Continue straight past a side trail to MA 57 on the right and through a seasonally wet area. Buck River, emanating from headwaters near the Monterey town line, soon comes into view on the right, paralleling the highway. Sandisfield's post office is barely visible through the trees.

Bear left at a discontinued trail at the property boundary, remaining on Clam River Loop Trail and heading away from Buck River, which merges with Clam River about a quarter-mile downstream. A few birches grow in the understory of an old pine plantation. Big-tooth aspen, named for its serrated, toothlike leaf edges, is adaptable to a variety of habitats, including stream edges and old fields. Continue along a stone wall to a sharp left turn on the banks of Clam River.

From headwaters at the Otis town line, Clam River flows southeast through Sandisfield to the confluence with the Farmington River East Branch in New Boston. The reserve protects 1.5 miles of frontage along this less known waterway. The name Clam River is derived from the river's population of eastern pearlshell mussels ("clam" is a misnomer), which thrive in pristine coldwater streams favored by trout and salmon, their host fish. Larvae attach themselves to fish gills in late summer and grow in the oxygen-rich environment until the following May or June, when they drop off. Distinguished by their rough black or dark brown shells, eastern pearlshells can live more than 100 years but are vulnerable to habitat disturbance and climate change. The upper Farmington River watershed hosts one of southern New England's largest mussel populations, along with several other snail and crayfish species. The state of Massachusetts annually stocks the Clam and Buck rivers with trout.

Follow the narrow footpath over another knoll and past a stone wall, then skirt a swampy area on the right. Shady hemlocks and pines offer welcome relief from summer heat, but be prepared for black flies, mosquitoes, and other biting insects. Continue along the riverbank upstream to a posted map at the intersection with Clam River Trail.

Turn right to continue north on Clam River Trail toward Hammertown Road (a left returns you to the trailhead for an easy 1.5-mile round trip). The trail initially follows a mostly level woods road, ideal for cross-country skiing, along the river's west banks. Look for tracks and droppings of white-tailed deer, which often use hemlock and pine groves as wintering areas. Moose also benefit from these extensive unbroken woodlands. Reach an impressively large old white pine with a broad base and six shooting trunks. Such specimens—known as "cabbage pines," "pasture pines," or "wolf trees"—colonized abandoned agricultural fields and then were likely infested by white pine weevils, causing the multiple trunks.

Bear left at an arrow marker, following the obvious path past a wet area where a hidden brook gurgles beneath mossy boulders. The well-drained soil sustains

Clam River, part of the Farmington River watershed, meanders through a hidden valley in the remote hills of Sandisfield.

wildflowers including red trillium, violets, and foamflower. Some American Indian tribes used foamflowers, named for their foamy-looking white flower clusters, for pain relief and other medicinal purposes. After another brook crossing, the trail—clearly delineated with blazes and directional markers— briefly rejoins the woods road, passes a viewpoint above the river, and winds past another stone wall. Diminutive winter wrens, difficult to see but easily identified by their long, warbling song, are year-round residents of these woods, especially around stream ravines.

As you progress north, the terrain becomes more rugged, though none of the sections are especially steep. Turn left at another marker to stay on Clam River Trail, and ascend the moderately steep valley slope for about 0.25 mile, heading away from the river. The path levels off in a wet area with a lush growth of violets. Veeries, small migratory thrushes that often nest along wooded riverbanks, have a distinctive (haunting to some) song of descending flutelike notes. Cross another brook, and then climb easily through a pine grove.

After 1.2 miles on Clam River Trail (1.9 miles overall), reach a posted map at the junction with Hammertown Loop. Turn right to begin a 1.6-mile circuit on Hammertown Loop. Descend to Clam River on a switchback, which mitigates the steep grade. Pass through a growth of hobblebush, a shrub often found along stream banks and in rich, moist woods. Bear left to begin what is arguably the hike's most scenic segment, a pleasant 0.5-mile stretch following gently rolling terrain along the hemlock-lined riverbank. Pass a narrow, rocky chasm and the stone remains of an old mill, another artifact of past land use. Clam River and the other Farmington River watershed tributaries powered many mills and tanneries during the nineteenth century, which was a time of economic prosperity in the region. Several mossy brooks cascade down the slopes above the river. Painted trillium, another characteristic species of moist ravines, emerges in May.

Shortly after passing a stone foundation, the footpath ends at Hammertown Road, a few hundred feet downstream from a bridge over Clam River. Make a sharp left to continue the loop, following Hammertown Road (very light traffic, unmaintained in winter) uphill past a pullout and trail map on the left. Along the way you'll pass several brooks you crossed on the lower portion of the loop. Jack-in-the-pulpit, distinguished by its curved, hoodlike flower (the "pulpit") and long leaves, blooms along the road edge in spring, as do yellow violets, red trilliums, and other wildflowers.

After 0.7 mile on Hammertown Road, turn left at a metal gate and kiosk with another posted map, and follow a woods road east past a wet area and the large stone foundation of a former country home. Continue along a stone wall lined with tall old sugar maples to the end of the loop at the junction with Clam River Trail at 3.5 miles overall. Turn right and retrace your steps south along Clam River Trail. The mostly downhill segments make for a fairly quick return to the riverside. When you rejoin Clam River Loop Trail, stay straight on a gentle climb through hemlock-hardwood forest for a few hundred feet to the intersection at the start of the circuit. Turn right to return to the town hall annex's parking area.

DID YOU KNOW?

Berkshire Natural Resources Council, MassWildlife, and the U.S. Department of Agriculture Natural Resources Conservation Service coordinated a 25-acre timber harvest off Hammertown Road (not visible from the hiking trails) in 2013 and 2014. The project provides habitat diversity for wildlife, including endangered New England cottontail rabbits. Some red oaks were left as seed trees.

MORE INFORMATION

Open year-round. Access is free. Skiing, biking, leashed dogs, and hunting are allowed. There are no restrooms. The Hammertown Road trailhead (not maintained in winter) is 1.5 miles east of the road's intersection with MA 57. Berkshire Natural Resources, Council 20 Bank Row, Pittsfield, MA 01201 (413-499-0596; bnrc.org/trails-and-maps/top-berkshire-trails/clam-river).

NEARBY

Sandisfield State Forest protects 4,200 acres of northern hardwood forests and wetlands, including 35-acre York Lake. Created by the Civilian Conservation Corps in the 1930s, the lake offers paddling, fishing, and an easy 2.2-mile loop trail. The York Lake entrance is at the intersection of MA 183 and East Hill Road in New Marlborough (mass.gov/locations/sandisfield-state-forest-york-lake).

41

EAST MOUNTAIN AND ICE GULCH

This out-and-back hike on the Appalachian Trail combines splendid views of the Housatonic Valley and Taconic Range with the cooling breezes emanating from the rocky cleft known as Ice Gulch. The return offers a second opportunity to take in the stunning vistas.

DIRECTIONS

From the intersection of US 7 and Castle Street at the traffic signal in downtown Great Barrington, follow US 7 south 1.25 miles. Turn left on Brookside Road (which becomes Brush Hill Road and then Homes Road—labeled Home Road on some maps—in Sheffield) and continue 2.0 miles to the Appalachian Trail crossing. Parking is available off the pavement on the left. *GPS coordinates*: 42° 09.286′ N, 73° 20.469′ W.

TRAIL DESCRIPTION

Follow the white-blazed Appalachian Trail (AT) eastward on a gentle ascent into woods of sugar maples, hickories, black birches, and massive white pines. Canada mayflower (wild lily of the valley) graces the forest floor. Note the dead wolf pine with large spreading branches on the left that matured in what was once an open field. A residence is visible to the right, but the trail soon veers left, away from it (please stay on the footpath). Chunks of quartzite dot the ground; witch hazel and striped maple compose the understory. The AT meanders through this woodland but soon begins climbing more steeply.

Arrive at gneiss boulders and a ledge outcropping covered with flaky brown rock tripes (lichens). The route leads up a stone staircase, the first of several. The soil and hence the vegetation change dramatically. Soil in pine/oak woodlands like this is drier and more acidic. Chestnut oak and root sprouts of American chestnut, as well as lowbush blueberry,

LOCATION
Sheffield and Great Barrington, MA

RATING
Moderate

DISTANCE
7.2 miles round trip

ELEVATION GAIN
680 feet

ESTIMATED TIME
4-4.5 hours

MAPS
USGS Great Barrington; Appalachian Trail Conservancy Map of AT in MA and CT, MA sections 7-9

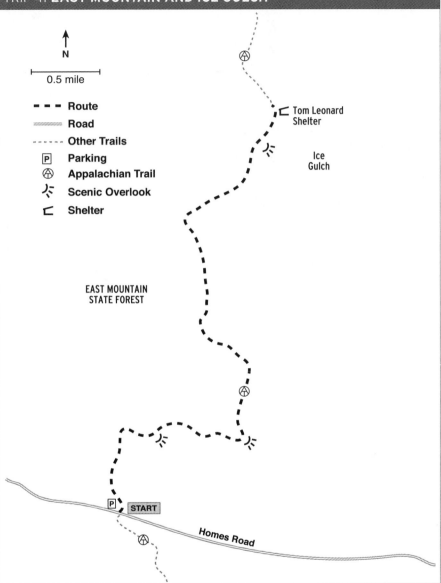

live in this sandy soil. A sharp turn to the right is indicated by a log across the trail ahead (watch for the white blazes). Climb along a ledge outcropping and turn right to amble over it. Listen for the *drink-your-tea* song of the eastern towhee.

At 0.6 mile, stride up a steep, sloping gneiss outcropping (use caution when wet), and glance back for screened views of the Taconics and Mount Everett. But better views await you. Huckleberry shrubs border the rock and soon become ubiquitous. Distinguish this blueberry relative by its resinous, sticky leaves, and pinkish, rather than white, flowers. In late May or early June, you'll detect the

Cool air and a peaceful atmosphere emanate from the boulder-filled ravine known as Ice Gulch.

sweet smell of mountain azaleas and their pink blossoms. Another pink flower to watch for this time of year is lady's slipper, an orchid.

The trail undulates under oaks and reaches a split boulder. Cross a short wooden span over the spring-fed stream flowing through the gap. Leathery bracken ferns now line the path. This forest has shorter-stature oak and red maple, but you'll soon pass taller trees in woodland with witch hazel in the understory. Winterberry, a native ground cover with shiny leaves and bright red fruits, is loaded with fragrant oil of wintergreen. Listen for the slow *beer-beer-bee* refrain of breeding black-throated blue warblers in late spring and early summer. They're partial to mountain laurel for nest sites.

Chestnut oaks dominate again atop the rocky spine of East Mountain. As the trail levels out, look for a low gneiss ledge on your right, and take in the fabulous views from atop it (but be mindful of the sharp dropoff). The expansive scene across the Housatonic Valley to Mount Everett is exhilarating. Continue to follow the undulating AT north, past another split boulder; descend into a gully watered by a spring at 1.3 miles, and climb out. Arrive at another open vista atop an exposed ledge shared by two pitch pines. On a clear day, the views southwest to New York's Catskills are striking.

Pass another exposed boulder-top viewpoint at 1,790 feet (not as stunning as the previous two), briefly scramble over another outcropping, and reach a narrow woods road. Walk right 40 feet, then bear left. Wild sarsaparilla blooms here in late spring. Cross a moss-lined flow under an oak canopy and continue on the undulating path. White oaks briefly mix with other oaks. Stride around a big, slanting boulder to screened views of the Taconics, and listen for the ethereal, flutelike song of the hermit thrush. Drop into a damp spot where the rich, black soil beneath oaks nourishes wild geranium and interrupted fern. Soon, the closed canopy includes yellow birch, a northern hardwood. Oaks still dominate, and some, among a jumble of big boulders, are an impressive size. After a short climb, enter an area where mountain laurel and huckleberry proliferate. The first hemlocks make an appearance in a shallow cleft, while a bit farther, cinnamon fern fills a swale on the left. Negotiate more rocks, stride along a jutting ledge, and then walk through a seepage area. At 3.5 miles, a blue-blazed side path leads down to the Tom Leonard Shelter. Enjoy a pleasant vista just beyond the shelter on the left.

Follow the AT left for another 0.1 mile, across a brook, up and through a tight squeeze in the ledge, and along a sheer cliff face. The trail bears right for an evocative view of Ice Gulch, but be careful of the dropoff! The boulder-filled ravine is shaded by hemlocks. (*Caution*: Climbing into the gulch is unsafe and not recommended.) This is the turnaround point for the hike, so you may want to linger a bit to enjoy the cool air and peaceful atmosphere. When you're ready to start back, retrace your steps along the well-blazed AT to the trailhead and your vehicle, 3.6 miles distant.

DID YOU KNOW?

Tom Leonard was an AT Ridgerunner who passed away suddenly in 1985 at a young age. The lean-to shelter bearing his name was built in 1988 by volunteers of the Appalachian Trail Committee of AMC with materials flown to the site via helicopter by the Air National Guard.

MORE INFORMATION

Open year-round; no fee. Biking is not allowed. The Appalachian National Scenic Trail is managed by the National Park Service and maintained by volunteers of the Appalachian Mountain Club's Berkshire Chapter (amcberkshire.org/at; at@amcberkshire.org). East Mountain State Forest is managed by the Massachusetts Department of Conservation and Recreation (413-442-8928; West Regional Office, P.O. Box 1433, 740 South Street, Pittsfield, MA 01202).

NEARBY

For a picnic meal after your hike, give the Bistro Box a try. It's a little roadside stand with tasty treats, including fresh milkshakes made with local ice cream. After returning to US 7, turn left and drive south a short distance to 937 South Main Street (US 7) in Great Barrington. The stand is open seasonally on Monday, Tuesday, and Sunday, 11 A.M. to 4 P.M.; Thursday, Friday, Saturday, 11 A.M. to 7 P.M.; and closed Wednesdays (413-717-5958; thebistrobox.rocks).

42

JUG END STATE RESERVATION AND WILDLIFE MANAGEMENT AREA

Bucolic meadows with a stunning backdrop of ridges clothed in mixed woodlands beckon hikers to enjoy a landscape that evokes a time before commercial development. This is a great hike to take with young children, and a fine place to bird-watch or cross-country ski.

DIRECTIONS

From the intersection of US 7 and MA 23/MA 41 in Great Barrington, turn onto MA 23/MA 41 and drive south for 4.0 miles. Turn left onto MA 41 South (at Mill Pond), and in 0.1 mile turn right onto Mount Washington Road. Follow it for 1.7 miles to Jug End Road on the left. Stay on Jug End Road for 0.5 mile and turn right into the large gravel parking area. *GPS coordinates*: 42° 08.904′ N, 73° 26.995′ W.

TRAIL DESCRIPTION

Blue-blazed Jug End Loop Trail begins at the far (south) end of the parking area near the concrete footing and ruins of the former massive cattle barn and silo. (The barn was turned into a hotel in 1935.) A brief climb leads to an old woods road; turn right, following blue blazes. Sugar maple, white ash, and black cherry form a canopy. Signs of former habitation include daffodil and yew plantings and lengths of rusty barbed wire. A substantial stone wall dissects the meadow below to your right. An old apple orchard is up the slope to your left.

On the right, columnar big-tooth aspens rise before an easy, rolling descent, and a sizable sugar maple stands on the same side. Reach a field on the left bordered by apple trees. Walk easily along its right perimeter, passing trees heavy with pinkish-white blossoms in early May. The flowering apples attract buzzing pollinators and birds that feed on insects.

LOCATION
Egremont, MA

RATING
Easy

DISTANCE
2.9-mile loop

ELEVATION GAIN
365 feet

ESTIMATED TIME
1.5 hours

MAPS
AMC Massachusetts Trail Map 2; USGS Egremont; Massachusetts Department of Conservation and Recreation map: mass.gov/files/documents/2017/01/sh/mwashington.pdf

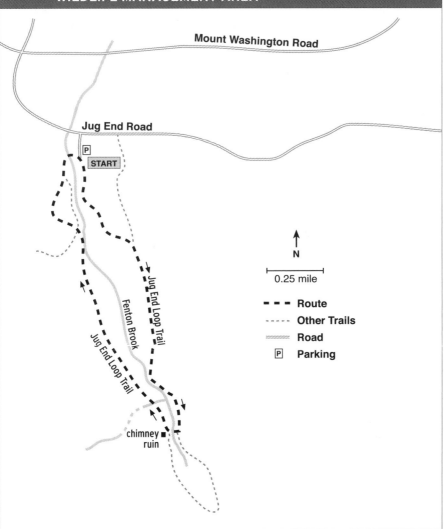

Reenter deciduous woods of maple, cherry, ash, and birch that shade tall witch hazel shrubs. Cross two small streams and soon arrive at a dark wall of planted Norway spruces. The path skirts the spruce plantation. No plant life exists in the total shade of the spruces, in contrast to the shrubs thriving in the forest opening. On your left is a brushy tangle of raspberry canes, cherry tree saplings, Japanese barberry shrubs, and multiflora roses. Chestnut-sided warblers prefer early successional habitats like this. Listen for their *pleased, pleased, pleased to meetcha* refrain in late spring and early summer. Native grapevines and the vines of Oriental bittersweet, an invasive exotic, crowd the trail. Oriental bittersweet invades fields, edges, and woodlands, often forming dense growths that can smother native trees and shrubs. The grapevines cause no harm to the supporting trees.

You are soon surrounded by deciduous woodland of aspens, maples, ashes, and a few white pines. At a more open mowed field, the path hugs the woodland edge, where oaks, maples, and white birches—the latter in a row—flourish. As you pass through a bowl bordered by ridges, the fine view from your right (west) to left includes Mount Whitbeck, Mount Sterling, and, beyond the radio towers, Mount Darby. A number of ski runs once cut the slopes of Sterling (elevation 1,980 feet). Following Jug End Loop Trail, bear left, reenter broadleaf woodland with some pine, and bear right onto an old woods road. More old barbed wire remains here.

When you are back in the forest, notice the copious sugar maple seedlings along a road—sometimes wet—cut deeply into the earth from years of use. Reach a mowed meadow on a hillside. (Some New England farmers joke that their cows have longer legs on one side of their bodies to graze on these hill-sides.) Shad trees (juneberry) show white-petaled blossoms before they produce leaves in late April along the field margins. Pass a marble boulder near a big, spreading sugar maple and continue past the end of a line of trees separating this meadow from another beyond it. The path continues to follow the upper field edge, and the sound of water flowing in the valley soon fills the air.

Head back into the forest and over a series of bog bridges across soggy ground. Here, you may find American woodcocks, which are chunky "shorebirds" with long bills perfectly suited to extract earthworms from moist soil. Below to the right is a shaded hemlock gorge from which the sound of flowing water is now unmistakable. As you walk among the hemlocks in summer, the cooler micro-climate results from their deep shade. Hard, gray schist litters the road. Red trillium blooms in spring around an old cellar hole on the right just before Fen-ton Brook comes into view.

At the fork in the road, marked with a sign for the lower loop, bear right and follow blue blazes and stones to cross Fenton Brook at 1.5 miles. When the trail turns right, many hikers are probably surprised by the ruins of a stone fireplace and chimney in the midst of a hemlock forest. This was once a cabin of a popular resort called Jug End. Follow the old roadway under hemlock, ash, black birch, yellow birch, red maple, and oak to where mountain laurel appears. (If you have time for a longer hike, the upper loop offers an optional 1.2-mile extension.)

Descend easily on the old road to cross a rocky feeder stream on stones. One chunk of milky-white marble has been elegantly polished by the flow. During your gradual downhill ramble, you cross a handful of minor feeder streams. This open forest of maturing hemlocks—some tall and straight—is evocative, but soon sugar maple and white ash once again dominate. Violets—yellow, white, and purple—adorn the woods, and jack-in-the-pulpit holds forth under his canopy of maroon and green. Likewise, nonflowering plants, such as Christ-mas, sensitive, and lacy maidenhair ferns, grace the forest floor.

Jug End Loop Trail skirts a large, sloping meadow, beyond which rises a ridgeline clothed in mixed hardwoods.

A rock wall on the left once kept in sheep. Approach Fenton Brook and bear left, then right at another old roadway. Reach a brushy field, and at a Y intersection, turn right to continue on Jug End Loop Trail. A view of the ridge again appears as the path continues to follow the brook downstream. Cross a short wooden span over a tiny flow to arrive at a T intersection. Little yellow warblers and Baltimore orioles pour out their songs from perches in late spring and early summer.

Instead of following the blue-blazed trail to the right, turn left and make a short detour along the field edge, bearing right to reach an obvious grassy track. In addition to offering fine views, meadows and other open areas provide habitat diversity for a variety of wildlife along the interface between field and forest. Bear right at the grassy track, reach another Y intersection, and turn right again. Rejoin blue-blazed Jug End Loop Trail and follow it left, downstream, along Fenton Brook, past ancient Norway spruces as well as other ornamentals—forsythia, arbor vitae, and rhododendron. Turn right to cross the sturdy wooden bridge and return to your vehicle.

DID YOU KNOW?

The somewhat-odd name Jug End is actually derived from the German word Jugend, meaning "youth." For 40 years, beginning in the 1930s, the property was a booming year-round resort and ski area known as Jug End, which no doubt appealed to young people in the vicinity.

MORE INFORMATION

Open sunrise to sunset year-round. Access is free. Parking is permitted for day use only. Pets must be on a 10-foot-maximum leash, attended at all times; owners must have proof of current rabies vaccination. Carry in, carry out rules apply. Motorized vehicles and alcohol beverages prohibited. Hunting permitted in season. Mount Washington State Forest, 165A East Street, Mount Washington, MA 01258 (413-528-0330; mass.gov/locations/jug-end-state-reservation-wildlife-management-area).

NEARBY

Mill Pond, at the intersection of MA 23 and Mount Washington Road, is a favorite spot of area bird-watchers because it attracts an interesting variety of waterfowl and other birds that prefer wet habitats. Common gallinule, a rare breeder in Massachusetts, related to the American coot, has nested in the area. Pull off the pavement onto the wide gravel shoulder; there is no formal parking area. Viewing is best done from your vehicle with binoculars.

43

BASH BISH FALLS

A tale of two trails: One option is an easy stroll to Massachusetts's most spectacular waterfall with a short, steep climb for a fine view of Bash Bish Gorge, New York's Harlem Valley, and the distant Catskill Mountains. The other is an out-and-back ascent to another overlook on South Taconic Trail. Both pay ample dividends.

DIRECTIONS

From the junction of US 7, MA 23, and MA 41 in Great Barrington, take the combined MA 23 and MA 41 west for 3.9 miles to Egremont, where MA 41 splits off to the left (MA 23 continues straight). Follow MA 41 along the shore of Mill Pond, and then bear right onto Mount Washington Road (called East Street in Mount Washington). Drive for an additional 7.6 miles, following signs for Bash Bish Falls, to the signed intersection with Cross Road and turn right (Church of Christ chapel is on the opposite corner). Cross Road intersects West Street. Bear right on West Street, which becomes fairly steep and winding. At the bottom of the hill, bear left to cross Wright Brook and turn left immediately onto Bash Bish Falls Road. Follow it for 2.4 miles into New York (passing the Bash Bish Falls State Park parking area in Massachusetts along the way), where it becomes NY 344, to the large, paved lower parking area of Taconic State Park on the left. *GPS coordinates*: 42° 07.020′ N, 73° 30.460′ W.

TRAIL DESCRIPTION

At the parking area, two kiosks feature a detailed map and information about the locale's fascinating tourism and iron industry history. Walk down the gravel road bordered by hemlocks and sugar maples. Tall, autumn-blooming

LOCATION
Mount Washington, MA;
Copake Falls, NY

RATING
Easy to Moderate or
Moderate (depending on
route)

DISTANCE
2 or 3.8 miles round trip

ELEVATION GAIN
470 or 900 feet

ESTIMATED TIME
1.5 or 2.5 hours

MAPS
AMC Massachusetts Trail
Map 2: C1; USGS Copake (NY),
USGS Bash Bish Falls;
Massachusetts Department
of Conservation and
Recreation map:
mass.gov/files/documents/
2017/01/sh/mwashington.pdf;
Taconic State Park map:
parks.ny.gov/parks/
attachments/TaconicCopake
FallsAreaTrailMap
-NorthernSection.pdf

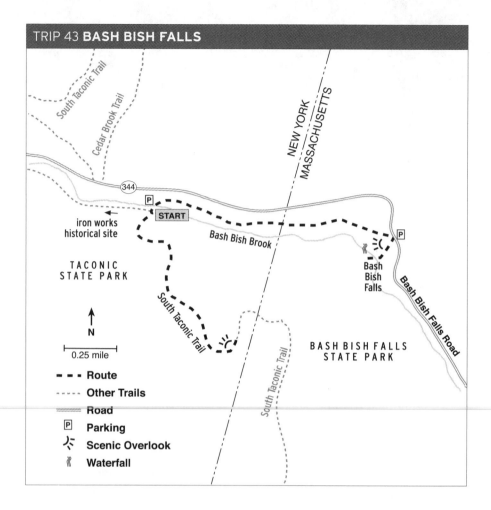

South Taconic Trail

Cedar Brook Trail

344

iron works
historical site

START

Bash Bish Brook

NEW YORK

MASSACHUSETTS

P

Bash
Bish
Falls

Bash Bish Falls Road

TACONIC
STATE PARK

South Taconic Trail

South Taconic Trail

BASH BISH FALLS
STATE PARK

N

0.25 mile

- - - **Route**
- - - - **Other Trails**
===== **Road**
P **Parking**
ﻵ **Scenic Overlook**
《 **Waterfall**

witch hazel shrubs line both sides of the path as it follows Bash Bish Brook closely upstream. The frothy green water flows with a thunderous roar after rains or snowmelt. Shiny, platy schist protrudes from the roadway and lines the stream; the route leads gently down to brook level, so you can take a closer look. Large red oaks, black oaks, and white ashes dot the hillside on your left, while the north-facing slope is shaded by hemlocks.

Just after a bench, a jutting schist boulder on the left offers eastern phoebes small shelflike platforms upon which to build their moss-covered nests. But the brook's roar makes it almost impossible to hear birdsong. As the trail climbs gently to a second bench, hardwoods intermix with hemlocks. The precipitous slope of Bash Bish Mountain, loden-green in hemlock attire, flanks the far side of the gorge. The path becomes a little rougher as it leads high above the surging stream. Note some large red oaks on the left. In winter, black-capped chickadees and tiny golden-crowned kinglets, hanging from the hemlock boughs in search of insects, may be among the few birds you'll find. After about fifteen minutes, reach the Massachusetts border and Bash Bish Falls State Park.

Continue a gentle ascent on the obvious gravel road, skirting denser hemlock growth. Reach an intersection with a short gravel service road that leads left, up to a metal gate and the highway. Stay straight, guided by the roar of the falls, and arrive at a kiosk with a donation pipe at a viewing area bordered by metal railings. Admire the falls from above, and then walk down native stone steps for a closer look at the spectacle at 0.75 mile. Be extremely careful when conditions are icy or wet! Bash Bish Falls, Massachusetts's most impressive waterfall (about 60 feet), plunges in twin streams around a jutting granite outcropping into an icy, green pool. "No Swimming" signs alert visitors to the potential danger.

Angular slabs of schist surround the pool. In wet seasons, a feeder brook slants down the high-gradient slope from the left, adding its flow. Water tumbling over the falls originates from springs 1,300 feet up, in the Mount Washington State Forest. In winter, windblown mist artistically coats tree branches with ice. Climb up the steps and turn left to walk back the way you came. After about 150 feet, turn right onto the 0.3-mile trail to the Bash Bish Falls State Park entrance. (This blue-blazed trail is the shortest route to the falls, but there is a 300-foot elevation gain.) Walk up wooden steps, then rock steps, and turn right onto a former woods road that angles up the steep valley slope.

Follow triangular blue blazes and cross a couple of seasonal flowages under impressive hemlocks, sugar maples, and ashes. Ascend fairly steeply toward the head of the ravine past schist boulders—some blazed with blue paint—to a twin-log bridge across the upper reaches of the feeder brook. The path continues to ascend under towering hemlocks that impart a primeval forest feel. Some are nearly 3 feet in diameter. Cross an intermittent drainage on rocks, and walk a short distance on railroad-tie steps through a small stand of white birch to a kiosk and the paved upper parking lot. The kiosk informs visitors about the presence of the endangered eastern timber rattlesnake.

Head right, along the edge of the lot, and turn right at metal fencing at 1.1 miles to semi-scramble along the fence and up schist bedrock to a viewpoint above the gorge. Atop the crag are white pines, shrub-sized oaks, and a lone pitch pine. Common polypody ferns fill the crevices of the upturned schist, which contains milky quartz veins. From the vantage points along the metal railing (use caution), enjoy splendid vistas west down the gorge to the Harlem Valley and the distant Catskill Mountains. The falls are audible but not visible from here; the green mound of Bash Bish Mountain (1,890 feet) looms to the left, and oak-clothed Cedar Mountain (1,883 feet) forms the opposite wall of the gorge. (*Note:* Bash Bish Gorge Trail, formerly leading to Bash Bish Mountain and connecting with South Taconic Trail, has been permanently closed due to hazardous conditions, making a loop hike no longer possible.)

Retrace your steps about 1.0 mile past the falls to the lower parking area. When you return to the trailhead, there are several options for exploring this

A thunderous roar alerts you to the proximity of Bash Bish Falls's impressive 60-foot split drop into a clear pool.

unique area. Described here is an out-and-back climb to a scenic lookout on a segment of the long-distance South Taconic Trail, which passes through Taconic State Park and adjacent Mount Washington State Forest in Massachusetts. Iron Works Trail, leading to the Copake Iron Works historical site, is a worthwhile diversion (see final paragraph).

On the west side of the parking area, pick up the white-blazed South Taconic Trail on the campground access road. Turn left, heading southbound, away from NY 344. (Cedar Brook Trail, leading 1.0 mile to a waterfall on Cedar Brook, begins on the north side of the highway.) Cross a bridge over hemlock-shaded Bash Bish Brook at the junction with Iron Works Trail on the right. Continue past the overflow parking area to the campground entrance.

Turn right at a brown shower building and follow South Taconic Trail uphill along a cascading tributary stream. After a few hundred feet, bear left, away from the stream, and continue ascending the valley slope, passing a twin-trunked tulip tree. The deciduous trees here are significantly taller than those growing along the ridge top, where the soil is much thinner and less hospitable. The trail levels out in a hemlock-shaded, bowl-like depression carpeted in spots by the long vines of the three-leafed hog peanut, a member of the bean family.

Pass the Taconic State Park boundary and bear left, making a steep ascent over rocks to a Y intersection at 0.9 mile, just west of the Massachusetts state line. Note an outcropping on the right covered with rock tripes, lichens that green up after absorbing moisture, and polypody fern. Blueberry and wintergreen border the path.

At the junction, turn left down a rocky blue-blazed side path leading about 200 feet to a partially open outcropping. Enjoy splendid long-distance views north and west to the alternating farm fields and forested ridges of the Harlem Valley, the village of Copake, and the Catskills well beyond. Look for turkey vultures and ravens soaring past.

The ridge top's upland forest communities include groves of mixed hemlocks, white pines, and hardwoods and predominantly broadleaf woodlands. Thin soil on the bony slopes doesn't allow trees to grow very tall. Identify chestnut oak by its blocky bark and wavy-edged leaves. In fall, pines shed a third of their needles.

Return to the Y junction and resume walking on South Taconic Trail, which continues south along the ridge to Bash Bish Mountain's 1,890-foot wooded summit and Alander Mountain, about 3 miles from the trailhead (an option for a longer day hike). To complete this outing, retrace your steps down to the campground road. Watch your footing on the upper portion of the trail as you maneuver over rocks that may be slippery when wet.

At the bridge over Bash Bish Brook, consider taking a short detour on Iron Works Trail to the nearby Copake Iron Works Historic District, a designated National Heritage Area. The easy, level path parallels the brook downstream, passing interpretive stations at a charcoal exhibit and mill pond before reaching the iron works site in 0.3 mile.

DID YOU KNOW?

Legend has it that Bash Bish Falls takes its name from a beautiful Mahican princess named Bash Bish, who was sent over the falls in a canoe to her death as punishment for suspected adultery. Whether true or not, the story adds romantic appeal to an already evocative scene.

MORE INFORMATION

Taconic State Park (New York) is open sunrise to sunset, year-round, weather and conditions permitting. Access is free. The campground is open from the first Friday in May through the first weekend in December. Dogs must be on a 10-foot-maximum leash at all times. Motor and wheeled vehicles are prohibited. Taconic State Park, P.O. Box 100, Copake Falls, NY 12517 (518-329-3993; parks.ny.gov/parks/83/details.aspx).

Bash Bish Falls State Park (Massachusetts) is open from sunrise to a half hour after sunset, year-round. Access is free. Pets are permitted on a 10-foot-maximum leash; owners must have proof of current rabies vaccination. Swimming, diving, rock climbing, and alcoholic beverages are prohibited. Bash Bish Falls State Park, Falls Road, 143 East Street, Mount Washington, MA 01258 (413-528-0330; mass.gov/locations/bash-bish-falls-state-park).

NEARBY

The Copake Iron Works Historic District visitor center is open daily during daylight hours. A museum in the former engine house, featuring an extensive collection of artifacts and docent-led guided tours, is open 2 to 4 P.M. weekends Memorial Day to mid-November. The self-guided Iron Works Heritage Trail links many historical sites and other trails. A restored narrow-gauge railroad is scheduled to open after 2020 (518-329-3993 [Taconic State Park]; friendsoftsp .org/iron-works-museum).

44

UPPER RACE BROOK FALLS AND MOUNT RACE

A hike of superlatives: a spectacular series of waterfalls, a stupendous laurel bloom mid-June to early July, and superb views from the southern Taconic ridgeline on Mount Race make this one of the most picturesque outings in the Berkshires.

DIRECTIONS

From the junction of US 7, MA 23, and MA 41 in Great Barrington, take the combined MA 23 and MA 41 south-west for 4.1 miles to where MA 41 splits off from MA 23 in Egremont. Turn left and follow MA 41 along the Mill Pond shore for 0.1 mile, and then bear left to stay on MA 41 (Mount Washington Road bears right). Drive for 4.9 more miles (passing Berkshire School on the right at 3.1 miles) and park in a paved pull-off area to the right of the trail-head. *GPS coordinates*: 42° 05.368′ N, 73°24.667′ W.

TRAIL DESCRIPTION

Sign in at the kiosk trail register. A large topographic map of the route and other information is posted here. Paper trail maps may also be available. (*Note*: You may encounter black bears and, occasionally, endangered timber rattlesnakes along this route, so be watchful.) A non-native mulberry tree near the kiosk produces sweet fruit relished by birds and mammals. Turn left and follow blue-blazed Race Brook Falls Trail down an initially eroded path and cross a shallow brook on stepping-stones. The trail bears left and is built up in a wet area under white ashes and sugar maples. Cross a rill and skirt the edge of a field on a narrow path through grasses, bedstraws, red clovers, and daisies in summer. A few red cedars are scattered about.

Enter a shaded hemlock forest. As the path widens, note the presence of white pines, maples, and oaks—red, white,

LOCATION
Sheffield and Mount Washington, MA

RATING
Strenuous

DISTANCE
6.2 miles round trip (7.2 miles including out-and-back spur to Lower Race Brook Falls)

ELEVATION GAIN
1,625 feet

ESTIMATED TIME
4 hours

MAPS
AMC Massachusetts Trail Map 2; USGS Bash Bish Falls; Massachusetts Department of Conservation and Recreation map: mass.gov/files/documents/2017/01/sh/mwashington.pdf

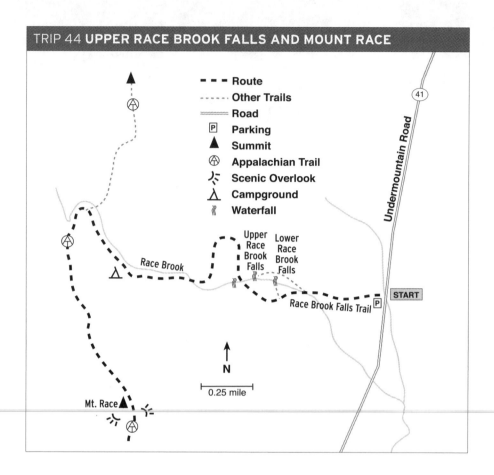

Route
Other Trails
Road
P **Parking**
▲ **Summit**
Ⓐ **Appalachian Trail**
Scenic Overlook
Ⓐ **Campground**
Waterfall

41

Undermountain Road

Upper Lower
Race Race
Brook Brook
Falls Falls

Race Brook

Race Brook Falls Trail P START

N

0.25 mile

Mt. Race ▲

and chestnut. Chestnut oak sports wavy-edged leaves. The trail climbs gradually and then levels out. At a signed intersection with a side path to Lower Race Brook Falls, you have the option now or on the return of adding a mile to the route by bearing right on the 0.5-mile out-and-back trip to Lower Race Brook Falls (see final paragraph).

From the intersection, Race Brook Falls Trail continues left and uphill through hardwood-hemlock woods and mountain laurel shrubs toward the Appalachian Trail (AT), 2.0 miles away. Reach a moss-coated gneiss boulder along cascading Race Brook, guarded by sizable hemlocks. Bear right along the water for a short distance and then descend to the brook, crossing it on stones. On the opposite bank, turn left, then right, to begin the ascent. Hemlock roots crisscross the wide, well-blazed trail as it climbs higher and more steeply above the brook, which rushes along perhaps 60 feet below. American chestnut continues to root-sprout decades after blight effectively removed this magnificent species from southern New England's woodlands. As you move farther from the stream, a leafy forest of red maple, black birch, and oak forms a canopy over laurel thickets.

Reach a signed intersection for Lower Falls Loop Trail on the right, but stay straight on Race Brook Falls Trail up toward the falls campsite. The grade increases again, highlighted by ledge outcroppings. Switchback to climb the slope. The path follows the steep hillside contour but logs and rockwork ensure the path's integrity. In this mixed deciduous-evergreen forest, the songs of scarlet tanager and hermit thrush intermingle. The hemlocks look sickly, perhaps the result of hemlock woolly adelgid infestation. These minute insects, aphids, have already killed thousands of acres of hemlocks in southern New England, and they continue to spread north.

Catch a glimpse of one of Race Brook's numerous cascades through the many rough-barked trunks of chestnut oaks on the right. The slope above you is strewn with boulders. An informal path on the right approaches the base of the falls, but footing is potentially hazardous, so tread carefully. The falls cascade down layered gneiss bedrock into a clear, green pool. Back on Race Brook Falls Trail, pass below a massive hemlock on the left and cross Race Brook—shallow here—on stones. Use caution, as rocks are often slippery when wet. Partway across, take in the view of the high falls from a large, flat rock. This is one of the most impressive falls in the Berkshires.

Pass through a narrow gap between gneiss boulders and continue moderately upward under a leafy canopy. Listen for the loud, effervescent refrain of the tiny winter wren, a familiar species of wooded ravines. Turn left, and ascend rock steps past a 25-foot-high ledge bedecked with leafy rock tripes, lichens that turn green when wet. Additional steep climbing is followed by a few switchbacks and then a walk through abundant laurel. Even without the blossoms, this is a very pretty section.

The route levels out and turns left through more mountain laurel. Enjoy peekaboo views of the Housatonic Valley through the trees. The sound of fast-moving water presages your return to Race Brook, where cooling breezes prevail in summer. Turn right to closely follow the crystal-clear mountain brook upstream, and then turn left to cross the brook on a double-log bridge. Water striders skate across the glassy surface of pools. Emerald-green mosses coat the damp stones. Walk along the opposite bank and pass a pair of windblown trees. Their shallow roots easily separated from the tilted bedrock upon which they grew.

At a sign for Race Brook Falls Campsite, bear left on Race Brook Falls Trail and climb toward a long, low, wall-like outcropping, turning right before reaching it. Bear left and then right past wooden tent platforms to a map board and campsite register. A privy stands nearby. You have covered 1.8 miles, and the AT is but 0.2 mile farther. Walk up under maple, beech, oak, and hemlock, and then bear left and ascend schist stone steps. As the trail levels out and reaches a junction with the AT, you find even more amazing laurel in mid-June to early July. At the junction, turn left (south) onto the white-blazed AT to head toward Mount Race, 1.1 miles distant on a sometimes-steep route. (Mount Everett's summit is 0.8 mile north via the AT.) Carefully cross a wet spot on stones,

Hikers gaze out over the Housatonic River valley from the thrilling Mount Race escarpment.

cushioned by a bit of highly absorbent sphagnum moss, and climb again. A bit of scrambling is required, but nothing major. The wheezy *drink-your-tea* refrain of the robin-sized black, white, and rust-colored eastern towhee indicates you've entered a shrubbier habitat.

The path follows bedrock outcroppings—some showing the polished gouges formed by the abrasive force of thick glacial ice. The white flowers of tiny three-toothed cinquefoil bloom in early summer in sunlit spots. The trees of this ridge-top woodland are short, owing to the thin soil and a brief growing season. Before long, the first pitch pines appear, and then patches of huckleberry. The pines take on a bonsai appearance. Add the luxuriant laurel, lowbush blueberry, and shrubby bear oak, and the scene is somewhat reminiscent of a Japanese garden. The trail remains fairly level amid more laurel (the state flower of nearby southern neighbor Connecticut).

Reach an outcropping some 20 feet high and climb it via natural rock steps. The gneiss melted and recrystallized under tremendous heat and pressure. These rock layers now stand on end. (The Taconic Mountains are among the oldest in North America and resulted from the collision of tectonic plates hundreds of millions of years ago.) Enjoy panoramic views from atop the rounded rock promontory of Mount Race at 2,365 feet. An official USGS benchmark once marked the summit; only a 0.75-inch-diameter hole remains. Looking back in the direction you came, the rounded form of Mount Everett is about 2 miles north along the AT corridor. To the right is the saddleback form of Mount

Greylock, and New York's 4,000-foot-high Catskills form a blue ridgeline far to the west. Face south and look left to view the Twin Lakes lying across the state line. Short-needled pitch pines no more than 6 feet tall make for a pleasing dwarf forest on this bony spine laced with white quartz swirls. For a more expansive vista, continue south and down along the AT, approximately 250 feet past a large rock cairn. From there the views are truly inspiring.

When you're ready to descend, retrace your steps to Race Brook Falls Trail on the right. Watch carefully for the blue blazes, as some turns can be missed, especially at the last major brook crossing.

If so inclined, turn hard left when you reach the signed intersection in a flat area under hemlocks for the 0.5-mile spur to Lower Race Brook Falls. The detour is worth the effort. The spur path leads gradually uphill through mixed woods to a spot amid huge boulders that offers a view of the lower falls. Retrace your steps to Race Brook Falls Trail after enjoying the charming cascade.

DID YOU KNOW?

Some of the head-high pitch pines you brush against as you make your way along the bony Taconic ridgeline are more than 100 years old. Scant soil and harsh weather conditions severely limit their growth rate. Similar pitch pines on nearby Mount Everett have been dated at nearly 200 years of age!

MORE INFORMATION

Open sunrise to sunset, year-round. Access is free. Pets must be on a 10-foot-maximum leash and attended at all times; owners must have proof of current rabies vaccination. Motorized vehicles, mountain bikes, horses, and alcoholic beverages prohibited. Hunting allowed in season, except along the AT corridor and near campsites. Fires are allowed only in designated areas. Mount Washington State Forest, 165A East Street, Mount Washington, MA 01258 (413-528-0330; mass.gov/locations/mount-washington-state-forest).

The AMC Berkshire Chapter's Appalachian Trail Management Committee is responsible for maintenance, management, and protection of the nearly 90 miles of the AT in Massachusetts; volunteers do this work, with assistance from the Massachusetts Department of Conservation and Recreation. Massachusetts AT Committee, Berkshire Chapter AMC, P.O. Box 2281, Pittsfield, MA 01202 (amcberkshire.org/at; at@amcberkshire.org).

NEARBY

The Shays' Rebellion monument in Sheffield commemorates an armed revolt by indebted farmers against the state and wealthy merchants after the American Revolution. A final bloody battle with government militia was fought here in February 1787, during which the rebels were routed. Captain Daniel Shays, a veteran of the Revolution, was one of the rebellion's leaders. The monument stands along the Appalachian Trail at the intersection of Egremont and Rebellion roads in Sheffield.

45

GUILDER POND AND MOUNT EVERETT

Guilder Pond is locally renowned for its profuse mountain laurel bloom, while ancient, pitch pine-topped Mount Everett, the highest point in southern Berkshire County, offers sublime vistas.

DIRECTIONS

From the intersection of US 7, MA 23, and MA 41 in Great Barrington, take the combined MA 23 and MA 41 west for 4.1 miles and turn left at Mill Pond in Egremont to follow MA 41 for 0.1 mile to Mount Washington Road on the right (becomes East Street in Mount Washington). Drive for 7.5 miles and turn left at the sign for Mount Everett State Reservation. Follow the gravel entrance road for 0.1 mile to an iron gate. Park along the right side of the gravel turnout. It is possible to drive all the way to Guilder Pond Picnic Area below Mount Everett's summit when the road is open seasonally and start the hike from there, but this trip begins at the lower entrance road gate. *GPS coordinates*: 42° 6.220′ N, 73° 27.091′ W.

TRAIL DESCRIPTION

From the iron gate and a donation pipe at the bottom of the gravel access road, stroll steadily uphill on the gravel road through a mixed forest of oak, maple, birch, beech, white pine, and hemlock. Mountain laurel is in evidence almost immediately, especially from late June to early July when it flowers. Some bushes are more than 12 feet tall. The road winds under a canopy of shading eastern hemlocks, as does Guilder Brook a bit farther on the left.

After about 0.9 mile, pass one end of Guilder Pond Trail on the left and arrive at its namesake water body. At 2,042 feet above sea level, Guilder Pond is either the second- or third-highest natural water body in the commonwealth. Many sources place it second, but Tilden Swamp in

LOCATION
Mount Washington, MA

RATING
Moderate

DISTANCE
4.2 miles round trip

ELEVATION GAIN
825 feet

ESTIMATED TIME
2.5-3 hours

MAPS
AMC Massachusetts Trail Map 2; USGS Bash Bish Falls; Massachusetts Department of Conservation and Recreation map: mass.gov/files/documents/2017/01/sh/mwashington.pdf

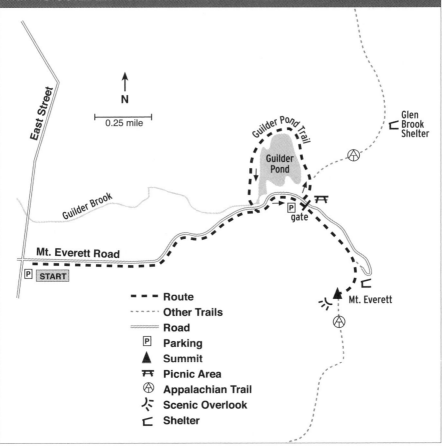

Pittsfield State Forest, flooded by beavers in the mid-1990s, may be a few feet higher (2,150-foot Berry Pond, also in Pittsfield State Forest, is the highest). Patches of sweetgale, leatherleaf, and sphagnum moss have colonized the shore. Black whirligig beetles gyrate on the water's surface in summer. Regardless of elevation, the pond is a beautiful sight, especially when fringed with pink and white laurels in early summer; later you'll walk completely around it. For now, continue on the gravel road another 0.2 mile to Guilder Pond Picnic Area, which has toilet facilities.

At the far-left end of the picnic area is the other access for Guilder Pond Trail, which you'll use upon your return. But first, follow the white-blazed Appalachian Trail (AT) at a large sign (maps may be available at the kiosk on the right) up into beech, maple, yellow birch, and oak woodland on a steady incline. After just 0.1 mile, reach the gravel summit road and turn left. Walk 100 feet and turn right to continue on the AT, which leads up on a rocky path. Striped maple (moosewood) is an abundant small tree here. Wood sorrel (with cloverlike leaves and white, pink-veined summer blossoms), *Clintonia* (blue-bead lily), and Canada mayflower also grow in the rich soil.

The summit road parallels a footpath on the left. The AT bears right, climbs a short distance, turns left, and ascends a stone "stairway" adjacent to rocky outcroppings. Blue-green spinulose wood ferns soften the sharp angles below yellow birch and mountain ash.

At a short, rocky side path, bear left to a bench and shelter in a grassy clearing that offers an expansive vista all the way to Mount Greylock, 37 miles north. When you look at this mountain from a distance, it's easy to imagine how its other name—Saddleback Mountain—came to be.

Return to the AT, which resumes its uphill climb before leveling out briefly. Mountain azaleas put on quite a show in May. In late June and early July, mountain laurel (Connecticut's state flower), festooned with clusters of white and pink flowers, crowds the path. The modest leaves of trailing arbutus (Massachusetts's state flower) beneath the laurel are easy to overlook. The hike is so close to the Connecticut border here, it's fitting that the two state flowers are in such close proximity as well. Adding much to the overall ambience are shrubby red maple, mountain ash, wild raisin, huckleberry, and lowbush blueberry. The latter two offer tasty treats as well.

After the wooden sign indicating 0.1 mile to the summit, tread over schist bedrock that stands on end due to the collision of continental plates hundreds of millions of years ago when these mountains formed. The thin soil atop the bedrock provides nourishment for bear oak (or scrub oak), also found on Cape Cod. Its tough, leathery leaves and tiny acorns limit water loss in this harsh environment. At a blue blaze on the right, step up onto a ledge outcropping and viewpoint to gaze eastward over the Housatonic Valley, the Berkshire Plateau beyond, and the Twin Lakes just over the Connecticut–Massachusetts border. You might even be able to identify the sloping meadow on Hurlburt's Hill (Trip 48).

Continue on the AT, which soon reaches the site of the former summit fire tower at 2,624 feet (signage erroneously indicates the height as 2,602 feet), surrounded by short, stiff-needled pitch pines. Only the concrete footings remain. The tower, erected in 1915, fell into disrepair and was removed by helicopter in 2003. The summit is an unusual and fragile environment; please remain on the trail and bedrock to avoid trampling the vegetation. Studies of the summit vegetation have revealed that some of the gnarled dwarf pitch pines are between 100 and 200 years old—an old-growth forest in miniature! Views of the bluish ridgeline of New York's Catskill Mountains—50 miles to the west-southwest—are yours to enjoy.

After taking in the panoramic vistas, retrace your steps down to Guilder Pond Picnic Area, but turn right to follow the joint AT/Guilder Pond Trail, marked with both white and blue blazes. Ignore the almost-immediate unmarked side path on the left, and continue straight through northern hardwoods blended with hemlocks, oaks, and laurels. At the Y intersection, where bog bridges lead

Guilder Pond, one of the state's highest water bodies, presents a lovely sight at any time of year.

through a seasonally damp area, turn left to follow blue-blazed Guilder Pond Trail. Based on their girth, some hemlocks appear to have attained an advanced age. The needle-cushioned path undulates through and around old mountain laurels that tower over your head. This woodland is filled with the songs of vireos, warblers, and thrushes in summer.

After passing through a fern glade dominated by New York fern (the fronds taper to a point at the bottom as well as the top), ascend a rocky ledge on stone steps that bring you to a viewpoint that looks out across the pond to the rounded "Dome of the Taconics," as Mount Everett is known. A beaver lodge is visible on an island in the pond, but you may be surprised to see stumps cut by industrious beavers quite high up the slope. However, hemlocks and oaks are not among their preferred foods. Continue past a ledge that runs parallel to the trail. The schist of the bedrock along the shore is laced with the white veins of milky quartz.

To your left are a concrete water control structure, wooden decking, and a black plastic culvert that transports water under an old beaver dam to the pond's outlet stream—Guilder Brook. Water from this side of the mountain eventually finds its way into the Hudson River. Cross a single-log span over Guilder Brook and rejoin the gravel entrance road at the end of the 0.8-mile loop. Turn right and walk about 1 mile back to your vehicle.

DID YOU KNOW?

Mount Everett is named for Edward Everett, the fifteenth governor of Massachusetts, who served from 1825 to 1835. The name was suggested by geologist Edward Hitchcock in 1841. Up until that time, the mountain was known as "Bald Mountain" or "the Dome."

MORE INFORMATION

Open sunrise to sunset, year-round. Access is free. Toilet facilities are available at Guilder Pond Picnic Area. Pets permitted but must be on a 10-foot-maximum leash; proof of rabies vaccination required. Motorized off-road vehicles and alcoholic beverages are prohibited. Mount Everett State Reservation, 143 East Street, Mount Washington, MA 01258 (413-528-0330; mass.gov/locations/mount-everett-state-reservation).

The AMC Berkshire Chapter's Appalachian Trail Management Committee is responsible for maintenance, management, and protection of the nearly 90 miles of the AT in Massachusetts (P.O. Box 2281, Pittsfield, MA 01202, amcberkshire.org/at, at@amcberkshire.org).

NEARBY

Pick organically grown blueberries, in season, at Blueberry Hill Farm, 100 East Street, in Mount Washington. The farm's 10 acres contain three varieties of highbush blueberries. Bring your own containers. Visit the farm's Facebook page for dates and hours of operation and other information (413-528-1479; austinfarm.com).

46

ALANDER MOUNTAIN TRAIL

Alander Mountain is one of the most scenic summits in the Berkshires. Throw in a roaring mountain brook and attractive mixed woodland alive with birds, and you have a real winner.

DIRECTIONS

From the intersection of US 7, MA 23, and MA 41 in Great Barrington, turn onto the combined MA 23 and MA 41 and drive southwest for 4.1 miles. Turn left onto MA 41 South at Mill Pond, and in 0.1 mile, turn right onto Mount Washington Road (becomes East Street in Mount Washington). Follow it for 9.1 miles (past the entrance to Mount Everett State Reservation) until you come to the Mount Washington State Forest headquarters on the right. Follow the driveway around to the right and the large gravel parking area. *GPS coordinates*: 42° 5.185′ N, 73° 27.725′ W.

TRAIL DESCRIPTION

Trail maps are available at the trailhead kiosk. Hikers are asked to sign in and out. A donation pipe is to the left of the kiosk. Walk across the mowed field, where lowbush blueberries and tiny, four-petaled bluets attract pollinators in spring. Hunts Pond, with its resident Canada geese, lies serenely in a bowl to the left. Enter woods of eastern hemlock, where Canada lilies bloom in May. The route follows blue-blazed Alander Mountain Trail. Listen for the *weeta-weeta-weeteo* song of the black, yellow, and white magnolia warbler and for the buzzy notes of the black-throated green warbler in spring and early summer. After strolling through mixed woods, amble down through a second field, where fiery wood lilies brighten the brushy meadow in July. Your destination is visible 2.0 miles to the west.

At the far end of the meadow, cross a wooden bridge over Lee Pond Brook and turn right onto an old roadway.

LOCATION
Mount Washington, MA

RATING
Moderate

DISTANCE
5 miles round trip

ELEVATION GAIN
790 feet

ESTIMATED TIME
3-4 hours

MAPS
AMC Massachusetts Trail Map 2; USGS Bash Bish Falls, USGS Copake (NY); Massachusetts Department of Conservation and Recreation map: mass.gov/files/documents/2017/01/sh/mwashington.pdf

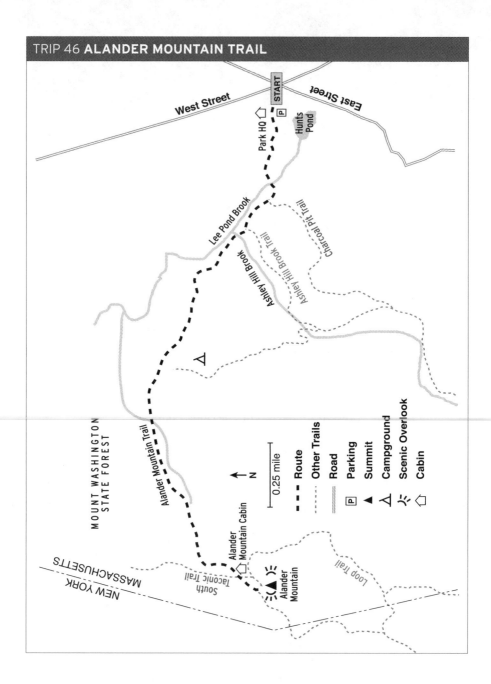

A stone foundation lies adjacent to the brook. At 0.5 mile, stay straight at the intersection with Charcoal Pit Trail on the left. This forest was clear-cut between the late 1700s and mid-1800s to make charcoal—fuel for the many iron furnaces in the area. Note the significant yellow birch on the left, perhaps one of the first to grow back after the last clear-cut. The bark of young trees is much brassier. At a signpost, reach the junction with Ashley Hill Brook Trail on the left; that trail leads south to Connecticut, but you will remain on blue-blazed Alander Mountain Trail.

A short descent through hemlocks brings you to cascading Ashley Hill Brook (first audible from some distance away), just above its confluence with another high-gradient stream. Cross a well-built wooden bridge over the roaring flow. The water has polished the schist bedrock to a silvery patina.

Arrive at the stone remnants of a millrace, which once conveyed water to a mill's water wheel. Across the stream, water cascades down small falls to join the main flow. Alander Mountain Trail now ascends along an old woods road under the dense shade of deep-green hemlocks as the slope drops off sharply to the right. Shade-tolerant American beech, recognizable by its smooth gray bark, joins the conifers, along with yellow birch and red oak. Striped maple, black birch, and black cherry all also grow here. Striped maple has green bark, and, black cherry has scaly bark, while that of young black birch can be identified by its dark, shiny bark.

A sign on the right indicates that the primitive campground is 0.5 mile away. Alander Mountain Trail continues on level ground through mixed woodland, where little spring beauty blooms in early May with five delicate white petals veined with pink, but then steepens as you bear left. Former heavy use and flowing water have eroded the rocky road. The rocks are schist, the tough material that makes up the Taconic Mountains. At 1.3 miles, a side path leaves to the left, uphill toward the primitive campground. Continue straight on the main trail and soon find yourself among mountain laurel shrubs. Laurel boughs support the nests of black-throated blue warblers in spring and summer. Listen for their *beer-beer-bee* songs during the breeding season. After crossing a generally dry, stony streambed, the trail follows a short stretch of brook through a shallow hemlock gorge.

Cross a small stream on rocks. Pass more laurel and enter a maple and oak forest. The small stream is now on your left. Reach a landing that may be a former charcoal-making site. One clue is that the earth is black from years of use. This is a good spot to pause for a moment; the trail turns right and climbs sharply from here. Head uphill and bear left under hemlocks in an especially attractive woodland. A tiny, handmade metal sign affixed to a hemlock warns that the stream is the last source of water during the dry season. (Should you use it, be sure to purify it first!)

Walk up through lush laurel and along a ledge outcropping that parallels the trail on the right. Ahead sits a cabin where hikers may spend the night. Wood smoke aroma permeates the structure, and a rock tied to a rope serves as a clever counterweight that closes the door behind you. The cabin was originally built in the early 1920s for observers at the fire tower that stood on Alander's summit around 1928 to 1930. The tower was dismantled and moved to Washburn Mountain in Copake Falls before being relocated again to Beebe Hill. A few feet

A group of hikers enjoy a snack and expansive three-state views from Alander's open summit.

beyond the cabin, Alander Mountain Trail joins South Taconic Trail. Turn right to follow both trails up over steplike schist outcroppings. Reach an intersection with a small rock cairn and sign. Turn left through brushy scrub oak (bear oak) and bear right toward the splendid open rock summit of 2,239-foot Alander Mountain at 2.5 miles. The footings of the former fire tower are still obvious on the banded schist.

Lowbush blueberry and glossy-leafed bearberry both produce delicate, whitish, bell-like blossoms in May. Listen for the hoarse *chewink* call and the sweet whistled *drink-your-tea* song of the eastern towhee, a large black, white, and rust-colored member of the sparrow family. Gaze skyward for migrant hawks in spring and fall, and see vultures all in every season except winter.

This summit is the most open and, arguably, the most spectacular in the region, and it offers wonderful views of the Catskill Mountains, some 45 miles to the west (right). Nearby, behind you, is the rounded form of Mount Everett (Trip 45). To your left is an undulating wooded ridge with three bumps. Mount Ashley is on the left, Mount Frissell is in the middle, and Mount Brace (at the New York–Connecticut state line) is on the right. Note the rock cairn on Brace Mountain's open summit. Ahead, below you, lies the Hudson River valley. New York's Route 22 is the ribbon of blacktop that runs south and north along the western side of the Taconics, one of this country's oldest mountain ranges, at approximately 400 million years. When you're ready to descend, retrace your steps and follow the blue blazes, but be sure to turn right at the small cairn in the trail.

DID YOU KNOW?

This area of the southern Taconics was disputed by early Dutch and English colonists. Violence ensued following the murder of an English settler over a land claim in 1755. Forty proprietors subsequently established a plantation on the range in an attempt to legally control the land. The town of Mount Washington was established in 1779.

MORE INFORMATION

Open sunrise to sunset, year-round. Access is free. Pets must be on a 10-foot-maximum leash and attended at all times; owners must have proof of current rabies vaccination. Motorized vehicles and alcoholic beverages prohibited. A portable toilet is available at the parking lot. Mount Washington State Forest, 165A East Street, Mount Washington, MA 01258 (413-528-0330; mass.gov/locations/mount-washington-state-forest).

NEARBY

Mount Washington's diminutive town center, at the intersection of East Street and Cross Road, includes the historical First Church of Christ (116 East Street) and the town hall/library (118 East Street). The church hosts a popular annual fair on the first Saturday in August.

FEEDING THE FIRES OF INDUSTRY

In the mid-nineteenth century, Massachusetts was only 25 percent shaded by a forest canopy. Fully 75 percent of the state was devoid of tree cover. Beginning in earnest during the previous century, the ancient forests that had greeted the first white settlers were systematically cut. Early colonists used timber for house construction and firewood, and they cleared the land for agricultural use, to be sure, but not until the Industrial Revolution did the wholesale clear-cutting of Massachusetts woodlands move into high gear.

Early in the life of the young nation, the Berkshires were the center of a booming iron industry. In his book *Exploring the Berkshire Hills: A Guide to Geology and Early Industry in the Upper Housatonic Watershed,* historian and geologist Ed Kirby chronicles this little-known period when America's industrial epicenter was right in Massachusetts. Iron was discovered in 1731, and eventually there would be 43 blast furnaces processing locally mined ore. The iron was used to manufacture cannons and cannon balls for the American Revolution and, later on, wheels for railroad trains. Not until large quantities of a higher-quality grade ore were discovered in the upper Midwest did the prominence of the Berkshire industry diminish.

The fires of the mammoth Richmond Furnace, which had once operated 24 hours a day, went out for good in 1923. The fuel that fired the blast furnaces was not coal, but locally produced charcoal (made from wood), which was more abundant and therefore cheaper. Thousands upon thousands of forested acres were cleared to make charcoal to feed the insatiable furnaces.

Charcoal making was a laborious proposition. Workers called colliers cut up to 30 cords of wood that required seasoning for a year to dry it. Later, the colliers constructed a mound from the cords of wood in the shape of a wigwam, which was covered with ferns and sod to slow the combustion process, while vents at the base of the mound controlled airflow. The smoldering mound was tended for four weeks as the wood slowly transformed into charcoal.

Of course, at first, the furnaces burned charcoal from the abundant woodlands close at hand, but as those supplies were exhausted, sources farther away from the furnaces were required. Eventually, with local forests decimated, people had to import charcoal from elsewhere, making it more expensive than coal. But by then the landscape had virtually been laid bare. Today's woodlands are only now recovering from the far-reaching effects of the iron industry.

47

LIME KILN FARM WILDLIFE SANCTUARY

This biologically diverse property in the Housatonic Valley boasts rolling hayfields with magnificent vistas and hardwood forest alive with songbirds, almost in the shadow of Mount Everett and the Taconic Range. This is a fine walk for families with small children.

DIRECTIONS

From the north: From the center of Sheffield, at the U.S. Post Office, travel south on US 7 for 1.1 miles. Turn right on Silver Street (blue-and-white sanctuary sign) and follow it for 1.1 miles to the sanctuary entrance and crushed-stone parking lot (room for twelve vehicles) on the right.

From the south: From US 7 at the Connecticut border, drive north on US 7 for 3.6 miles to Silver Street on the left (blue-and-white sanctuary sign), and follow the directions above. *GPS coordinates*: 42° 04.963′ N, 73° 21.766′ W.

TRAIL DESCRIPTION

From the parking lot, there is a wonderful view of Mount Everett (elevation 2,624 feet), 3 miles away. The sanctuary information sign includes a map with trail information (paper copies are available as well) and a donation box. Blue blazes indicate the outbound travel route, with yellow ones indicating the return route.

Amble under a canopy of apple trees down a former dairy farm lane—with a hayfield to the right and marsh to the left—where sweet flag thrives. This relative of jack-in-the-pulpit has greenish-yellow flower spikes the size and shape of your pinkie and cattail-like leaves. Pink-flowering hairy willow herb fills the wetland in summer. Arrive at a former farm pond on the left, just before a trail junction.

Here, the circuit portion of Lime Kiln Loop begins. Continue straight up on the path into another hayfield,

LOCATION
Sheffield, MA

RATING
Easy

DISTANCE
1.8 miles round trip

ELEVATION GAIN
135 feet

ESTIMATED TIME
1.5 hours

MAPS
USGS Ashley Falls;
Mass Audubon map:
massaudubon.org/content/
download/6946/127691/file/
limekiln_trails.pdf

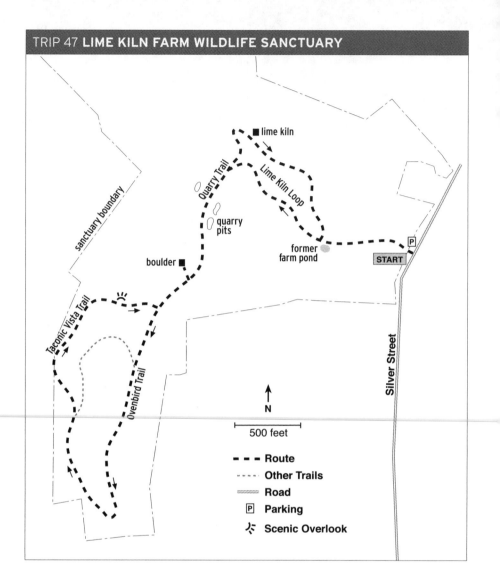

lime kiln

Quarry Trail

Lime Kiln Loop

sanctuary boundary

quarry pits

boulder ■

former farm pond

START

P

Taconic Vista Trail

Ovenbird Trail

Silver Street

N

500 feet

- - - Route
---- Other Trails
═══ Road
P Parking
⚞ Scenic Overlook

following blue blazes and passing weathering marble outcroppings on the right. Marked by a signpost, the path soon bears right and briefly enters regenerating woody vegetation that includes columnar eastern red cedars (junipers) and invasive exotic autumn olive trees that sport silvery-red fruits. Emerge into the field again, turn right, and then bear left at another signpost. Follow the broad path over soggy ground, and pass a small quarry area on the left, largely hidden by woody growth.

The trail leads gently uphill and passes several corky-barked hackberry trees, unusual in these parts. Two species of butterfly caterpillar—hackberry emperor and tawny emperor—feed exclusively on hackberry leaves. Bear left and look for

The rounded mass of Mount Everett, the highest point in the southern Berkshires, presents a picturesque image from the sanctuary's parking lot.

the concrete footings of a former trestle on the right, over which marble rock was conveyed to the top of the lime kiln (not visible from here). A few feet farther, a wooden bench provides a fine spot for a snack as you survey a large, sloping hayfield and its Taconic Mountains backdrop. Sanctuary hayfields are cut annually by a neighboring dairy farmer, but not until late summer, giving grassland-nesting birds time to breed.

At this point, Lime Kiln Loop turns right and follows the field edge down past the lime kiln and back to the parking lot; turn left instead to follow Quarry Trail, a wide former roadway. Pass a monument to the three women who formerly lived on the property and are responsible for its donation as conservation land in 1990. Reenter the woodland edge and soon bear left. Reach several former marble quarry pits. The largest is often filled with water and may serve as a vernal pool. Red-and-yellow blossoms of columbine grace the path's borders in June.

Continue along the wide, grassy path, where Oriental bittersweet vines drape the trees. This invasive exotic is a real curse as it strangles native trees and robs them of sunlight. In fall, the yellow fruit husks split open, revealing bright-red-orange fruits that are consumed and spread by birds, such as cedar waxwings and robins. Before long, enter deciduous woodland and arrive at signed Boulder Spur on the right. Walk a short distance down this side path for a close look at an imposing angular glacial erratic. A bench faces the Taconics.

Back at Quarry Trail, turn right to continue. At 0.5 mile reach a junction with Taconic Vista Trail on the right, where a 0.8-mile loop begins. Continue straight on Ovenbird Trail—an old farm road passing through mixed woodland that includes hemlock and white pine. Keep straight at an intersection where Ovenbird Trail splits to form a loop. Interestingly, yellow-rumped warblers nest among the pines on the left, although they are much more apt to choose high-elevation nest sites in the Berkshires.

Ovenbird Trail eventually turns right and makes its way along the property line. This path through woodland of oak, black birch, big-tooth aspen, hemlock, and witch hazel parallels a linear ledge outcropping rising on the right. At a signed junction, bear left on Taconic Vista Trail, leaving the Ovenbird Trail loop. Follow Taconic Vista Trail as it winds over and around the end of the ledge softened by moss. Even after heavy snowfall, the ground is relatively bare below the hemlocks because their dense foliage intercepts and holds much of the fluffy white stuff. These hemlocks are threatened by hemlock woolly adelgids, aphids that continue to gradually spread across the Berkshires, especially in years with mild winters.

After passing a large fallen hemlock trunk cut to make way for the trail, walk through a patch of Christmas fern before turning right to follow an old barbed wire fence line up into mixed woodland that includes yellow birch. At a signpost marked "Vista," turn left and walk a few feet to the upper edge of a hayfield that affords a stunning view north and west of the Berkshire Hills and Taconic Mountains. This field is loaded with butterflies and dragonflies in summer.

Continue on the main path gently uphill. Taconic Vista Trail soon rejoins Quarry Trail. Turn left and follow the yellow blazes back to the monument to the property donors and the junction with Lime Kiln Loop on the right.

Instead of turning right to retrace your steps past the bench, however, stay straight and walk along the large field edge down to a signpost. After leaf fall, the 40-foot-high lime kiln, a concrete cylinder, is visible to your right. At the signpost, turn right and approach the former kiln. Built in 1909, this enterprise lasted only three years before it was abandoned. Marble rock was dumped in the top and cooked at 1,400 degrees to drive out all the moisture. The rock was reduced to powdery lime, used in agriculture and many industrial applications. (Be sure to stay clear of the kiln and adjacent structures.)

Past the kiln on the left stand two enormous hemlocks that must be several hundred years old. Continue to follow Lime Kiln Loop along an old road lined by prickly ash shrubs. While the shrub is not an ash at all, the branches are certainly prickly—avoid contact with them. Walk along the left margin of another field and turn right where a couple of deciduous conifers—American larches (tamaracks)—stand. Their needle tufts turn yellow in fall before dropping off.

Pass a shrubby wetland on your left, where alder flycatchers nest in summer. Their breeding "song" is a rapid, hiccuping *fee-bee-o*.

In summer and fall, American woodcocks sometimes flush from beneath the brushy growth to the right of the path just before Lime Kiln Loop ends near the farm pond. When you complete the loop, turn left to stroll back to your vehicle.

DID YOU KNOW?

Lime Kiln Farm (248 acres) is part of the much larger 13,750-acre state-designated Schenob Brook Area of Critical Environmental Concern (ACEC), established in 1990. The Schenob Brook ACEC and its associated wetlands make up one of the most significant natural communities in Massachusetts, featuring the largest continuous calcareous seepage marsh (open, nonforested wetland with scattered shrubs), the finest examples of calcareous fens in southern New England, and more than 40 state-listed rare species.

MORE INFORMATION

Open dawn to dusk, year-round. Access is free, but donations are appreciated. The site has no toilet facilities. Dogs, vehicles, hunting, fishing, trapping, and collecting are prohibited. The property is owned by Mass Audubon and managed by Mass Audubon's Pleasant Valley Wildlife Sanctuary, 472 West Mountain Road, Lenox, MA 01240 (413-637-0320; massaudubon.org/get-outdoors/wildlife-sanctuaries/lime-kiln-farm).

NEARBY

Sheffield Covered Bridge, destroyed by fire in 1994 and rebuilt in 1998, is a 93-foot-long lattice truss bridge across the Housatonic River. It's one of only seven historical covered bridges remaining in Massachusetts. The original, constructed in 1854, was the oldest covered bridge in the state until it burned. The bridge, open only to pedestrian traffic, is 0.8 mile north of the center of Sheffield, on the east side of US 7.

48

BARTHOLOMEW'S COBBLE RESERVATION

Long beloved by botanists and fern enthusiasts, Bartholomew's Cobble offers terrific bird-watching and wildflower-viewing opportunities, interesting geology, and fabulous panoramic views from the crest of Hurlburt's Hill.

DIRECTIONS

From the center of Sheffield (at the U.S. Post Office), follow US 7 south 1.7 miles to the intersection with US 7A. Turn right onto US 7A and follow it 0.4 mile. Turn right on Rannapo Road, cross the railroad tracks, and drive 1.5 miles to Weatogue Road on the right. Turn right on Weatogue Road and continue 0.1 mile to the reservation's gravel parking area on the left. *GPS coordinates*: 42° 03.452′ N, 73° 21.042′ W.

TRAIL DESCRIPTION

Check in at the visitor center or, if the center is closed, examine the kiosk with map at the trailhead to the left. Trail maps are available at the visitor center (inside and out). Trail intersections are signed.

From the kiosk, walk left and follow Eaton Trail, a short path that leads up the smaller cobble, past junipers (eastern red cedars). Cobbles are composed primarily of erosion-resistant quartzite rock and softer marble. The amalgamation of these two rock types and the soils they produce gives rise to great botanical biodiversity here. Note the large rock outcroppings, capped by polypody ferns, on both sides of the trail. Delicate maidenhair spleenwort, just one of 43 ferns and allied species to be found in this botanist's wonderland, thrives at the base of the rocks. Reach the top and enjoy a screened view of the Housatonic River valley from a well-placed wooden bench.

LOCATION
Sheffield, MA

RATING
Moderate

DISTANCE
3.5 miles round trip

ELEVATION GAIN
310 feet

ESTIMATED TIME
2–2.5 hours

MAPS
USGS Ashley Falls; The Trustees of Reservations map: thetrustees.org/ assets/documents/ places-to-visit/trailmaps/ Bartholomew-s-Cobble -Trail-Map.pdf

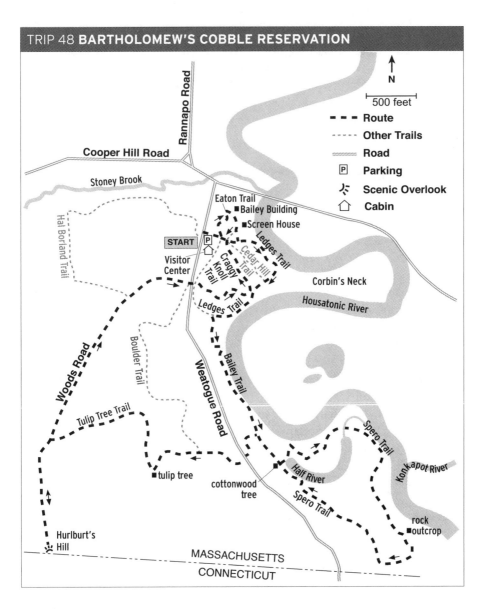

Bear left and proceed downhill, still under junipers, to the old Bailey Building, a former museum. Bear right under white pines on a wide path, and soon arrive at a three-way split. Continue straight ahead (the middle branch), where invasive garlic mustard dominates in spring. Turn left on red-blazed Ledges Trail at an intersection shaded with eastern hemlocks and white pines, and head toward the Housatonic River. The larger of two moss-and-fern-covered quartzite cobbles hems in the path on the right. Steps lead down to the edge of the floodplain, where spring's rising waters deposit silt. This flat pasture, nearly encircled by the river, is known as Corbin's Neck. One day it may be cut off by the flow and become an oxbow pond. Watch for fish-hunting ospreys here during their spring and fall migrations; you can see bald eagles in winter.

In early spring, look for the pleated leaves of false hellebore rising from the silt, and find the dainty pantaloons of dutchman's breeches closer to the cliff face. The latter are ephemeral wildflowers that bloom in midspring, before unfurling tree leaves shade the ground. White ashes predominate, and maples are present too. Bear right and climb a bit to the Cedar Hill Trail intersection under large oaks; continue left on Ledges Trail, which skirts the larger cobble. After a few steps up, note the massive white ash, more than 3 feet in diameter, on the right. Past Corbin's Neck, follow Ledges Trail above and adjacent to the Housatonic and along a marble-and-quartzite cliff face topped by junipers. Sinewy ironwood, hop hornbeam (both have hard wood) and birch clothe the slope down to the water's edge.

At a small clearing at 0.3 mile, turn left onto blue-blazed Bailey Trail and cross a small brook. Skunk cabbage and red osier dogwood thrive in the moist soil. A "hairy" poison ivy vine snakes up a black cherry tree on the right. A bit farther, large wild grapevines hang from the trees. Follow the river downstream, cross a few small feeder streams, and walk beneath some sizable white pines until you reach the Spero Trail/Tulip Tree Trail junction. Continue straight, following Spero Trail (also blue blazed) under more towering pines. Listen for the sweet trill of pine warblers during spring and early summer. Shallow pools dot the floodplain in spring.

At 0.7 mile, arrive at Half River, an oxbow pond that was once part of the river's main stem. Here, the Spero Trail loop begins. A cottonwood of truly monumental proportions dominates the intersection. This giant, hollow at its base, is more than 6 feet in diameter. Turn left and tread through a floodplain dominated by silver maples tolerant of periodic inundation, and then walk along the edge of a wet meadow, the site of recent floodplain forest restoration work. Depending on how wet the meadow is, it may not always be passable. If the trail is flooded, backtrack to the giant cottonwood tree and turn left, then return along that stretch of Spero Trail.

Climb out of the floodplain and bear left at the signed fork to remain on Spero Trail. An angular schist outcropping juts from the oak woodland on the left. Schist is considerably harder than the eroded marble bedrock that underlies the river valley. Enjoy a wonderful view south into Connecticut upon reaching another meadow, and then begin another gradual climb on Spero Trail into a forest of hemlock, pine, and black birch. The cooling effect of deep evergreen shade is readily apparent under hemlocks as you close the loop and arrive back at Half River. Check the protruding logs for basking painted turtles.

After crossing a boardwalk spanning a trickle, find yourself once more among quartzite boulders. Striking emerald-green mosses pad the surface of one low, vertical rock face on the left. Maidenhair fern and round-lobed *Hepatica* do well in the nutrient-rich soil at the bottom of the slope a bit farther along. When you

The larger of two moss- and fern-capped quartzite cobbles is skirted by Ledges Trail.

reach the giant cottonwood, continue straight for a short distance to the intersection with Tulip Tree Trail on the left.

Begin a 0.9-mile trek to Hurlburt Hill, ascending moderately through pines and hemlocks to gravel Weatogue Road. Cross it and follow Tulip Tree Trail up into rocky, mixed woodland of oak, ash, hemlock, and pine. Turn left at the intersection with Boulder Trail to remain on Tulip Tree Trail. After traversing a series of bog bridges, marvel at a massive tulip tree more than 3 feet in diameter, with a spreading crown. This imposing species, near its northern range limits in the southern Berkshires, is the largest species of our eastern forests. The path may be a bit muddy here during wet weather. Bits of rusted barbed wire and a luxuriant growth of invasive Japanese barberry and multiflora rose bushes indicate former disturbance by humans and livestock.

As you enter a small field, be on the lookout for wild turkey and ruffed grouse, two game birds that thrive in a mosaic of habitats. Bear left and walk up to Tractor Path, an old farm road. Turn left to follow it steadily up an obvious mowed path toward the summit of Hurlburt's Hill. Bluebird nest boxes on wooden posts flank the trail. A splendid view awaits as you ascend the hillside hayfield. Near the crest at 2.5 miles, two wooden benches facing north offer a magnificent

180-degree vista: unobstructed views of Mount Everett (Trip 45) and the southern Taconics to the northwest and East Mountain (Trip 41) to the northeast. This is also a fine site from which to spot southward-migrating hawks in fall. An interpretive panel identifies both distant landscape features and the hawks that one might see. A stone monument just to the right marks the state line.

Retrace your steps down the hill, past the intersection with Tulip Tree Trail, and enter pine, hickory, ash, and cherry woods with Japanese barberry and another invasive exotic: winged euonymus. Both escaped from cultivation long ago. A few old apple trees along the field edge produce fruit for deer and other wildlife. Continue steadily downslope and cross Weatogue Road at 3.2 miles. Cross Ledges Trail and continue straight on Craggy Knoll Trail. Walk under junipers—some dead—up to the top of the larger cobble. Ledges heavily padded with mosses and ferns rise on the left. The rock has been intriguingly eroded over eons. In late spring, the delicate pink blossoms of Herb-Robert are ubiquitous. Finally, descend rather steeply from the promontory around a quartzite boulder, reaching the intersection with Cedar Hill Trail and Ledges Trail. Turn left here to return to the visitor center.

DID YOU KNOW?

Today's twin cobbles originated some 500 million years ago. During those ancient times, layers of sediment (quartzite is metamorphosed beach sand, and marble is metamorphosed limestone composed of the shells of sea creatures) were pushed upward. The property is named for farmer George Bartholomew, who purchased the land in the late nineteenth century.

MORE INFORMATION

Trails open sunrise to sunset, year-round. The museum and visitor center are open year-round; hours vary seasonally (call 413-298-3239, ext. 3013, for details). Entrance fees: Nonmember adults, $5; children ages 6 to 12, $1. No fee for Trustees of Reservations members. Pets and mountain biking are not permitted. Public programs are presented on a regular basis. Bartholomew's Cobble, 105 Weatogue Road, Ashley Falls, Sheffield, MA 01222 (413-229-8600; thetrustees .org/places-to-visit/berkshires/bartholomews-cobble.html).

NEARBY

Visit historic Ashley House, built in 1735, on nearby Cooper Hill Road. Also owned by The Trustees of Reservations, it is on the National Register of Historic Places. The home was the residence of Colonel John Ashley, who amassed a 3,000-acre estate in the eighteenth century. It was also the residence of Mum Bett, an enslaved African American who sued Ashley for her freedom in 1781 and won, effectively ending slavery in Massachusetts. The grounds are open daily year-round; the house is open for tours on Fridays in July and August, 10 A.M. to 2 P.M. (413-298-3239, ext. 3016; thetrustees.org/places-to-visit/berkshires/ashley-house.html.)

49

SAGES RAVINE AND BEAR MOUNTAIN

A journey into a charming chasm—a veritable mile of delights—contrasts with a short but tough climb to Connecticut's loftiest perch, offering sublime views.

DIRECTIONS

From the intersection of US 7, MA 23, and MA 41 in Great Barrington, turn onto the combined MA 23 and MA 41, and drive southwest for 3.9 miles. Turn left onto MA 41 South (at Mill Pond) in Egremont. Follow MA 41 for only 0.1 mile before bearing right to Mount Washington Road. Follow Mount Washington Road (its name later changes to East Road) for 11.4 miles, past the entrances to Mount Everett State Reservation (7.3 miles) and Mount Washington State Forest (8.8 miles). The last 2.3 miles are on gravel. A small parking area, with space for about five vehicles, is on the left, approximately 100 feet beyond the 1906 granite marker signifying the Massachusetts–Connecticut border. Be sure not to block the metal gate. The road may be closed in winter. Additional parking space is 150 feet back the way you came. *GPS coordinates*: 42° 02.959′ N, 73° 28.011′ W.

TRAIL DESCRIPTION

From the parking area, walk around the metal gate on wide, grassy Undermountain Trail (also known as Northwest Road), marked with blue blazes. Showy mountain laurel (the Connecticut state flower) is profligate to the right, while dense ferns—tall interrupted fern and shorter New York and hay-scented ferns—populate a glade on the left. At the trail fork, stay left to remain on Undermountain Trail and cross a feeder stream on stones. The right fork leads to AMC's Northwest Camp, wonderfully situated on a rise under hemlocks. Sages Ravine Brook soon

LOCATION
Mount Washington, MA; Salisbury, CT

RATING
Strenuous

DISTANCE
3.9 miles round trip

ELEVATION GAIN
915 feet

ESTIMATED TIME
2.5–3 hours

MAPS
USGS Bash Bish Falls; AMC Massachusetts Trail Map 2; Massachusetts Department of Conservation and Recreation map: mass.gov/files/documents/2017/01/sh/mwashington.pdf

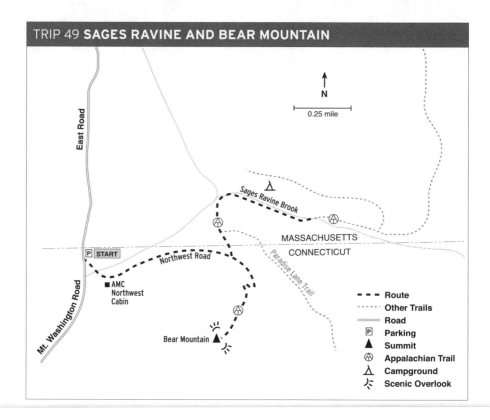

comes into view to your left, and the forest diversifies into mixed hemlock and beech woods, and then virtually pure deciduous growth.

It doesn't take long to come upon the first cascade on the old built-up roadway, but this is only a teaser. Cross a plank bridge over another feeder stream just before the narrowing path turns rocky and the grade increases through laurels. American beech sprouts, striped maples, and laurels fill the space between yellow and black birches, then maples, ashes, and oaks. Soon you're treading on level ground through open woodland along the base of Bear Mountain, which you'll climb later. Multitrunked oaks hint at past logging.

A sign on the left announces that you've entered the 500-foot-wide Appalachian Trail (AT) corridor, and within moments you reach the fabled footpath. Here, you have a choice. Turn right to scale Bear Mountain first or turn left to visit Sages Ravine. For the latter, turn left and stride downhill under a mixed evergreen-deciduous canopy to arrive at a wooden sign that states, "You are entering a very fragile environment. Please camp at designated sites only. Help this area to recover from overuse and abuse. Thank you." Here, blue-blazed Paradise Trail diverges to the right; turn left to continue on the white-blazed AT as it proceeds moderately downhill through a thick stand of striped maple saplings and over stone steps toward Sages Ravine Brook.

The grade eases along the brook, where the path bears right and runs along steep ledge faces. The next mile or so is without doubt one of the loveliest stream strolls in the region. Spinulose wood fern blankets the lower reaches of the mountain as you arrive at a long, double-split-log bridge leading across the stream to hemlock-shaded Sages Ravine Campsite. But instead of crossing the bridge, continue straight ahead on the AT, now a rocky, narrow path edging the brook. Pools that harbor native brook trout are interspersed with little cascades. Some "brookies" here attain all of 6 inches in length.

At one point, a large pool is hemmed in by sheer ledge. As you proceed downstream, the scene becomes progressively more enchanting, so take your time moving through the ravine. American yew caps boulders. Wood sorrel, with cloverlike leaves, thrives in patches on the forest floor under hemlocks. A high-gradient tributary empties into Sages Ravine Brook, and a laurel shrub marks the confluence. The AT climbs jauntily above the rock-lined chasm. From above, you can see that the water has scoured the sides of the vertical walls.

Cross a flow that bounces precipitously down the right slope from one rock ledge to the next in multiple cascades. It's only a sideshow to the main act, but a delight nonetheless. These rocky tributaries cause the main stream to flow with even more gusto. Work your way down through angular schist boulders. The battlements of a formidable ledge rise above on the right slope. The path descends to the brook's bank again at a 3-foot-high falls, and the volume of water charging down the ravine is impressive. Delight to another plunge where the brook makes a serpentine bend under hemlocks. This second cascade, which is actually split into two, is more than 12 feet high. Viewed upstream from an elevated location, the falls align themselves into a truly sublime scene. Note the trough to the right that the torrent has gouged into tilted bedrock during flood events.

After reaching a lofty height of about 45 feet above the churning flow, descend on expertly constructed stone steps to a cool microclimate. Here grows long beech fern, a small fern identified by its bottom two leaflets, which point downward. A sign affixed to a tree on the right welcomes hikers to Connecticut. (You are actually in Massachusetts here, but only about 1,000 feet north of the state line.) The AT crosses the brook on large stones, but this is the turnaround point for this portion of the hike. The good news is that you'll have a second opportunity to revel in the many delights of Sages Ravine. Retrace your steps to the signed intersection with Undermountain Trail, where you first began hiking on the AT.

Now it's time for a very different hiking experience. If your energy level is low by this point, put off the ascent of Bear Mountain's steep north face for another day, as it gains more than 500 vertical feet in 0.3 mile. Otherwise, make sure you have enough drinking water and forge on, following the white-blazed AT as it bears left along the slope contour under a deciduous canopy. Descend, and then climb a series of stone staircases over slanting bedrock. The path zigzags up the steep gradient. Negotiate rock ledges that have some easy handholds to

Gazing up Sages Ravine Brook from an elevated perch reveals a series of falls and cascades in a sublime setting.

aid your progress. White blazes are few heading up, and the going can be tricky, so watch your footing; this hike is certainly not recommended during icy or wet conditions.

A few herbaceous dogwoods—bunchberries—have gained a foothold in the scant soil, while mountain azalea, common polypody fern (the little one clinging to rocks), and lowbush blueberry eke out a living in sun-dappled spots. The first pitch pines appear on the right, as does more laurel, loaded with blossoms in late June and early July. Ascend more bedrock, but not as steeply. Glaciers scoured this stone some 14,000 years ago. If you have a compass—and you should—note that the grooves line up north–south, the direction of the flow of the glacier's mile-thick ice sheets.

An evocative pine-resin aroma wafts in the air of sunny gaps as you near the summit. Blueberry and related huckleberry shrubs (note huckleberry's shiny resin dots on the undersides of its leaves) populate the area, as do gray birches, oaks, and cherry trees. A stone tower, appearing as a giant rock cairn, sits atop Bear Mountain, the highest summit (2,316 feet) entirely within Connecticut's boundaries. The tower has been rebuilt three times.

Climb the mound of schist flagstones from the back for sublime views—some stones are loose, so tread carefully. To the near north are Mount Race (Trip 44) and Mount Everett (Trip 45) along the AT, while the Housatonic River valley and Twin Lakes in Connecticut lie seemingly at arm's length to the east. On a completely clear day, portions of five states—Massachusetts, Connecticut, New York, Vermont, and New Hampshire—may be visible. When you're ready to leave, retrace your steps to Undermountain Trail on the left and follow it back to your vehicle.

DID YOU KNOW?

A plaque placed on the summit tower in 1885 refers to Bear Mountain as being the highest point in Connecticut. It has since been discovered that the actual high point (highest elevation) is on the south slope of Mount Frissell at 2,380 feet. The summit of that peak is across the border in Massachusetts.

MORE INFORMATION

Camping is permitted only in designated areas. Carry in, carry out rules apply. Motorized vehicles, horses, hunting, and fires are prohibited. Appalachian Mountain Club Connecticut Chapter, Northwest Camp Committee (ct-amc .org/nwcamp; nwcamp@ct-amc.org). Appalachian Trail Conservancy, P.O. Box 807, Harpers Ferry, WV 25425, appalachiantrail.org.

NEARBY

The site of the boyhood home of African American intellectual and civil rights leader W.E.B. DuBois (1868–1963) is just south of the MA 71 intersection along MA 41/MA 23 in Great Barrington. Designated as a National Historic Landmark, the site contains foundation remnants of DuBois's grandfather's home, where DuBois spent his first five years; an informational kiosk and self-guided interpretive trail; and a commemorative boulder. The 5-acre property was donated to the state in 1987 and is administered by Housatonic Heritage and the University of Massachusetts Amherst (duboisnhs.org).

50

ROUND MOUNTAIN, MOUNT FRISSELL, AND BRACE MOUNTAIN

This rugged but fairly short out-and-back trek offers a unique opportunity to traverse three distinctive summits in three states. Attractions include many scenic views, Connecticut's highest elevation, and a three-state historical boundary marker.

DIRECTIONS

From the junction of US 7, MA 23, and MA 41 in Great Barrington, follow the combined MA 23 and MA 41 west for 3.9 miles to South Egremont. At Mill Pond, turn left and follow MA 41 for 0.1 mile, then turn right onto Mount Washington Road. Follow Mount Washington Road (which becomes East Street in the town of Mount Washington) for 11.4 miles, passing the entrances to Mount Everett State Reservation on the left at 7.3 miles and Mount Washington State Forest on the right at 8.3 miles (stay straight at the Union Church). The last 2.3 miles are on gravel. Parking is available at the trailhead and a small lot on the left, about 100 feet beyond the Connecticut state line. *GPS coordinates*: 42° 02.959′ N, 73° 28.011′ W.

TRAIL DESCRIPTION

The southern Taconic Mountains' many natural treasures include Round Mountain, Mount Frissell, and Brace Mountain, a trio of rolling summits clustered along the three-state boundary of Massachusetts, Connecticut, and New York. Mount Frissell is well known for its unusual distinction of being Connecticut's highest elevation even though its summit is in Massachusetts. This hike combines Mount Frissell Trail, which traverses several steep and rocky areas on Round Mountain and Mount Frissell, and a segment of South Taconic Trail leading to Brace Mountain. You can turn back at any point for a shorter

LOCATION
Mount Washington, MA; Salisbury, CT; Millertown, NY

RATING
Moderate to Strenuous

DISTANCE
4.4 miles round trip

ELEVATION GAIN
1,425 feet

ESTIMATED TIME
3.5 hours

MAPS
AMC Massachusetts Trail Map 1; USGS Bash Bish Falls; Massachusetts Department of Conservation and Recreation map: mass.gov/files/documents/2017/01/sh/mwashington.pdf

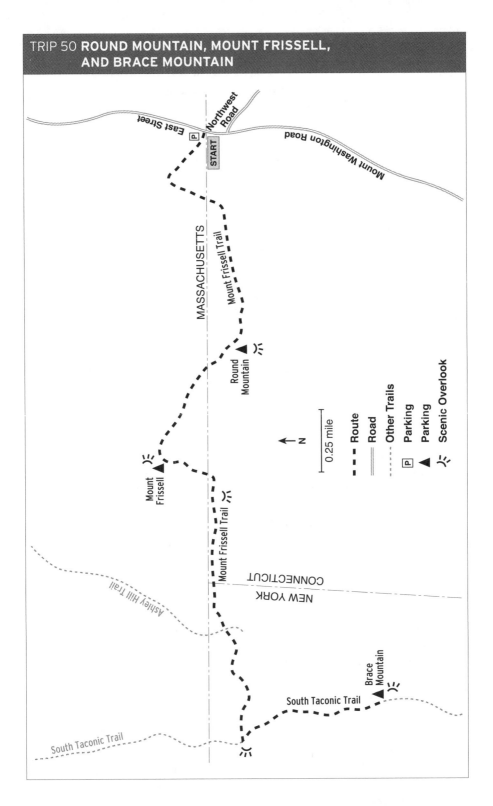

outing (1.2 miles round-trip for Round Mountain, 2.2 miles for the Connecticut high point and vista on Mount Frissell, and 2.8 miles for the three-state marker).

From the trailhead on the west side of East Street, follow red-blazed Mount Frissell Trail into the woods and along the south side of a swampy area, where yellow and chestnut-sided warblers breed in spring and summer. Evergreen eastern hemlocks and mountain laurels shade the rocky path before you enter hardwood forest dominated by red oak and chestnut oak, characteristic of the southern Taconic Mountains. Watch for black-throated blue warblers, with calls sounding like *sir-sir-sir-please,* in and around shrubby growths.

Bear left, entering Connecticut at the first of several state line crossings, and begin ascending at an initially gentle grade. Painted trilliums, named for their three-part white flowers with pink markings, bloom in May and then produce scarlet berries (mildly toxic to humans) in late summer and early autumn. After a 0.4-mile warm-up, the character of the hike changes rather abruptly as you begin a steep, rocky ascent of Round Mountain's eastern slope. Carefully work your way around and over several sections of exposed rock (free hands are helpful in places). Near the crest of the climb, gaze back for a fine view overlooking nearby Bear Mountain and the hills to the east.

Continue through stunted scrub oaks and birches and abundant blueberries, all well adapted to the ridge top's thin soil, to the 2,289-foot summit at 0.6 mile. The blueberries display tiny, white bell-shaped flowers in spring before the tasty fruits ripen in summer. Several outlooks offer fine views across the region, including nearby Mount Frissell and Brace Mountain, your next destinations, to the west-southwest. Other landmarks include Mount Everett and Mount Race to the north, Mount Greylock on the distant northern horizon, and Riga Lake and the Mount Riga Forest Preserve to the south. The oak forests on the surrounding slopes show mostly russet hues when fall foliage peaks in middle to late October. Common yellowthroats, easily identified by their *witchity-witchity-witchity* song, frequent the shrubby vegetation during spring and summer.

Continue west on Mount Frissell Trail, descending to the narrow gap (less than 100 feet wide) between Round Mountain and Mount Frissell, through growths of paper birches and mountain laurels. Look for pink lady's slippers blooming along trail edges in late spring. These orchids are well-adapted to a variety of habitats with acidic soils. Make another steep (but thankfully short) 0.1-mile ascent of Mount Frissell, crossing back into Massachusetts about halfway up the slope. When the grade levels, take a moment to catch your breath and enjoy another easterly view to Round Mountain and Bear Mountain. At the wooded 2,453-foot summit, a trail register in a metal box is just off the trail on the right. Tiger swallowtail butterflies frequent the hilltops and open woods of this area in spring and summer.

Follow Mount Frissell Trail as it curves left (south) down to an open ledge with splendid 180-degree southerly views of Riga Lake and the surrounding hills. At the state line, a USGS survey marker and another trail register denote Connecticut's highest elevation at 2,380 feet. Many "highpointers" (see "Did

Round Mountain's summit, offering views of the surrounding southern Taconic Mountains, is one of many scenic overlooks on Mount Frissell Trail and South Taconic Trail.

You Know," below) hike the trail just to reach this spot. Bear Mountain, roughly 1.5 miles to the southeast, is Connecticut's highest summit at 2,316 feet.

Continue west along the Massachusetts–Connecticut state line through more shrubby ridge-top vegetation. Two openings along the path afford westerly views to New York and the distant Catskill Mountains. From the second lookout, carefully descend another section of exposed rock. The terrain is much gentler from this point to Brace Mountain. Pink and white blooms of mountain laurel, which thrives in dry, rocky, oak woods, peak in June here.

At 1.4 miles, reach a stone pillar at the boundary of Massachusetts, New York, and Connecticut, one of 65 places in the United States where three states meet. (Because of a long-standing historical dispute over the location of Connecticut's western border, only Massachusetts and New York are marked on the monument, which was erected in 1898.) Enter New York's Taconic State Park and pass the signed intersection with Ashley Hill Trail, which leads north into adjacent Mount Washington State Forest.

Bear right and follow Mount Frissell Trail past a discontinued trail and a boulder capped with lichens and Canada mayflowers. Ascend easily past blueberry shrubs and over exposed rock up to the Taconic ridge's western escarpment. The *drink-your-tea* call of eastern (or rufous-sided) towhees is a familiar sound in shrubby growths and thickets during spring and summer. In mountain settings, they're most common on mild south- and west-facing slopes. Mountain azaleas and pink lady's slippers add splashes of color to forest edges in late spring.

At 1.8 miles, reach Mount Frissell Trail's western terminus at the junction with long-distance South Taconic Trail. Straight ahead is a westerly view across farm fields in the Harlem Valley to the Catskills. Alander Mountain's summit is 3.7 miles north of the intersection. Turn left and follow white-blazed South Taconic Trail along the ridge toward Brace Mountain, just 0.4 mile away on a well-maintained path. Pass the junction with an unmarked woods road, leading southeast approximately 1.5 miles to East Street, on the left. Nannyberry, a shrub in the viburnum family with tiny, white flower clusters and blue-black berries, grows in rocky uplands and forest edges.

A gentle climb to Brace Mountain's grassy, open top completes your three-summit, three-state trifecta. The 2,311-foot peak, capped by a large rock cairn and windsock, is the highest point of South Taconic Trail and New York's Dutchess County. Enjoy sweeping vistas in all directions, including the Catskills and Hudson River valley to the west, Bear Mountain on the east side of the range, Alander Mountain to the north, Mount Frissell and distant Mount Greylock northeast, and the southern end of the Taconic uplands to the south. Westerly breezes provide welcome relief on hot summer days. Brace Mountain is a popular destination for hang gliders and paragliders, thanks to the thermal currents along the ridge and its gradual topography.

The summit marks the end of this out-and-back hike (you can extend the trip by exploring South Taconic Trail, but be sure to save enough time and energy for the return). Retrace your steps to Mount Frissell Trail and turn right to return to the trailhead, crossing back over Mount Frissell and Round Mountain. Use caution descending the steep sections. The return route entails roughly 475 feet of elevation gain, but the last 0.4-mile segment is easy after you descend Round Mountain.

DID YOU KNOW?

"Highpointing"—ascending to the highest natural elevations within geographic areas, such as states, countries, or continents—became popular in the late nineteenth century. Arthur Marshall was the first known person to reach the highest points of all 48 continental states. His quest began at Mount Rainier in Washington State in 1919 and ended at Hoosier Hill in Indiana in 1936.

MORE INFORMATION

Open sunrise to sunset, year-round. Access is free. No restrooms are available. Biking, skiing, leashed dogs, and hunting are allowed. Mount Washington State Forest, 165A East Street, Mount Washington, MA 01258 (413-528-0330; mass.gov/locations/mount-washington-state-forest). Taconic State Park, 253 Route 344, Copake Falls, NY 12517 (518-329-3993; parks.ny.gov/parks/83/details.aspx).

NEARBY

Kenver Ltd., at 39 Main Street (MA 23) in South Egremont, is the Berkshires' largest winter sports store. Contact the store for seasonal operating hours (413-528-2330; kenver.com).

INFORMATION AND RESOURCES

CAMPING

From Mount Greylock's upper slopes to secluded backcountry sites in the southern Taconic Mountains, the Berkshires offer a variety of options for campers. Public campgrounds generally offer basic amenities, including restrooms, showers, swimming, beaches, boat launches, and picnic areas. In addition to the public sites listed below, there are many privately owned campgrounds that offer extra features, such as playgrounds, family activities and events, and RV hookups.

The camping season generally runs from May to September or mid-October; specific dates vary by location. Reservations for Massachusetts state forest and park campgrounds can be made anytime from six months to one day in advance through Reserve America (reserveamerica.com). For all campgrounds, public or private, be sure to contact the management ahead of time to confirm availability and amenities.

BEARTOWN STATE FOREST

69 Blue Hill Road
Monterey, MA 01245
413-528-0904; mass.gov/locations/
beartown-state-forest

Twelve primitive sites at Benedict Pond (some universally accessible); no showers or flush toilets; available year-round, campground office open mid-May to mid-October.

CLARKSBURG STATE PARK

1199 Middle Road
Clarksburg, MA 01247
413-664-8345; mass.gov/locations/
clarksburg-state-park

Forty-five sites at Mausert Pond.

MOHAWK TRAIL STATE FOREST

175 Mohawk Trail (MA 2)
Charlemont, MA 01339
413-339-5504; mass.gov/locations/
mohawk-trail-state-forest

Forty-seven seasonal sites, six log cabins available year-round, near Cold River and Mahican-Mohawk Trail.

MONROE STATE FOREST

Tilda Hill Road and River Road
Florida, MA 01247
413-339-5504; mass.gov/locations/
monroe-state-forest

Three primitive shelters at Dunbar Brook, Ridge, and Smith Hollow; no facilities.

MOUNT GREYLOCK STATE RESERVATION

30 Rockwell Road
Lanesborough, MA 01237
413-499-4262; mass.gov/locations/
mount-greylock-state-reservation;
mass.gov/location-details/
camping-at-mount-greylock

Eighteen sites (four-person limit) and nine group sites (twelve-person limit); reservations required Memorial Day weekend to Columbus Day. Off-season camping available November to mid-May (first-come, first-served, no fee, registration recommended). Five primitive shelters at Deer Hill, Wilbur's Clearing, Bellows Pipe, Peck's Brook, and Mark Noepel (first-come first-served, twelve-person limit, no fee, registration recommended). Bascom Lodge at the summit offers accommodations and meals for up to 34 people; open mid-May to late October.

MOUNT WASHINGTON STATE FOREST AND MOUNT EVERETT STATE RESERVATION
165A East Street
Mount Washington, MA 01258
413-528-0330; mass.gov/locations/
mount-washington-state-forest

Wilderness camping allowed year-round at designated sites and lean-tos (see map at mass.gov/files/documents/2017/01/sh/mwashington.pdf); first-come, first served, no fee, five-person limit.

OCTOBER MOUNTAIN STATE FOREST
317 Woodland Road
Lee, MA 01238
413-243-1778; mass.gov/locations/
october-mountain-state-forest

Forty-three sites, three yurts; open mid-May to mid-October.

PITTSFIELD STATE FOREST
1041 Cascade Street
Pittsfield, MA 01201
413-442-8992; mass.gov/locations/
pittsfield-state-forest

Thirteen sites at Berry Pond at summit, nineteen sites at Parker Brook, six sites at Bishop Field. Group sites at Bishop Field (twenty-person limit) and Lulu Brook (50-person limit).

SAVOY MOUNTAIN STATE FOREST
260 Central Shaft Road
Florida, MA 01247
413-663-8469; mass.gov/locations/
savoy-mountain-state-forest

Forty-five seasonal sites, four log cabins available year-round, at South Pond.

TACONIC STATE PARK COPAKE FALLS CAMPGROUND
253 NY Route 344
Copake Falls NY 12517
518-329-3993;
parks.ny.gov/parks/83/details.aspx

One-hundred and six sites, including 70 tentsites and three cabin areas, at state line near Bash Bish Falls, South Taconic Trail, and Copake Iron Works Museum.

TOLLAND STATE FOREST
410 Tolland Road
East Otis, MA 01029
413-269-6002; mass.gov/locations/
tolland-state-forest

Ninety-three sites and RV facilities at scenic peninsula on Otis Reservoir, open mid-May to mid-October.

OTHER STATE PARKS

NATURAL BRIDGE STATE PARK
McAuley Road
North Adams, MA 01247
413-663-6392; mass.gov/locations/
natural-bridge-state-park

Marble arch bridge on Hudson
Brook; open weekends Memorial
Day-Columbus Day; parking fee.

WAHCONAH FALLS STATE PARK
North Street
Dalton, MA 01226
413-442-8992; mass.gov/locations/
wahconah-falls-state-park

Forty-eight-acre park at scenic
Wahconah Falls; picnic area; open
year-round; free.

OUTFITTERS

AMC BERKSHIRE CHAPTER
413-256-1301;
amcberkshire.org/boat-rental

Whitewater and quiet water canoes
and kayaks for rent.

ARCADIAN SHOP
91 Pittsfield Road (US 7/20)
Lenox, MA 01240
413-637-3010; arcadian.com

Bike, cross-country ski, snowshoe
rentals; outdoor clothing, accessories.

BARRINGTON OUTFITTERS
289 Main Street
Great Barrington, MA 01230
413-528-0021;
barringtonoutfitters.net

Outdoor gear, shoes, clothing,
furniture.

BERKSHIRE BIKE AND BOARD
29 State Road
Great Barrington, MA 01230
413-528-5555;
berkshirebikeandboard.com

Bike rentals and service.

BERKSHIRE OUTFITTERS
169 Grove Street
Adams, MA 01220
413-743-5900; berkshireoutfitters.com

Cross-country ski, bike, canoe, kayak
rentals; outdoor gear and accessories.

BERKSHIRE U DRIVE BOAT RENTALS
1651 North Street
Pittsfield, MA 01201
413-281-4196;
berkshireudriveboatrentals.com

Canoe, kayak, and boat rentals. On
Pontoosuc Lake.

CLARKE OUTDOORS
163 US 7
West Cornwall, CT 06796
860-672-6365; clarkeoutdoors.com

Canoe, kayak, and raft rentals;
paddling gear. On Housatonic River.

CRAB APPLE WHITEWATER
2056 Mohawk Trail
Charlemont, MA 01339
800-553-7238;
crabapplewhitewater.com

Rafting tours on Deerfield River.

DICK'S SPORTING GOODS
635 Merrill Road
Pittsfield, MA 01201
413-395-0870;
dickssportinggoods.com

Wide selection of outdoor apparel, equipment, footwear.

THE GREAT OUTDOORS
78 Main Street
Charlemont, MA 01339
413-339-8373;
thegreatoutdoors.business.site

Outdoor and sporting goods and accessories, tube rentals, river shuttles and parking. On Deerfield River.

KENVER LTD.
39 South Main Street (MA 23)
South Egremont, MA 01258
413-528-2330; 800-342-7547;
kenver.com

Bike rentals, outdoor gear and accessories.

NATURE'S CLOSET
61 Spring Street
Williamstown, MA 01267
413-458-7909; naturescloset.net

Outdoor apparel, accessories, and footwear.

ONOTA BOAT LIVERY
463 Pecks Road
Pittsfield, MA 01201
413-442-1724; onotaboat.com

Canoe, kayak, boat, and pontoon rentals. On Onota Lake.

SKI FANATICS
145 North Main Street (Route 7)
Lanesborough, MA 01237
413-443-3023; skifanatics.com

Ski and snowboard rentals.

ZOAR OUTDOOR ADVENTURE RESORT
7 Main Street
Charlemont, MA 01339
800-532-7483; zoaroutdoor.com

Kayaking, rafting, rentals, tours, and instruction. On Deerfield River.

SKI AREAS

BERKSHIRE EAST MOUNTAIN RESORT
66 Thunder Mountain Road
Charlemont, MA 01339
413-339-6618; berkshireeast.com

Downhill skiing, whitewater rafting
on Deerfield River, zip line tours, tree
house trail and adventure park,
mountain biking.

BOUSQUET SKI AREA
101 Dan Fox Drive
Pittsfield, MA 01201
413-442-8316; bousquets.com

Downhill skiing, water slides,
adventure park, disc golf.

CANTERBURY FARM
1986 Fred Snow Road
Becket, MA 01223
413-623-0100; canterbury-farms.com

Groomed ski and snowshoe trails, ice
skating, equipment and kayak
rentals, lessons; near October
Mountain State Forest.

JIMINY PEAK MOUNTAIN RESORT
37 Corey Road
Hancock, MA 01237
413-738-5550; jiminypeak.com

Downhill skiing, aerial adventure
park, mountain biking.

MAPLE CORNER FARM
794 Beech Hill Road
Granville, MA 01034
413-357-8829; maplecornerfarm.com

Groomed cross-country ski and
snowshoe trails, rentals, lessons;
blueberry picking in summer.

NOTCHVIEW (THE TRUSTEES OF RESERVATIONS)
Route 9
Windsor, MA 01226
413-684-1048; thetrustees.org/
places-to-visit/berkshires/notchview

Twenty-five miles of groomed and
ungroomed ski trails, snowshoeing,
rentals and food at Budd Visitor
Center. Open year-round; skiing and
snowshoeing daily 8 A.M. to 4:30 P.M.
December to April.

OTIS RIDGE
159 Monterey Road
Otis, MA 01253
413-269-4444; otisridge.com

Downhill skiing and lessons.

SKI BLANDFORD
41 Nye Brook Road
Blandford, MA 01008
413-848-2860; skiblandford.com

Downhill skiing and lessons.

SKI BUTTERNUT
380 State Road
Great Barrington, MA 01230
413-528-2000; skibutternut.com

Downhill skiing, rentals, lessons.

INDEX

ABOUT THE AUTHORS

René Laubach retired in 2014 from Mass Audubon's Berkshire Wildlife Sanctuaries, which he directed for nearly 30 years. He is also co-author of *AMC's Best Day Hikes in Connecticut*, has written seven books on natural history, and has written for *AMC Outdoors, Audubon, Sanctuary*, and many other publications.

John S. Burk is an outdoor writer, photographer, and historian from central Massachusetts. His other books include AMC's *Massachusetts Trail Guide* and *AMC's Best Days Hikes in Central Massachusetts*.

ABOUT AMC IN WESTERN MASSACHUSETTS

AMC has a long-standing commitment to the forests, land, and rivers of western Massachusetts. With more than 3,400 members, AMC's Berkshire Chapter is integral in conservation and trail maintenance efforts in the region. The chapter offers hundreds of activities such as hiking, mountaineering, paddling, snowshoeing, and family outings.

AMC also manages properties in western Massachusetts. The Upper Goose Pond Cabin, located on the Appalachian Trail and run exclusively for thru-hikers and section hikers, is owned by the National Park Service and managed by volunteers from AMC's Berkshire Chapter. AMC's Noble View Outdoor Center in the Pioneer Valley accommodates groups of many sizes in cottages and campsites. The 360-acre property features 50-mile views over the Connecticut River valley and trails suitable for hiking, snowshoeing, and cross-country skiing.

Members maintain local trails—including the Appalachian Trail, Metacomet–Monadnock Trail and New England Trail—lead outdoor skills workshops, and promote stewardship of the region's natural resources. AMC also offers a Teen Volunteer Trail Crew program in the Berkshires. To view a list of AMC activities across the Northeast, visit activities.outdoors.org.

AMC BOOK UPDATES

AMC Books strives to keep our guidebooks as up-to-date as possible to help you plan safe and enjoyable adventures. If we learn after publishing a book that relevant trails have been relocated or route or contact information has changed, we will post the updated information online. Before you hit the trail, visit outdoors .org/books-maps and click the "Book Updates" tab.

While hiking, if you notice discrepancies with the trip descriptions or maps, or if you find any other errors in the book, please let us know by submitting them to amcbookupdates@outdoors.org or to Books Editor, c/o AMC, 10 City Square, Boston, MA 02129. We will verify all submissions and post key updates each month. AMC Books is dedicated to being a recognized leader in outdoor publishing. Thank you for your participation.

BE OUTDOORS™

Since 1876, the Appalachian Mountain Club has channeled your enthusiasm for the outdoors into everything we do and everywhere we work to protect. We're inspired by people exploring the natural world and deepening their appreciation of it.

With AMC chapters from Maine to Washington, D.C., including groups in Boston, New York City, and Philadelphia, you can enjoy activities like hiking, paddling, cycling, and skiing, and learn new outdoor skills. We offer advice, guidebooks, maps, and unique eco-lodges and huts to inspire your next outing.

Your visits, purchases, and donations also support conservation advocacy and research, youth programming, and caring for more than 1,800 miles of trails.

Join us!
outdoors.org/join

AMC's Best Day Hikes in Central Massachusetts

John S. Burk

Spotlighting 50 of the best day hikes in central Massachusetts (west of Boston and east of the Berkshires), this indispensable guide covers the wild beauty of Franklin, Hampshire, Hampden, and Worcester counties, including Royalston Falls, Mount Holyoke, the historic Mohawk and Keystone Arches trails, and more. Whether hiking with kids, dogs, skiing, or snowshoeing, this guide provides the important information you need when exploring the trails of this scenic region.

$18.95 • 978-1-62842-094-4 • ebook available

Massachusetts Trail Guide, 10th Edition

Compiled and edited by John S. Burk

Thoroughly updated with 30 new trails, the tenth edition of AMC's comprehensive trail guide to the Bay State covers more than 390 treks, from Cape Cod to the Berkshires. Get elevation gain, mileage, and driving directions for hikes of all lengths and skill levels, including Mount Greylock and the Appalachian Trail.

$24.95 • 978-1-62842-020-3

New England Trail Map & Guide

AMC Books and Connecticut Forest & Park Association

This two-map set is the perfect day-hiker's companion to the entire 215-mile New England National Scenic Trail, extending from Long Island Sound in Connecticut to the Massachusetts–New Hampshire border. The map and guide pairs two topographical trail maps—one for each state—with relevant information, such as safety tips, Leave No Trace guidelines, natural history, and more.

$14.95 • 978-1-62842-015-9

The Unlikely Thru-Hiker

Derick Lugo

Derick Lugo, a young black man from New York City with no hiking experience, had heard of the Appalachian Trail, but he had never seriously considered attempting to hike all 2,192 miles of it. And yet, when he found himself with months of free time, he decided to give it a try. With an extremely overweight pack and a willfully can-do attitude, Lugo tackles the trail with humor, tenacity, and an unshakeable commitment to grooming that sees him from Georgia to Maine.

$19.95 • 978-1-62842-118-7 • ebook available